TWENTIETH-CENTURY FURNITURE DESIGN

D1119212

Twentieth-Century
FURNITURE DESIGN

KLAUS-JÜRGEN SEMBACH
GABRIELE LEUTHÄUSER
PETER GÖSSEL

TASCHEN
KÖLN LISBOA LONDON NEW YORK PARIS TOKYO

Illustrations on the cover:
Gerrit Rietveld, modern replica of the "Zig-Zag" chair, designed in 1934
Pierre Chareau, living hall in the "Maison de Verre" in Paris, 1932
Frontispiece: tubular steel furniture by P.E.L. England, 1933

© 1991 Benedikt Taschen Verlag GmbH
Hohenzollernring 53, D-50672 Köln
Editor: Dr. Angelika Muthesius, Cologne
English translation: Irene Quaile-Kersken, Cologne
Selection of illustrations and lay-out: the authors
Typesetting: Utesch Satztechnik GmbH, Hamburg
Reproductions: Repro Ludwig, Zell am See
Printed in Germany
ISBN 3-8228-0276-X

CONTENTS

ACKNOWLEDGEMENTS

Abitare, Cologne, Mr. Giusi Timpanaro
Architectural Digest, Los Angeles, Mrs. Wright
Architectural Collection of the Technical University in Munich, Prof. Winfried Nerdinger
Artek, Helsinki, Mr. Ben Af Schulten
Artemide GmbH, Düsseldorf, Mrs. Megger
Dr. Paul Asenbaum, Vienna
Association des amis de la maison de verre, Paris, Madame Vellay Dalsace
Badisches Landesmuseum Karlsruhe, Dr. Irmela Franzke
Herr Rudolf Baresel-Bofinger, Heilbronn
Baumeister-Archiv, Stuttgart, Mrs. Felicitas Karg-Baumeister
K.Barlow decorative arts, London, Mr. Albrecht Widmann
Bauhaus-Archiv, Berlin, Mrs. Sabine Hartmann
Porzellanfabrik (Porcelain Factory) Weiden Gebr. Bauscher, Mr. Karlheinz Sammet
Bayer AG Leverkusen, publicity department, Mrs. Kampf
B&B Italia, Como
Mr. Janos Frecot, Berlin
Madame Maria de Beyrie, Paris
Library of the "Landesgewerbeanstalt", Nuremberg, Mrs. Erna Missbach and Frau Heidrun Teumer
Bieffeplast, Padua
Bildarchiv Foto Marburg, Dr. Brigitte Walbe
Bildarchiv Preussischer Kulturbesitz, Mrs. Klein
Mr. Bruno Bischofberger, Zürich
Blattmann Metallwarenfabrik AG, Wädenswill, Switzerland
Mr. Andreas Brandolini, Berlin
Austrian Federal Ministry for Economic Affairs, Vienna, Dr. Peter Barenzahn
Casa-Möbel, Munich, Mr. Horst Franke
Cassina, Meda/Milan, Mrs. Anna Casati
Castelli GmbH, Munich, Mr. Franco Duca
Prof. Achille Castiglioni, Milan
Catedra Gaudi, Escola Tecnica Superior d'Arquitectura, Barcelona, Prof. Juan Bassegoda Nonell
Mrs. Beth Cathers, New York
Cor Sitzkomfort Helmut Lübke GmbH & Co., Rheda-Wiedenbrück
Det Danske Kunstindustrimuseum, Copenhagen
Dux International, Trelleborg, Mrs. Margaretha Svenning
Ecart International, Paris, Mrs. Beatrice Villa
Eidgenössische Technische Hochschule, Zürich, Institute for the History and Theory of Architecture
Christian Farjon France, Aubusson
Fondation Le Corbusier, Paris, Madame Evelyne Trehin
Fondazione Lucio Fontana, Milan
Mr. Klaus Frahm, Hamburg
Galerie Paolo Curti, Brescia

Galerie Geitel, Berlin
Galerie Yves Gastou, Paris
Galerie Kaess-Weiss, Stuttgart
Galerie L'Arc en Seine, Paris
Galerie Frantisek Sima, Nuremberg
Galerie Vallois, Paris
Galerie Stefan Vogt, Munich
Galerie Jordan-Volpe, New York
Mrs. Astrid Gmeiner, Vienna
Mrs. Sophie Renate Gnamm, Munich
Gufram, Cirie-Torino
Habit, Ulrich Lodholz GmbH, Leverkusen
Fritz Hansen, Allerød, Mrs. Anette Rasmussen
Johannes Hansen, Søborg, Mr. Poul Hansen
Verlag Gerd Hatje, Stuttgart
Hedrich Blessing, Chicago, Mr. Michael O. Houlahan
Mr. Keld Helmer-Petersen, Copenhagen
Dr. Georg Himmelheber, Munich
Historisches Museum der Stadt Wien, Vienna
Hochschule für angewandte Kunst (College of Applied Arts),
    Vienna, Dr. Erika Patka
Prof. Hans Hollein, Vienna, Mrs. Madeleine Jenewein
Hunterian Art Gallery, The University, Glasgow, Mrs. Pamela
    Robertson
Institute for Building History, University of Karlsruhe, Dr.-Ing. Immo
    Boyken
Institute for the History of Medicine, Freie Universität Berlin, Prof.
    Rolf Winau
Mrs. Lillian Kiesler, New York
Knoll International, Murr/Murr, Mr. Wolf Kaiser
Alexander Koch Verlagsanstalt, Leinfelden-Echterdingen
Mr. Rainer Krause, Bad Essen
Mathsson International, Värnamo, Mr. Henry Thelander
Loos Archives, Vienna, Dr. Bösel
Design Ingo Maurer GmbH, Munich, Mrs. Jenny Lau
Memphis Milano, Milan
Galerie Metropol, Vienna, New York
Metropolitan Museum of Art, New York, Mrs. Mary F. Doherty
Mobilia Nuremberg, Mr. Joachim Warm
Musée d'Art Moderne de la Ville de Paris, Paris, Madame Jac-
    queline Lafargue
Musée de l'Ecole de Nancy, Nancy
Musée Horta, Brussels, Madame Françoise Dierkens-Aubry
Museum für Kunst und Gewerbe, Hamburg, Dr. Rüdiger Joppien
Museum für Kunsthandwerk, Frankfurt am Main, Dr. Hildegard
    Hoos
Museum für Zeppelingeschichte, Friedrichshafen, Mr. Heinz Urban
Museum Bellerive, Zürich, Mrs. Heidi Kühnel
Museum of Modern Art, New York, Mr. Richard L. Tooke

Mr. Eckart Muthesius, Berlin
The National Trust for Scotland, Glasgow, Mr. Findlay McQuarrie
Die Neue Sammlung, Munich, Dr. Hans Wichmann
Nordenfjeldske Kunstindustrimuseum, Trondheim
Österreichisches Museum für angewandte Kunst (Austrian Museum
    of Applied Arts), Vienna
Österreichische Nationalbibliothek (Austrian National Library),
    Vienna
Thomas Pedersen and Poul Pedersen, Arhus
Pentagon, Cologne, Mrs. Sabine Voggenreiter
Prestel-Verlag, Munich, Mr. Peter Stephan
Rudolf Rasmussens Snedkerier, Copenhagen
Prof. Dieter Rams, Kronberg im Taunus, Mrs. Rose-Anne Fryda
Rat für Formgebung (Design Council), Frankfurt, Mrs. Asmoneit
Mr. Bill Rothschild, New York
Galerie Rotor, Amsterdam, Mr. Johannes Teutenberg
Royal Commission on the Ancient and Historical Monuments of
    Scotland, Edinburgh, Miss McGaw
Werner Schmitz Collectionen GmbH, Düsseldorf
de Sede of Switzerland, Klingnau
Smithsonian Institution, Freer Gallery of Art, Washington D.C.
Sonnabend Gallery, New York, Mr. Lawrence Beck
Sotheby's, Dept. for Applied Arts, London, Mrs. Lucy Dexter
Stadtmuseum, Munich, Dr. Hans Ottomayer
Stedelijk Museum, Amsterdam, Mrs. Daalder-Vos
Studio 65, Turin, Mr. Franco Audrito
Mr. Paul Swiridoff, Schwäbisch Hall
Syndikat, Bonn, Mr. George Hoitz
Walter Dorwin, Teague Associates, New York, Mrs. Aileen Gaughan
Tecno spa Deutschland GmbH, Munich, Mrs. Cattanes
Tecta, Lauenförde, Mr. Axel Bruchhäuser
Tecnolumen Walter Schnepel GmbH, Bremen
Tennessee Valley Authority, Knoxville TN, Mr. William S. Lee
Gebr. Thonet GmbH, Frankenberg, Mrs. Jutta Sachsenröder
Triennale di Milano, Milan, Dr. Ferrucio Dilda
Union des Arts Décoratifs, Paris, Madame Sonia Edard
USM Haller U. Schärer Söhne GmbH, Bühl/Baden, Mrs. Jutta
    Breinling
Vereinigte Werkstätten, Munich
Victoria and Albert Museum, London
Vitra GmbH, Weil am Rhein, Mrs. Martina Arnegger
Westfälisches Landesmuseum für Kunst und Kulturgeschichte,
    Münster, Mrs. Waltraud von Kries
Wilde & Spieth, Esslingen
Monsieur L. Wittamer de Camps, Brussels
WK-Gesellschaft für Wohngestaltung mbH, Leinfelden-Echter-
    dingen
Zanotta spa, Nova Milanese, Mrs. Patrizia Scarzella
Mrs. Ingeborg von Zitzewitz, New York

7

The Crystal Palace at the Great Exhibition in London, 1851

PROLOGUE

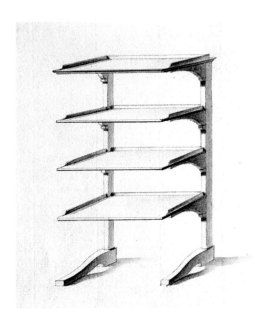

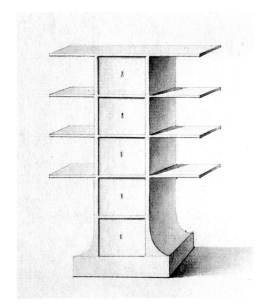

Josef Danhauser, sketches for a set of shelves and a chiffonier (right), Vienna, around 1820. Josef Danhauser ran a furniture factory in Vienna, which already employed 130 workers by 1808. He designed all the furniture produced in his workshops himself.
Österreichisches Museum für angewandte Kunst, Vienna

Gottlieb August Pohle, school drawing for an adjustable writing stand, Vienna 1806.
Österreichisches Museum für angewandte Kunst, Vienna

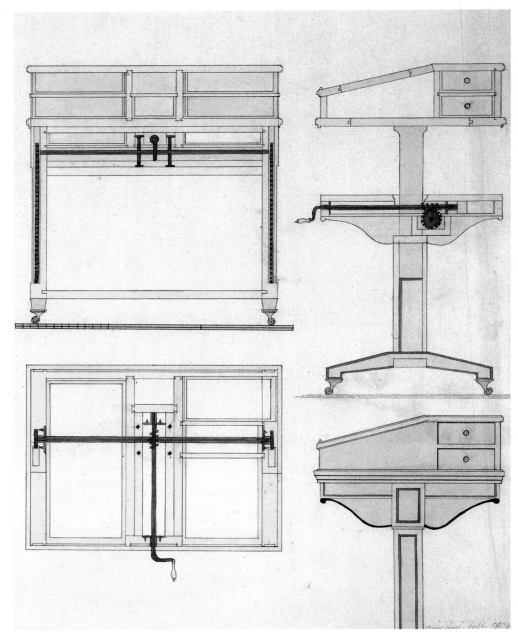

A history of twentieth-century design will repeatedly find itself recognising traditions and identifying revivals, reeditions, and new discoveries, which are based on models dating far back into the nineteenth century. One cannot avoid realising that many designs which we are tempted to regard as 'original' today were actually anticipated to some extent during the nineteenth century. There seem to be two main factors which had a determining influence: firstly, the simple designs of the Biedermeier period or related movements in other countries, and secondly, the effects of industrialisation on our sense of style and on the use of materials. Whereas the progressive furniture designs typical especially of the Viennese Biedermeier style were soon forgotten and only rediscovered around 1900, the concept of industrial production increasingly came to influence development. It is a well-known fact that the mechanization which accompanied it was carefully concealed behind a pseudo-historical exterior. This undoubtedly detracted from the admirable ingenuity which was a characteristic of the nineteenth century. But then again, not everything which was thought up was actually of any use.

Unknown designer. Walnut chair with seat of webbed fabric, about 1825. A well-thought-out piece in every respect, extremely economical in its design. The number of components is kept to an absolute minimum. This type of chair has repeatedly served as a model for durable, traditional everyday furniture.
Bundesimmobilienverwaltung, Vienna

The stately rooms of aristocratic society before 1800 were, for the most part, empty rooms. Tables were only moved into the centre when required, and removed and sometimes even dismantled afterwards. The middle classes showed little interest in adopting the aristocratic style of interior decoration. Indeed, it would rarely have been possible for them to do so. The middle-class lifestyle moved away from the aristocratic model and first received a name of its own in the Biedermeier period. At the beginning of the nineteenth century, middle-class style was characterised by its straightforward practicality rather than by the desire to display wealth. These were poor times, but, as is so often the case, something new was born of necessity. People dispensed with ornamentation to a large extent or were forced by the pressure of circumstances to do without it. The prevailing trend in furniture was to have smooth wooden surfaces, with an attractive, highly-polished finish. The veneer was often inlaid in symmetrical patterns. The overt simplicity of the form was not a result of mass production, but born of sheer craftmanship. However, with the rise of the middle classes, the laws of the industrial society began to take effect.

Unknown designer. Rocking chair with an iron frame and red velvet covers (covers renewed), England, probably 1851. It is uncertain whether the chair was actually presented as early as 1851, or 11 years later at the next World Fair in London. Die Neue Sammlung, Munich

Competition became important not only between firms, but also between the buyers of furniture. The desire to keep up with other people's ostentatious display of wealth led to the rise of the art of "artistic" cabinet making. It came to be considered tasteful to emulate historical designs. Biedermeier furniture disappeared almost without trace. In 1904, the Viennese magazine *Hohe Warte* wrote in an article entitled "The educative properties of Biedermeier": "Museums dedicated to art history considered themselves above collecting this sort of thing and showing the lifestyle of our grandparents". The title of the essay shows that, at the beginning of this century, in the course of the various reform movements – Art Nouveau was only one – people were rediscovering simpler forms. But there could be no repetition of the original circumstances. The Biedermeier style went along with socio-political changes, whereas the reform movement at the turn of the century was a purely aesthetic one. Only a rich minority could afford to buy from the cabinet makers who worked in the "modern style", and so, in spite of great expectations, this line of development was cut short.

The honesty of the Biedermeier style and its preference for simple forms had all but vanished by 1835. Yet purist tendencies lived on. Although it no longer had any decisive influence, the basic trend of the nineteenth century could not be suppressed to the extent that functional furniture disappeared completely. One example is the iron rocking chair which was probably presented as early as the Great Exhibition in London in 1851. It was a highly economically designed piece of furniture, and contrasted strongly with the highly ornamented exhibits surrounding it. Its material put it into the category of "technical" furniture, related to the new iron architecture, which was used in various competing World Fairs.

The aim of these spectacular and surprisingly frequent World Fairs was to bring the conflicting trends of the age together for display under one roof. This made the differences particularly obvious. In 1851, for instance, the amazing glass structure of the Crystal Palace, where the exhibition was held, was in stark contrast to most of the products exhibited inside it. Arts and crafts products – including furniture – were smothered in a profusion of ornamentation, borrowed from every conceivable stylistic era. Many visitors suddenly became aware of this, in the midst of the vast display. This was just what Henry Cole had intended when he organised the Great Exhibition with the support of Prince

Michael Thonet, chair model No. 14, first shown 1859. At the Great Exhibition in London in 1851, Michael Thonet exhibited luxury furniture. In 1862, he first presented his "cheap consumer items". The furniture was produced in his factory in Koritschan in Moravia, mostly with machines he designed himself. Wooden rods, mostly of copper-beech, were made pliable by steam treatment. In the initial stages, the side of the wood which was stretched often split. Thonet avoided this with a new, improved method. The rod was attached to a sheet metal strip during the bending process. This meant that the material was only compressed, and excessive tension avoided. Gebrüder Thonet GmbH, Frankenberg

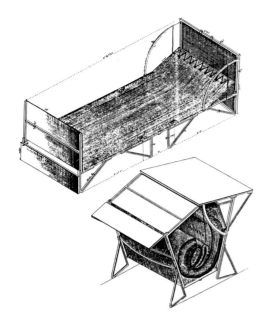

Albert and the Society of Arts. The high aesthetic standard set by Joseph Paxton's Crystal Palace demonstrated the tremendous creative powers which lay dormant beneath the surface of contemporary taste.

At that time, Owen Jones was in charge of the colour scheme for the exhibition building. He worked mainly with the primary colours, red, yellow and blue, which were thought to have particular spatial effects. The German architect Gottfried Semper played a major role in these considerations. He was in England at the time and participated in the project. Later, Semper's writings came to form a direct bridge to the German Arts and Crafts movement, which developed around 1900. But in the middle of the nineteenth century, there was still no chance of any lasting reform. In the years that followed, design in the modern sense of the word only occurred where the engineer had a decisive influence, for instance in fitting out railway carriages, hospitals or offices.

In this sector, America, the country of the pioneers, went into the lead. By about 1880, a wide variety of technical furniture had already appeared there. But the Europeans were not attracted to the ingenious swivel chairs, reclining

Unknown designer, drawing of a folding bed for the cells in Prussian prisons, around 1870.

chairs and convertible furniture which the Americans displayed at the World Exhibition in Philadelphia in 1876. Nevertheless, it was a French reporter who coined the term "Pullman Car Style", which was an extremely apt name. The railway carriage interior came to be the only continuous line of development for a type of furnishing which was at the same time mechanically excellent and comfortable. From then on, technical furniture only appeared in Europe where a particular function made it absolutely essential.

One exception was the bentwood furniture made by the Austrian Thonet company. It was progressive in every respect: simple in form, and cheap, thanks to a special production method. In a way, its unpretentious design represented a continuation of the Biedermeier style. But it did not try to conceal the fact that it was a product of the machine age. This type of furniture proved that industrial production techniques could manufacture furniture which did not date.

The cabinet maker Michael Thonet started out with a small workshop in the Rhineland. New opportunities opened up for him in Vienna, when he was given an order for the Palais Liechtenstein. Thonet's patron, Prince Metternich, per-

Unknown designer, doctor's armchair (left), which could effortlessly be converted into a chair for examination (right), Berlin, second half of the 19th century. The manufacturer of the chair was probably the Medizinisch-Polytechnische Union GmbH.

James Abbott McNeil Whistler, and the architect Jeckyll, the "peacock room", Princes Gate, England, 1887.
Jeckyll planned the room as a dining room. Narrow shelves along the walls were to allow the master of the house, Mr. Frederick Richard Leyland, to display his large collection of oriental porcelain. The wall which formed the background to these fittings was covered with expensive Spanish leather. One of Whistler's paintings was to be displayed in the same room. He found the leather too dark and suggested adding a few spots of colour. When Leyland agreed, Whistler began to brighten up the wall-covering with gold and blue and eventually painted the whole room. The architect is said to have gone mad when he saw the results of Whistler's work. The story says Whistler just shrugged his shoulders and said: "Yes, that's the effect I have on people". Freer Gallery of Art, Smithsonian Institution, Washington, D.C.

suaded him to move to Vienna. The reason for his interest was that Thonet had developed a process which made it possible to bend wood by steam treatment. In 1842, he was granted the privilege of being allowed to "shape and curve any type of wood – even the most brittle varieties – with his chemical and mechanical methods". But Michael Thonet was famous not only for his bentwood furniture, but also for his exquisite inlay work. One example was the round table which he exhibited in London in 1851. In 1856 he opened a large industrial factory, in which his chairs were machine-produced at such low costs that they could be widely distributed. In 1859, the famous Chair type No. 14 was developed. By 1910, fifty million of them had been manufactured. The company continued to grow even after Michael Thonet's death in 1871. Around 1900, 6000 workers were producing 4000 pieces of furniture per day. The basic principle was that the chairs had to consist of as few separate components as possible. These were then joined together with screws, which could be tightened up at any time.

But cheap consumer furniture, such as that produced by Thonet's production-line, or the Shakers' exemplary creations, were not able to oust prestigious historical furniture. There was still a strong preference for imitations of earlier styles, which industry had little difficulty in producing. All sorts of cheap substitutes were used to imitate expensive craftmanship. In 1900, the Darmstadt magazine *Innen-Dekoration* wrote: "Whereas the pieces produced to meet the demands of the rich were usually technically satisfactory, even if they left much to be desired from an artistic point of view and lacked creativity, furniture made for those who were not so well-off was terrible in every respect. The Biedermeier period, which was despised as a poor era, was artistically excellent, by comparison!..."

But the market for historical models had more to offer than the repertoire of outmoded European styles. A major discovery was Japan. Once more it was an exhibition which sparked off a fashion. In 1867, there was a Major Paris exhibition of the decorative art of Japan. It rapidly attracted the interest of numerous collectors, and the "Japanese cabinet" became a new feature of the luxurious home. The combination of simplicity and aesthetic sophistication was irresistible, and made people more critical of the prevailing jumble of styles.

The size of Japanese houses was determined by floor mats, which each measured 91 by 182 cm. These formed the basis for the ground-plan, which was put together like a sort of grid. The actual furnishings were planned down to the smallest detail, even from the point of view of hygiene. Anything that was superfluous was left out. The rest was light and could be carried around without any difficulty. Edward William Godwin and the American painter, James Abbott McNeill Whistler, were extremely successful in integrating elements of Japanese aesthetics into interior design to suit European requirements. Godwin's "artistic furniture", which was marketed by the factory owner William Wyatt, inspired numerous imitations. The first signs of an aesthetic reformation are undoubtedly to be discerned here.

Edward William Godwin, cabinet of black stained wood, Japanese vellum on the cupboard doors, England, around 1875. Godwin's frequently imitated furniture was first presented in 1877 in a catalogue by the factory-owner William Wyatt. Some of the pieces were designed much earlier. Victoria and Albert Museum, London

Furniture by the Shakers, mahogany rocking chair
and chair with black and white woven fabric
seats, New Lebanon, New York, around 1890
(top). Side table of dark stained pine, Hancock
Massachusetts, around 1860 and sewing box of
polished maple wood, Canterbury, New
Hampshire, around 1890 (bottom).
The Shaker Museum, Sabbathday Lake, Maine;
Shaker Community, Hancock, Massachusetts; The
Shaker Museum, Old Chatham, New York

The Shaker furniture can be seen as an individual
contribution to the history of modern furniture.
The Shakers were a religious community formed
in the United States towards the end of the
eighteenth century. They got their name from the
dances which were part of their services. In their
isolated and for the most part self-sufficient
communities, the Shakers emulated the model of
the early Christians, with common property, and
acknowledged the equality and freedom of all
men. One of their rules was celibacy. They
survived by taking in new members from outside.
As far as possible, they created all the objects
they needed themselves. Their requirements here
were as strict as in their religious life. The
Shakers' products – furniture, textiles, as well as
tools and machines – were characterised by their
high quality and formal austerity. The design of
the objects changed little, but, to meet the only
valid requirements – usefulness and durability –
they were continually improved and more or less
standardised. A typical example of the Shakers'
practical attitude was to be seen in a feature of
their homes: a horizontal board running round the
room, with hooks at regular intervals, where
clothes and tools could be hung up, and even the
chairs when the room was being cleaned.
Shaker furniture was sold all over the USA and
was widely used. The community was also open to
new ideas. When they displayed their goods at
the World Fair in Philadelphia in 1876, they found
out about Michael Thonet's bentwood method
and started to produce chairs using this
technique.

The English Arts and Crafts movement emerged in parallel to this development. It derived from the idealistic theories of John Ruskin. He regarded industrial production as the main enemy of proper design, and aimed at a return to craftmanship. Under his influence, William Morris then tried to put the idea of a new harmony based on the unity of art, craftmanship and society into practice. He was inspired to do this while building his own house. After finding a satisfactory form for the ground plan and exterior with the architect Philip Webb, he decided that none of the furniture available on the market was suitable, and so he and his friends made new designs for everything. Their joint work led to the formation of the first group of artist-craftsmen of its kind. They produced all sorts of utility goods, especially materials and wallpaper, of the highest possible standard, but also at high prices. Numerous other workshops followed, for instance those of Arthur Heygate Mackmurdo and Charles Robert Ashbee. In 1888 the numerous groups joined together to form the Arts and Crafts Exhibition Society. The Society's exhibitions also had a strong effect on the continent. Surprisingly, there, it was commercial enterprises like those of J. Littauer and L. Bernheimer in Munich which were the first to sell the new English furniture, even before the new German Arts and Crafts periodicals turned to the topic. These were based on the English journal *The Studio*, which was sold in Germany from 1893. It soon had 20,000 subscribers, which shows that British interior design had aroused great public attention. In Germany, Hermann Muthesius helped to spread the idea behind the British house. He studied contemporary British attitudes to housing design while he was an attache at the German Embassy there from 1896 until 1903. In his book *Das Englische Haus*, published in 1904, he commended the fact that "purely practical requirements always come first. An Englishman builds his house just for himself. He does not build it for prestige, just as he would never think of trying to impress people by the interior or the exterior of his house."

But apparently this concentration on good sense and simplicity was not enough to bring about radical change. That could not happen without an obvious aesthetic signal. For that reason, the new markedly artistic powers which were making themselves felt everywhere at the end of the century were, in a way, revolutionary. At least they had a strong liberating effect, and provided the signal people had been waiting for. The most imaginative steps towards overcoming the prevailing pluralism of styles actually happened in Belgium, a country which was particularly historicist in character. The architect and cabinet maker Gustave Serrurier-Bovy opened a shop in Liège in 1890, and sold not only William Morris's wallpaper and fabric, but also furniture from his own workshop.

In 1895, Henry van de Velde, who had worked mostly as a painter until that date, turned his attention to interior decorating. For his own house Bloemenwerf in Uccle near Brussels he designed chairs which already contained all the essential elements of his later designs: the emphasis on a functional structure, the elegant sweep of the main lines and the balanced composition of contrasting elements. On the one hand, they are still related to the furniture of the Shakers. On the other, they point forward to – and even beyond – the short but intense Art Nouveau period which was to develop from these origins.

Henry van de Velde, oak dining-room chair for the Bloemenwerf house in Uccle, near Brussels, 1895.
Museum Bellerive, Zürich

Entrance to the World Fair in Paris, 1900

ACT I

A NEW YEAR'S EVE CELEBRATION

THE CAST:

LEOPOLD BAUER
PETER BEHRENS
CARLO BUGATTI
EUGENE GAILLARD
ANTONI GAUDI
HECTOR GUIMARD
GEORGES HOENTSCHEL
JOSEF HOFFMANN
VICTOR HORTA
CHARLES RENNIE MACKINTOSH
JOSEPH MARIA OLBRICH
BERNHARD PANKOK
CHARLES PLUMET
RICHARD RIEMERSCHMID
TONY SELMERSHEIM
HENRY VAN DE VELDE

Victor Horta, the entrance hall of the Hôtel Tassel in Brussels, 1893.

The new awakening at the end of the nineteenth century was an artistic event which took place against the background of a capitalistic economic system, and which was subject to its conditions. The fact that Art Nouveau developed mostly in architecture and in arts and crafts demonstrates the commercial emphasis of the whole movement. The new style of art stimulated business. Everyone seemed to benefit from it: young artists, who felt they were being appreciated, the dealers who profited from them, manufacturers, who could execute their expensive designs, the public, which had a stimulating form of entertainment, and politicians, who could watch the national competition between avant-garde styles. For a while, even the advocates of a reformed lifestyle, whatever their philosophy, could rejoice. But their hopes of social change were dashed because of the prevailing production conditions and the emphasis on purely commercial considerations. Nevertheless, the century of bold engineers and capitalistic speculators, the century of grand opera, the great novel, the railway and the elevator ended ceremoniously, with a huge fireworks display, which at first appeared to represent a new beginning, but which later actually turned out to be a splendid close rather than a new start.

As mentioned above, business interests had a decisive influence on art. Belgium is a good example. During the last third of the nineteenth century, the country's economy was influenced to a large extent by foreign trade, both with its colonies and with North America. Industry was already highly developed at an early stage, and one of the export articles was prefabricated metal houses, which were delivered to the United States. Another important sector was the glass industry. From about 1870 onwards, there was an increase in the production of high-quality mirrors. These developments influenced architecture: numerous buildings were constructed of glass and iron. But social conventions stood in the way of any radical changes to the face of the city. An attempt to redesign Brussels along the lines used by Haussmann in Paris was unsuccessful. The middle classes in Brussels were simply not prepared to move into flats. Large multi-storey buildings did not become popular, as they did in other large European cities. Narrow town houses continued to be typical. The owners were often relatively young men, who had made their fortunes from the colonies, but were still keen on socialist ideas. They commissioned houses from friends of their own age who were architects, including Victor Horta. The socialist party, which was becoming increasingly influential, was also attracted to the revolutionary forms of Art Nouveau. This is demonstrated in a building of virtually programmatic importance, the Maison du Peuple. Henry van de Velde was also involved in this project. He was commissioned to provide the Party with graphic designs. The architecture of the new buildings was completely different from tradition, but since the façades were often no wider than six metres, the effect was not always very obvious from the outside. The long, narrow building plots made it necessary to have inside staircases with glass domes at the top. Victor Horta was particularly imaginative in making the best of this situation. The connecting rooms had high glass walls, or moveable partitions, which opened on the central hall, creating a strikingly bright effect. There was also a social aspect to this design. It suited the occupants' desire not so much to demonstrate wealth to the outside as to turn every building into a little theatre in its own right. Slim steel pillars also helped to create airy interiors, which demonstrated the cosmopolitan attitude of the builders, in spite of the small building areas.

In autumn 1893, those who went to adult evening classes in Antwerp could attend a series of lectures on the development of English arts and crafts. They heard a "Sermon to Youth", which the lecturer – Henry van de Velde – illustrated

Henry van de Velde, study at the Munich Secession Exhibition, 1899. The complete furnishings for this room, which contained a cabinet for prints, a filing cabinet and a screen as well as the furniture in the picture, was offered for 3,400 Marks at the time.

with fabrics and wallpapers by English masters. His wife Maria had bought them in London. The same year, van de Velde began to design his first furniture and to build a house of his own. At this time, he was visited by the Paris art dealer Samuel Bing and the German publicist Julius Meier-Graefe. Bing was searching for new talents for his Paris Gallery "L'Art Nouveau", and he was very impressed by what he saw in van de Velde's flat. He commissioned him to design four exhibition rooms. But when the gallery in the Rue de Provence was opened in 1895, the reaction from Paris critics was extremely negative. Bing was fortunate enough to be able to pass the furnishings on to the 1897 Dresden Arts and Crafts Exhibition. They were extremely successful there, and the path was clear for van de Velde to work in Germany. He soon developed his own style with the designs which followed. Henry van de Velde succeeded in designing some basic shapes for armchairs, chairs and tables, which he could re-use, or use with only minor variations, for similar orders. This was the case for instance with an armchair he developed in 1897. In the following year, he created a large desk for Julius Meier-Graefe, which was also exhibited – with slight changes – at the 1899 Munich Secession exhibition. Henry van de Velde successfully made the transition from private work to wider renown with two commissions in Berlin, where he had settled in 1900. The interior of the Continental Havana Compagnie's cigar shop and Haby's hairdressing salon were considered to be a sensation. Their creator, encouraged by his success, made an eloquent appearance in Germany and behaved a little like a Messiah. He believed he had found a new style – which is probably true – although the rational basis which he claimed for this corresponded more to his individual view than to consistent logic. From the very beginning, van de Velde had been concerned to provide a theoretical foundation for his work. For that reason, he not only designed a lot, but also wrote a lot. This gave him an unusual position amongst his contemporaries. He longed for a "rational" type of design which could exist without the arbitrariness of stylistic forms. The clear contrast between this and his designs resulted from the creative enthusiasm with which he strove to express his wisdom.

When the French President, Emile Loubet, opened the World Fair in Paris on April 14th, 1900, there were many disappointed faces. The fact that most of the pavilions were not completed was nothing unusual. But the event lacked any sort of common theme, linking the contributions from the various countries to one

Henry van de Velde, wallpaper design, 1899, in "Dekorative Kunst", III, 1899.

Henry van de Velde, comfortable padouk armchair with batik covers by the Dutch painter Jan Thorn-Prikker. The structural elements re-appear on the covers. It was first exhibited in the gallery "La Maison Moderne" in Paris. Nordenfjeldske Kunstindustrimuseum, Trondheim

Georges Hoentschel, "Salon des Eglantiers" in the decorative art pavilion at the World Fair in 1900. The theme of the room, which is varied throughout – on the mahogany chairs, tables and cabinets – is the wild rose motif, which gave the room its name. The painting on the wall is "L'Ile Heureuse" by Albert Besnard. In the adjoining hallway, partially visible in the background, there is a music cupboard by Alexandre Charpentier. Musée des Arts Décoratifs, Paris

single idea. From an architectural point of view, there was also little of interest, apart from the Métro, with Hector Guimard's imaginatively created entrance areas, which showed a successful combination of new technology and modern design. It prepared the guests for what was awaiting them in many of the exhibition rooms: the great entrance of Art Nouveau. Unfortunately the Belgians Victor Horta and Henry van de Velde were not able to attend. Rumour had it that they had not received any official support like that provided for the German participants. The French also had to appear without any subsidies, but Bing had gone to some lengths to set up his own small pavilion. Whereas in 1895 he had been brave enough to display Gallé glasses, Tiffany lamps and paintings and statues by Bonnard, Pissarro, Seurat, Toulouse-Lautrec, Beardsley and others in a room designed by a foreigner, this time he chose to present only interiors designed by French artist craftsmen: an entrance hall, dining room and bedroom by Eugène Gaillard, a parlour by Edouard Colonna, and a boudoir by Georges de Feure. While de Feure and Colonna remained fairly traditional, Gaillard displayed the élan of the new style in his room. His chairs were well-proportioned, which could not really be said of the matching cupboard. He failed in the attempt to provide an attractive design for such a large, box-shaped piece of furniture, in spite of prolific ornamentation. The room, with its opulent wall-paintings by the Spanish painter José-Maria Sert, had such a striking effect that the cupboard was lost in it. Gaillard's design was intended

Charles Plumet and Tony Selmersheim, dressing table, shown at the Paris World Fair in 1900. The exquisite furniture exhibited was bought firstly by well-off industrialists, such as Baron von Thyssen, who, for example, purchased a bathroom for his Landsberg estate, and secondly, the large European museums. For his museum in Hamburg, Justus Brinckmann ordered part of Hoentschel's room, some pieces by Eugène Colonna exhibited in Bing's salon, vases by Emile Gallé and presumably also this dressing table by Plumet and Selmersheim.
Museum für Kunst und Gewerbe, Hamburg

for a room with full-length windows instead of wall-paintings, which would have avoided the gloomy atmosphere. This situation tended to be typical of conditions at major exhibitions. The designer's concepts of intimate rooms were sacrificed in the interests of an excessive display of effects.

Meier-Graefe, who had opened his own gallery called "La Maison Moderne" in Paris in 1899, with similar intentions to those of Bing, did not display anything at the exhibition, but criticised the presentation of his acquaintance, Bing. He felt that the rooms exhibited were "almost too exquisite to use, apart from the fact that the number of people fortunate enough to be able to afford such extraordinary luxury was limited, even in France". He wondered "whether the path along which modern furniture is being sought here is not the wrong path". As an alternative, he valued the strong creative masculine hand in the work of Louis Majorelle, who represented the Nancy school, and was attracted to the comparatively restrained designs of Charles Plumet and Tony Selmersheim, because of their "solid simplicity". The works displayed firmly established France's reputation as a home of high-quality furniture design. As furniture designers were now daring enough to introduce bold, sweeping lines in their wooden furniture, it was not surprising that the bentwood furniture produced by the Austrian firms, Thonet and Kohn, attracted a lot of interest. Suddenly, the technique of bending wood turned out to be ideal for the new designs, and it seems surprising that it was rarely taken up outside of Austria.

Eugène Gaillard, dining room with wall-paintings by José-Maria Sert in the "L'Art Nouveau" pavilion, shown at the Paris World Fair, illustration from "The Studio", 1900.

Eugène Gaillard, dining-room chair made of polished walnut. Chair back of embossed leather, Paris, 1900. It was placed in the dining room of Bing's pavilion.
Museum für Kunsthandwerk, Frankfurt am Main

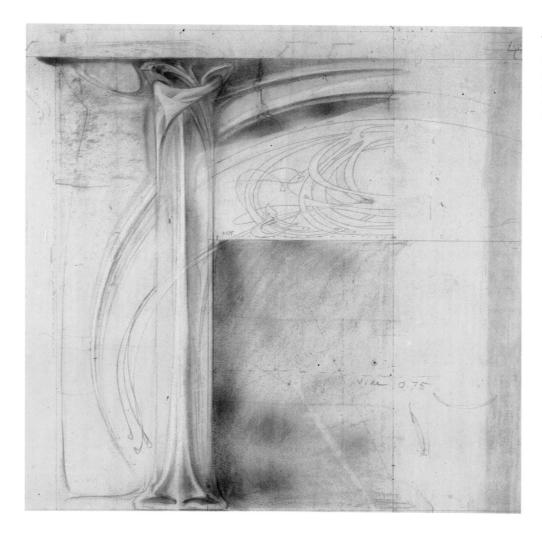

Hector Guimard, sketch for a fireplace for the Maison Coilliot in Lille, around 1903. The sinewy shape of the pillar and the sweep of the arch are reminiscent of the entrances to the Paris Métro, which Guimard designed at the turn of the century.
Musée des Arts Décoratifs, Paris

This evidence suggests that Art Nouveau was really a form of fashionable decoration rather than a true form of modern furniture design.

Austria's official contribution to the Paris exhibition was much more promising. It was presented as the Secessionist Style and involved an impressive combination of gracefulness and austerity. Josef Hoffmann's clearly ordered geometrical dining room furniture was a convincing advance on his earlier designs, which were still very close to the more rural "Brettel" style. Motifs of rectangles ans squares, which he often used later, appeared here in the cut glass windows of a heavy sideboard. The room had a prestigious touch, but it was in the style of the enlightened middle classes rather than aristocratic, and did not exclude playful elements.

In the main salon of the Austrian section, Joseph Maria Olbrich presented the "Salon for a Luxury Yacht". No expenses were spared. The materials included expensive types of wood, gold, silver, ivory, mother-of-pearl and silk. The room also had angled skylights in the ceiling, which made it very bright. Joseph Maria Olbrich's work was also to be seen in the German section. Like Henry van de Velde, he was one of the artistic immigrants, drawn to Germany by liberal circles. This was not the result of unselfish patronage. It was rather a question of prestige and promoting the economy. This made it possible for Olbrich, who had participated in the major transport and Danube canal projects as the assistant of Otto Wagner, to develop further in the artists' colony in Darmstadt. His "Darmstadt room" in Paris demonstrated how modern furniture could be designed at reasonable prices.

Further on in the German section, in "a dark corner", were the rooms of the artists in the Munich United Workshops for Artist Craftmanship. The group was formed for an exhibition in the Munich Glass Palace, and created its own company in 1898. The first members were Hermann Obrist and F. A. O. Krüger, as well as Richard Riemerschmid, Bernhard Pankok, Theo Schmuz-Baudiss and Bruno Paul. In the initial stages, the programme was to buy designs from young artists and pass them on to efficient craftsmen. Later, for financial reasons, the group opened its own factory. It was a great honour for this group to be invited to Paris by the Exhibition committee. It showed a growing understanding for the new artistic forces in Germany.

Riemerschmid was responsible for the overall organisation of the three rooms alloted to the Munich group. He himself designed the "room for an art lover", which had a particularly striking guilloche frieze. For the entrance to the room with the bay-window, Riemerschmid painted a sopraporte on the subject "the path of life". Unfortunately, the effect of the room was spoiled to a large extent by the presence of a bulky seating arrangement by Obrist. The connecting smoking room was designed by Pankok. The tense relation between the various components was reminiscent of a ship's cabin. But the effect of the room was lost, as it was badly lit, and had a dark wooden ceiling and subdued colour scheme. The third room was a hunting room by Bruno Paul. The large number of trophies hanging on the walls distinctly detracted from any impression of modernity.

Joseph Maria Olbrich, Salon for a luxury yacht at the Paris World Fair, 1900. The furniture was made of polished mahogany, stained in a greenish tint, the door-frames were decorated with mother-of-pearl roses and the walls were covered in embroidered silk, illustration from "Innen-Dekoration" XI, 1900.

Josef Hoffmann, dining room, illustrated in
"Innen-Dekoration" XI, 1900. It was first shown at
the 1899 Winter Exhibition in the Austrian Museum
for Art and Industry. At the 1900 World Fair in
Paris, it was again exhibited for the Viennese
Secession in the Palais des Beaux Arts, Avenue
Nicolas II. It was made by Anton Pospischil, who
did a lot of work for Hoffmann.

Josef Hoffmann, mahogany armchair, Vienna,
1899. A variant of the model shown above. The
form creates the impression of tensed muscles, the
shape of the back legs and the light metal feet
suggest a deer, poised to jump.
Galerie Metropol, Vienna, New York

31

Richard Riemerschmid, sketch for his room at the 1900 Paris World Fair, with an unusual guilloche frieze and the "way of life" sopraporte. Architektursammlung der Technischen Hochschule, Munich

Richard Riemerschmid first made a name for himself when he exhibited a music room, commissioned by a piano factory, at the Dresden Art Exhibition in 1899. For this room, he developed two of his best chairs: one with cleverly-designed supports to replace the armrests for the musicians, and one with armrests for the listeners. From the same basic idea, he designed a fabric-covered reclining chair. These unpretentious and logically designed pieces were the main surprise of the exhibition. The pale violet wallpaper and unusual lighting construction, in which the cables were also part of the decoration, helped to make the room appear unusually cool to Riemerschmid's contemporaries. At the same time, Riemerschmid was also working on a project which made him famous as an architect: the privately-run Munich theatre, opened in 1901, now known as the Kammerspiele, "the world's first completely modern theatre". Modern was certainly the word fot both the stage and the auditorium, with its three-dimensional design and the absence of chandeliers and gold decorations. At the World Fair in St. Louis in 1904, the German section showed six rooms by Olbrich, entitled "Summer Residence of an Art-Lover", and works by Paul, Behrens, Grenander, Riemerschmid and Pankok. As Pankok's room was designed to demonstrate the efficiency of Stuttgart's industry, those who commissioned it went to great lengths, and the interior of the room was as expensive as a whole house. The wall-covering included complex inlay-work, and the merlon-like top panels were decorated with the carved heads of animals. The door mounts were made of silver, the music cupboard was or-

Richard Riemerschmid, sketch for an armchair. It formed part of a music salon, which Riemerschmid showed at the Dresden Art Exhibition in 1899. Architektursammlung der Technischen Hochschule, Munich

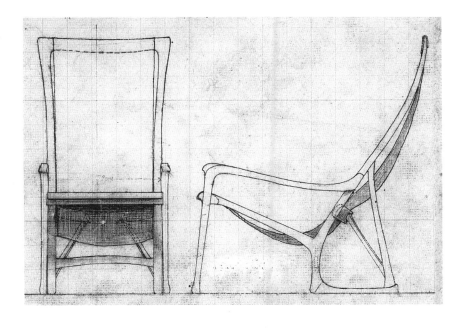

Richard Riemerschmid, oak music-room chair, also designed in 1899 for the Dresden Exhibition. Riemerschmid made the chair without arms to allow the musicians more freedom of movement. Instead, he used diagonal supports, which elegantly flow into the slant of the chair back. The design is unpretentious, nothing seems to be superfluous, all the details are constructively motivated. The chair was often declared to be the most successful German "Jugendstil" chair. Museum of Modern Art, New York

Richard Riemerschmid, music salon at the Dresden Art Exhibition, 1899. Looking from the musicians' podium to the window wall, illustration from "Dekorative Kunst" IV, 1899.

33

Bernhard Pankok, room commissioned by the Württemberg Commerce Association for the World Fair in St Louis, 1904. Afterwards, it was reconstructed at the Landesgewerbeanstalt in Stuttgart. It was later destroyed in an air raid – except for the grand piano.

namented with ivory reliefs. This collection of exquisite artistic craftwork was completed by a highly ornamental grand piano and coloured glass windows. The abundance of separate bizarre pieces, and especially the profusion of lights hanging from the ceiling, was reminiscent of an aquarium filled with exotic fish. In 1899, Grand Duke Ernst Ludwig of Hesse had invited seven artists to set up an artists' colony in the state capital, Darmstadt. He put the "Mathildenhöhe", a park above the town, at their disposal to experiment with. The colony was not to be a "school", but "a community of freelance artists, some of them mature and successful, others promising new talents…" They included the painter Hans Christiansen from Flensburg, the architect Joseph Maria Olbrich from Vienna, the painter, graphic artist and future architect Peter Behrens from Hamburg, the sculptor Rudolf Bosselt from the Brandenburg March, and the interior designer Patriz Huber from Stuttgart. The age of the first members of the

Bernhard Pankok, wardrobe, oak with cherry wood veneer, 1902, made by the Vereinigte Werkstätten (United Workshops) in Munich. There is a very imaginative relation between the strong, three-dimensional elements of the overall shape and the decorative picture on the panel, which is very successfully integrated by being focused inside a double frame. All the elements seem to complement each other, the wardrobe is like an organic creation. We can discern cloven feet, pointed ears, the contours of a rib cage, lungs and an active phallus.
Westfälisches Landesmuseum für Kunst und Kulturgeschichte, Münster

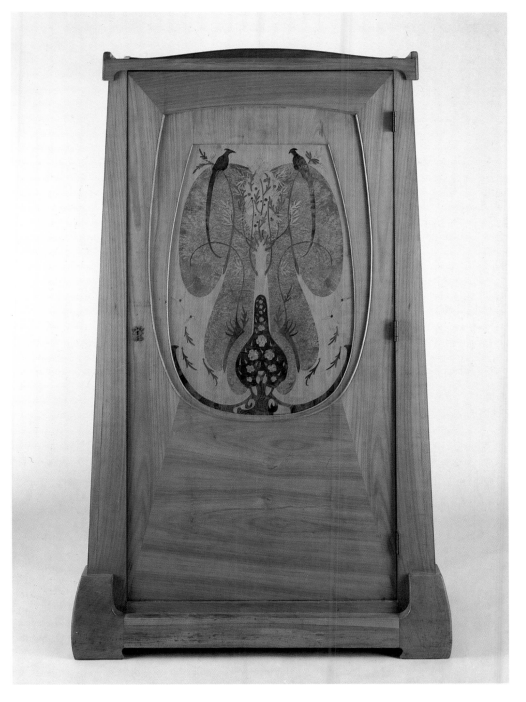

Peter Behrens, the dining room of his own house in Darmstadt, with furniture of white painted poplar, mahogany and ameranth wood, 1901, illustration from "Ein Dokument Deutscher Kunst", exhibition catalogue, 1901.

colony ranged from early twenties to early thirties. Olbrich became their unofficial leader.

From the very beginning, the colony planned an "exhibition of completely furnished houses" as its first joint effort. They stressed not only the "high idealistic value" of the project but also that it would benefit the economy of the town and the surrounding area. The exhibition was opened in 1901 under the ambitious title "A Document of German Art". All the buildings, except Behrens' house, were designed by Olbrich and furnished by the artists in the colony. In 1900, Olbrich wrote: "not a single square centimetre should contain any shape or colour which has not been inspired by the spirit of art".

A visitor to Behrens' house described just what an interior created according to these principles actually looked like: "... the whole chamber is in a sparkling white, intensified by an extremely delicate combination with silver. In a few, rare places, such as the cushions of the chairs, some of the wallpaper and the bases of the stemmed glasses, a contrasting deep, bluish red appears, which highlights the silvery white even further. Apart from this, amidst all the different lines of the ceiling and the crockery cupboards, in the decorations on plates and bowls, on the handles of the knives and spoons, in the crystal glass chandeliers, and even in the woven pattern of the exquisite table linen, in a hundred different places, the eye meets with the same motif, but it is an eternal theme with endless variations".

Next to the dining room was the music room, which had a much loftier effect. One had to go down a few steps to reach it. This individual variation in the height of the rooms also occurred in the upstairs section, where the low library room was next to a higher workroom, which made use of the roof gable. On the whole, Behrens' house was the most remarkable achievement of the exhibition, firstly from an architectural point of view, secondly for the overall artistic design. Behrens designed everything himself, down to the last porcelain plate, and the house was the beginning of his career.

An important role in the debate on room design was played by a competition announced by the Darmstadt journal *Zeitschrift für Innen-Dekoration* in 1900. It called for "individual artistic designs for the stately home of an art-lover", and offered prizes worth 8000 Marks altogether. The advertisment stated: "The only stipulation for the location of the building is that it shall be surrounded by a park. It should contain: Ground floor: a hall with an area of approximately 60 square metres. This should connect to 1 reception room, which also serves as a music room, which can be turned into a house stage for performances by removing or setting up partitions. It should be about 40 square metres, or both rooms together between 64 and 80 square metres; 1 study with a library, about 24

Peter Behrens, hexagonal tureen and large octagonal plate from a dinner service consisting of more than a hundred pieces, for the mayor of Hamburg, Mönckeberg, 1903.
Porcelain factory Weiden Gebr. Bauscher

Joseph Maria Olbrich, bedroom in Olbrich's house in the Darmstadt artists' colony, 1901. The drawing was published by Olbrich himself, as part of an extensive portfolio.

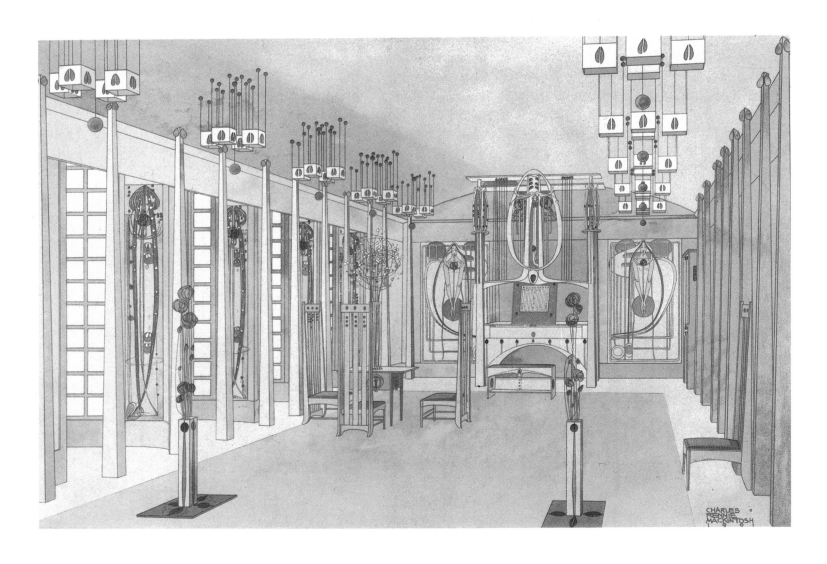

38

square metres; 1 room where the master can display works of art, about 28 square metres; 1 room for the lady, about 24 square metres; 1 breakfast room, about 20 square metres; 1 dining room, about 48 square metres, which can, if possible, be joined to the hall for performances; 1 pantry, 1 servants' room, cloakroom and toilet..." The rooms on the upstairs floor were similarly defined. Instructions were also given for the style of the drawings, the number and format of the sheets of paper, the building materials ("the architectural components, such as cornices, window and door surrounds etc., should be made of sandstone"), and the total costs were stipulated. Without furniture, heating and fittings, the upper limit was to be between 100,000 and 120,000 Marks.

Many prominent people were on the prize committee, but Henry van de Velde and Otto Wagner were unable to attend the decisive meeting. No first prize was awarded. A second prize went to the English architect Mackay Hugh Baillie-Scott. Three third prizes were awarded, including one to the Viennese designer Leopold Bauer. The contribution from the Scots architect, Charles Rennie Mackintosh, which is the most famous today, was purchased but did not receive a prize, as it did not contain the stipulated number of interior perspectives.

The Vienna Secession, which had been formed by a few innovators in 1897, aimed from the very beginning at the unity of all the arts. But it was not until its eighth exhibition in 1900 that it was really successful, with the building constructed by Olbrich. But what was still lacking was an interior design to match the architecture. Too many items remained just individual pieces.

Now, for the first time, the Viennese public was presented with works by Charles Ashbee, Charles Rennie Mackintosh, his wife Margaret Macdonald and the MacNair man-and-wife team. The exhibits by Ashbee and the workshops of the English Arts and Crafts movement were for the most part well-known, but the two couples from Glasgow had something new to offer. The

Drawings from the collection of designs submitted for the "House of an Art Lover" competition, published by Alexander Koch, 1901.

Charles Rennie Mackintosh, reception room and music room (top left)
Charles Rennie Mackintosh, dining room (bottom left)
Mackay Hugh Baillie-Scott, hall (top right)
Leopold Bauer, large dining room (bottom right)

Charles Rennie Mackintosh, modern replica of a high-backed chair, designed in 1897 for the Argyle Street Tea Rooms in Glasgow. The replica by Cassina shown here is made of ash instead of stained oak, but otherwise identical. Like all models for chairs in Italy, it was given a name: Argyle, after its original location.
Cassina, Meda/Milan

Charles Rennie Mackintosh, room design for the eighth Secession Exhibition in Vienna in 1900, with the painting "May Queen" by Margaret Macdonald. Here, Mackintosh presented a version of the "tea room chair" without a cushion.

room was dominated by two large paintings, which covered the upper parts of two opposite walls, above white panelling. The other exhibits were actually individual pieces, which Mackintosh had designed for other occasions. Nevertheless, all the elements combined successfully to form a whole, the much sought-after synthesis of the arts seemed to make a first appearance here in a truly spiritual design. A critic for the journal *Innen-Dekoration* saw the extensive friezes as representing "slim, stylised women", and suggested that their inspiration was to be found not only in the "ghostly realm of shades" but also in Japan.

The room appeared again with variations at the First International Exhibition of Modern Decorative Art in Turin in 1902. There, Mackintosh presented a group of white painted chairs, with unusually high backs, an element which he repeated in many of his chair designs.

Carlo Bugatti could be described as the *enfant terrible* of the Turin exhibition. His appearance was as eccentric as his designs, and his contemporaries had an explanation for this: "It runs in the family." His father, a fireplace manufacturer, had spent his life unsuccessfully – like most of those struck by the same idea – trying to construct a perpetual motion machine. Carlo Bugatti, a student of architecture, shared his fascination for all sorts of construction problems and also created furniture from 1880 onwards. Up to the turn of the century he opted for bold oriental-style designs. His works were decorated with tassels, little columns, latticework and marquetry in unusual combinations of materials such

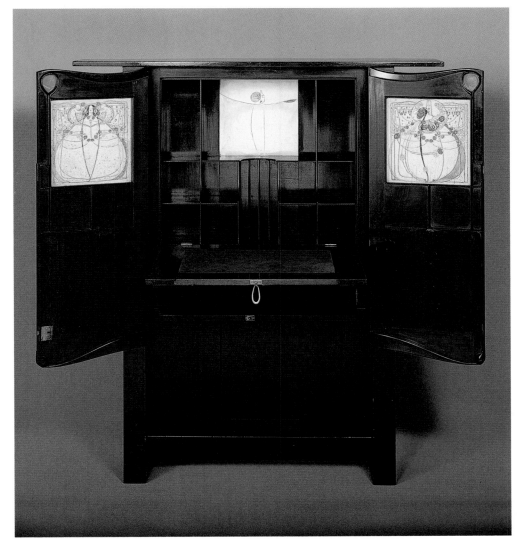

Charles Rennie Mackintosh, "The Rose Boudoir" at the "First International Exhibition of Modern Decorative Art" in Turin, 1902. The rose motif appeared in two paintings by Margaret Macdonald, entitled "The White Rose and the Red Rose" and "Heart of the Rose", on the end walls of the room. It reappeared in the doors of the writing cabinet, and was taken up again in the cloth covers for the white armchairs.
Illustration from the catalogue "The First International Exhibition of Modern Decorative Art in Turin".

Charles Rennie Macintosh, writing cabinet of dark-stained and polished maple wood with panels by Margaret Macdonald, closed (left), and opened (right), 1901. The delicate gesso panels on the outside of the doors are based on the theme of "weeping roses", those on the inside depict female figures with rose-petals: "The Awakened Rose" and "The Dreaming Rose". The back shows "The Spirit of Love", half rose-petal, half woman's face, with teardrops falling. The handles are also shaped like tears. The cabinet was probably made for the Viennese patron Fritz Wärndorfer and displayed at the international Arts and Crafts Exhibition in Turin.
Österreichisches Museum für angewandte Kunst, Vienna.

Carlo Bugatti, lady's desk and chair, shown at the First International Exhibition of Modern Decorative Art in Turin, 1902. Apart from the two discs where the legs cross, the wooden construction is completely covered with copper or parchment.
Alain Lesieutre, Paris

Carlo Bugatti, salon at the 1902 Turin Exhibition. Illustration from the exhibition catalogue.

as copper, wood, parchment, antilope skin and ivory. The surfaces were covered with Asian characters and small paintings. His furniture soon made a name for itself: people made a distinction between "ordinary oriental furniture" and "Bugatti-style". For the manufacture of his designs – which even made their way into the Waldorf-Astoria Hotel in New York in 1893 – Bugatti had his own workshop, where every model was first produced in clay or plaster.

The participants in the 1902 Turin exhibition had to fulfil a certain condition: only whole groups of new creations were to be presented. Bugatti designed four rooms, including the one referred to as the snails' room – a room for games and conversation –, a salon and a bedroom. Here, there were hardly any traces of oriental ornamentation. The designs were dominated by large, somewhat forceful forms, somehow reminiscent of magic charms. It was astonishing that an Italian should produce such "Germanic" objects. Play with small ornamental components had been replaced by elements which only revealed their function at a second glance. A glass cabinet was hidden behind an eye shape. Drawers appeared in unexpected places. A sculpture revealed itself to be a chair. Carlo Bugatti was awarded a "Diploma speciale d'Onore" for his exhibits, an honour which also went to Peter Behrens for his "Hamburg Hall of Power and Beauty" – another atavistic contribution.

It was interesting that with Art Nouveau, areas other than the main artistic centres began to make a name for themselves. This applies to Nancy, Darmstadt, Glasgow and especially of the home of Antoni Gaudí. His work is classified as part of the Catalan *Modernismo*. The background to this extensive cultural movement was the *Renaixensa*, the belief that Catalonia could regain its independence from Spain. Gaudí and those who commissioned him were passionate supporters of Catalan nationalism. One of Gaudí's main works is the Casa Batllo in Barcelona. From a distance, the house looks like a monstrous animal. The roof resembles the arched back. The façade is covered in round "scales" and shimmers in the sun like the skin of a reptile. There are no edges or

Carlo Bugatti, room for games and conversation, known as the "snails' room", at the Turin exhibition in 1902. The name comes from the unusual extension to the sofa. It forms a little cupboard in the shape of a snail's shell. Illustration from the exhibition catalogue.

Carlo Bugatti, two chairs from the "snails' room". These are not exactly the same as the ones exhibited in Turin, Bugatti probably made them later for a customer. Like the small desk, the wooden structure is completely covered in parchment and painted with red and gold insects. The amazing construction of the chairs is absolutely original. The perfection with which the parchment appears to cover the curves without showing any joins is astonishing.
Alain Lesieutre, Paris

Antoni Gaudí, dining room in the Casa Battló, designed for the textiles manufacturer, Josep Battló i Casanovas, in Barcelona, 1906. The chairs designed for the room are sculptures in wood, carved from solid oak.

corners, the whole surface of the wall is slightly waved. To enter the house, the guest first passes pillars, which are not unlike fat, clumsy feet. Inside, the impression that the building is alive and has been grown rather than made is even stronger. On the way to the master's quarters on the first floor, the visitor's hand strokes an oversized backbone – the wooden handrail along the staircase. After this, the dining room does not come as a surprise. The wall gradually joins the ceiling in a subtle arch. The walls appear soft, as if modelled in clay. Nothing is straight. The frames and partitions of the windows, the door frames and panels, everything runs in lightly sweeping curves.

ACT I

SCENE TWO
THE LADY'S ROOM

Bernhard Pankok, armchair for an elegant lady's room, 1900/01, manufactured by the Vereinigte Werstätten (United Workshops) in Munich. The chair, like the cabinet (top right) and the small desk (bottom right) was part of a "Lady's Salon", first exhibited by Bernhard Pankok at the Dresden Arts and Crafts Exhibition in 1901, then again in Turin, 1902.
Galerie Geitel, Berlin

Everything was supposed to be "small, coquettish, delicate and fragile" in ladies' rooms, according to a contemporary guide to matters of interior decoration. "Crystal candlesticks, . . . a dainty marble or bisque clock . . . and, the most important piece of furniture: a desk with the finest inlay work; also delicately designed cabinets for letters, precious trinkets and similar objects."

Bernhard Pankok, marriage room in Dessau, 1900/02, produced by the United Workshops in Munich. In 1900, Bernhard Pankok was commissioned for the interior decor of the new town hall, which had already been built. He tried to match the solemnity of the room's function but also to introduce a cheerful note.

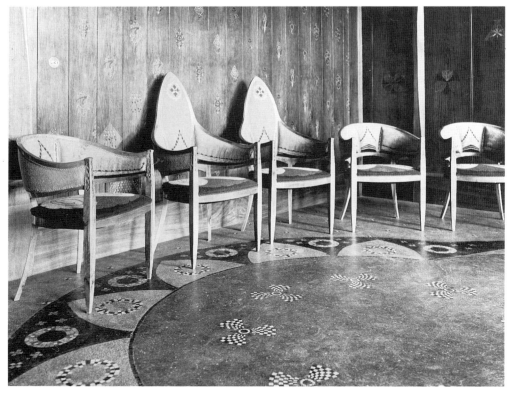

The success of social change increases with the number of areas of human life it affects. At the turn of the century, the feminist movement was beginning to evolve slowly, and to make its first hesitant attacks on male-dominated society. In the better-off circles, attention centred on the ridiculous style of prevailing fashion. Women also created rooms just for themselves, where they could meet without being disturbed by men. In Vienna, for instance, a special womens' club was set up. The interior was designed by Adolf Loos.

The typical rooms designed for women at this time were not an innovation in themselves. But the fact that they were popular locations for modern design makes them significant. The artistic movement met up with a social movement here, but the social position of the women who commissioned the rooms made it clear from the very start that the design would be subject to certain limitations. In a chapter on "Design, lay-out and furniture" in the *Handbook of Architecture* published in Stuttgart in 1902, Karl Weissbach describes the functions to be fulfilled by a lady's room at the turn of the century, and how it should be furnished: "Even in the homes of the upper middle classes, the lady of the house has her own room." Its function is "to provide her with a place where she can embark on some intellectual persuits, such as reading, music or even intricate handicrafts, when she is not occupied with her children, household tasks or social duties ... The furnishings should include a broad sofa, comfortable arm chairs and an elegant writing desk, with a small house library, which should contain not only her favourite authors, but also various other books of value to a housewife and mother. Reminders of her home and her youth should decorate the room, as well as some good works of art". The detailed description here may appear to be just a list of items, but no fact it provides a fairly exact outline of the degree of independence granted to the occupant of a lady's room around 1900.

Whereas architecture was the domain of the master of the house, the lady was allowed to demonstrate her sense of artistic appreciation with regard to the

*Bernhard Pankok, cabinet, 1900/01, produced by the United Workshops in Munich.
Staatliche Museen Preussischer Kulturbesitz, Kunstgewerbemuseum, Berlin (West)*

*Bernhard Pankok, lady's desk, mahogany and cherry wood, 1900/01, manufactured by the United Workshop in Munich.
Galerie Geitel, Berlin*

Joseph Maria Olbrich, design for a tea salon for the International Exhibition of Modern Decorative Art in Turin in 1902, illustrated in "Deutsche Kunst und Dekoration", XI. Olbrich, as the official Hessian delegate, had designed three interiors: the "Hessian" or "Blue Room", which was planned as a display room for Hessian trade and crafts, and a bedroom and a tea salon, furnished with pieces by the Glückert company.
Contemporary critics believed Olbrich's Turin works showed a shift in emphasis from his earlier designs: "The designing artist, Prof. J. M. Olbrich, is obviously attempting to free himself of certain extravagant tendencies and to find a similar language of forms, which allows his versatile gifts to show themselves to better advantage."

interior decoration. Likes and dislikes of particular designers were undoubtedly dependent to some extent on articles in the relevant periodicals. There were plenty which dealt with architecture, interior decoration and arts and crafts, such as *Deutsche Kunst und Dekoration, Dekorative Kunst, Innen-Dekoration, Art et Décoration* or *L'Art Décoratif,* to name just a few of the important ones. Some of them achieved an impressive circulation. The established English periodical *The Studio* was a model for the genre as a whole.

At the beginning of the century, one of *The Studio*'s favourites was undoubtedly Joseph Maria Olbrich from Vienna. In one of the 1904 issues, he was effusively celebrated as "the true leader, the real personification of modern tendencies", and as the "Prince of modern interior designers, the most powerful and productive amongst them".

Similar respect was enjoyed by the companies which manufactured the artistic designs and which demonstrated their perfect craftmanship at the large national and international exhibitions of the day. These included, for instance, the Vereinigte Werkstätten für Kunst im Handwerk (United Workshops for Artistic Craftmanship), which manufactured Riemerschmid's Music room for Dresden in 1899 and the exhibits for the 1900 World Exhibition designed by Riemerschmid, Pankok, Paul and Obrist. Their order books were filled with the famous names of contemporary society. Encouraged by their early successes in Paris and Vienna, Josef Hoffmann and Koloman Moser founded the Vienna

Joseph Maria Olbrich, two views of the library room in the home of the Grand Duke Ernst Ludwig of Hesse in the Old Castle in Giessen, 1906. The Grand Duke appreciated art and was famous as a patron. For the interior of his new palace, he had brought the Englishmen Ashbee and Baillie-Scott to Darmstadt in 1897. The rooms they created for him were praised highly and given a lot of publicity. To give the German arts and crafts movement a chance to come up to English standards, he founded an artists' colony in 1899. Joseph Maria Olbrich, the most prominent member of the colony, kept up his connection with it until he died in 1908, and also personally designed several rooms for the Grand Duke: 1902/03, the large music room in the "Neues Palais" in Darmstadt, 1906/07 the private chambers in the Old Castle in Giessen. In the park of the summer residence in Wolfsgarten near Langen, between Darmstadt and Frankfurt, Olbrich built a play-house for the little princess, Elisabeth of Hesse, in 1902.

Workshop in 1903, an association of artist craftsmen, who wanted to work directly for their customers without any middlemen. They got the idea from Charles Ashbee's furniture workshop in England, which they visited while on a joint educational trip. Charles Rennie Mackintosh, whom they had asked for his opinion on the project, wrote to them from Glasgow: "You are well-advised to embark on direct sales. You can carry out the greatest of works, that is, produce all sorts of articles for everyday use in the most splendid form." The banker Fritz Wärndorfer, who was to lose his whole fortune in this undertaking, became their financier. Workshops, drawing offices and sales premises were rented. The most modern machinery was bought for the workshops. Every product that left the house was marked WW for Wiener Werkstätte (Vienna Workshop), and bore the monograms of the designer and the craftsman. The painter Gustav Klimt, a member of the Secession, like Hoffmann and Moser, found this practice unnecessary. He felt that it was easy to tell who designed a piece anyway. "One only has to look at who is admiring it. If it's by Moser, it'll be women, if it's Hoffmann's, men."

Josef Hoffmann, oil and vinegar bottles with stand, glass and German silver, 1906, made by the Wiener Werkstätte (Vienna Workshop). Galerie Metropol, Vienna, New York

An author for the periodical "Deutsche Kunst und Dekoration" speculated in 1906 on the effect of the products of the Vienna Workshop: "One can well imagine that a person of good taste who is fortunate enough to possess one of these objects will, in time, experience a revolution in his environment, set in motion by this object, which will transform his surroundings and ultimately himself. It will happen again and again that someone who starts with a cigarette case or a vase cannot rest until he has a house to match it, with all the necessary accessories."

Leopold Bauer, room in the summer-house of a villa in Brünn, 1902, illustration from "Das Interieur" IV, 1903. The architect Leopold Bauer built a large house in Brünn and designed all the interior furnishings. The picture shows a room where one could rest after tennis, with a view of the court in the background. Its serenity and lightness was dazzling, even within the framework of the Viennese school.

Koloman Moser, armchair of wooden slats, painted beech, with a wickerwork seat, 1902, made by Prag-Rudniker Korbwaren, Vienna. Chairs of this sort were shown at the Vienna Seccession's major Klimt exhibition in 1903, and were used in the entrance hall of the "Westend" sanatorium in Purkersdorf in Austria, the first major commission for the Vienna Workshop. In contrast to the chair shown here, these also had small feet. Berta Zuckerkandl, an art critic and ardent admirer of Josef Hoffmann, had arranged the sanatorium commission via her brother-in-law, who was the director of it. The plan was to erect a new building for balneotherapy and other physical therapies, which should meet the highest standards in comfort and luxury. Hoffmann designed suitable extensive and extravagant lounges as well as treatment and other rooms. The cubic shape of the building reappeared in numerous pieces of furniture, for instance this wooden armchair.
Galerie Metropol, Vienna, New York

Josef Hoffmann, "Sitting-machine", armchair with adjustable back, blue and white painted beech and bentwood, 1905, manufactured by Jacob & Josef Kohn, Vienna. The spheres inserted at important joints on the frame – an element used by Hoffmann in a whole series of his designs – are reported to have served the function of increasing stability; but it seems more likely that they were only intended to give a decorative emphasis to the joints in the construction. A brass rod could be inserted between the spheres at the rear of the armrests to support the adjustable backrest in various positions. The colour scheme of this chair takes up the motif of blue and white borders used for the Purkersdorf sanatorium. It is also reminiscent of the façades of the houses which Josef Hoffmann built for Kolo Moser, Carl Moll and the Spitzer and Henneberg families in the fashionable "Hohe Warte" residential area of Vienna: light-coloured roughcast plastering was combined with red, yellow and blue-painted timber frames.
Galerie Metropol, Vienna, New York

Koloman Moser was not an architect, nor did he follow the course of other painters of the time, who progressed to house-building via arts and crafts. But he most certainly had a strongly developed gift for designing furniture. A flat completely furnished by Moser was described in the periodical *Dekorative Kunst* (Decorative Art) in 1904. It is not known who commissioned it; the author refers only to a young couple who had the flat furnished. It consisted of an outer room, cloakroom, drawing-, dining-, breakfast- and bedrooms, boudoir, kitchen and servant's room. Many of the pieces designed for it have survived, but they are now located in various places.

The common factor was their very rectangular shape, with large surfaces, broken up by inlay work in contrasting colours. The decorations were developed from floral motifs, which had a particular relation to the owners. Lily of the valley was the lady of the house's favourite flower, and dominated the decoration of the bedroom and boudoir. The breakfast room also contained a botanical motif: the inlay pattern was calyx shaped. The same form turned upside down re-appeared in the lampshades hanging from the ceiling. For the marquetry in the dining room, Moser took the noble title of the occupants as a motif and designed a stylised dove with an olive branch and a dolphin, which were used to decorate the surfaces of the sideboard and the smooth backs of the chairs. The lady's desk was particularly striking. It was placed in the breakfast room, and was constructed in such a way that the matching chair could be

Koloman Moser, sofa and table for a breakfast room, Vienna, 1904, illustrated in "Dekorative Kunst" XII, 1903/04. The picture was taken in the flat belonging to a young couple, completely furnished with Moser furniture.

Koloman Moser, buffet from the dining room of the same flat, Vienna, 1904. The cabinet veneer is elm root wood with an interesting grain. Square maple-wood panels are set into the doors of the lower part and the back of the upper part. The marquetry of these small areas, which uses mother-of-pearl, rosewood and maple wood, traces the outline of a dove with outspread wings, holding an olive branch in its beak. The insets on the pilasters show dolphins, who seem to be poised to jump into the water.
Badisches Landesmuseum, Karlsruhe

Koloman Moser, writing cabinet with integrated chair, Vienna, 1904, illustration from "Dekorative Kunst", XII, 1903/04. It was also in the flat of the same young couple. It stood in the breakfast room, opposite the sofa (left-hand page) and was designed for the lady of the house. The patterns of the marquetry reflected her love of flowers and plant motifs and was also used for the carpets. The Vienna Workshop had made a cabinet with a similar structure the year before for Fritz Wärndorfer. The idea was used again later with numerous variations.

pushed under the desk when it was closed, so that its even back formed a continuation of the desk front.

In Hill House, a villa which Charles Rennie Mackintosh designed in 1902 in Helensburgh in Scotland for the publisher Walter W. Blackie, all the lady's rooms were in one wing of the house. But the masculine and the feminine spheres met in the artfully designed bedroom: white painted furniture — which Mackintosh only designed for a brief period — formed a stark contrast to the austere fireplace and the famous dark chair, with its high, latticework back. It is placed between two white wardrobes in such a way that one could imagine it to be a silent servant, designed not to sit on but to hold a top hat, stiff collar and cuff-links. The wardrobes on either side, the bed alcove and the large mirror, by

Charles Rennie Mackintosh, modern replica of a chair, ash wood, stained ebony black, with an upholstered seat. The 1903 original was made of oak and stood in Hill House in Helensburgh, Scotland.
Cassina, Meda/Milan

Charles Rennie Mackintosh, sketch plan for the bedroom in Hill House, 1903. On the left-hand side is the bed, flanked by two bedside tables integrated into the head of the bed, which reaches almost to the ceiling, and a fitted cupboard. In the larger part of the room, the dark coloured chair with its ladder-style back was positioned between two wardrobes, opposite the wash stand. The easy chair and the sofa in the semi-rounded alcove were not actually manufactured.

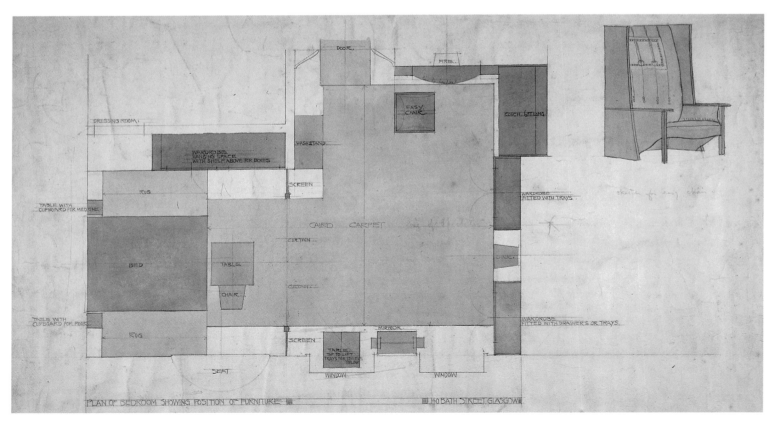

Charles Rennie Mackintosh, bedroom in Hill House in Helensburgh, Scotland, 1903. The photo shows the wall opposite the bed. Mackintosh left a broad recess, up to the height of the door lintel, and fitted two wardrobes. On the left there is a fitted couch, next to the fireplace.

contrast emphasise the feminine element of the room and produce an overall impression of brightness – in spite of the small window. The playful decorative scheme, which makes only occasional, but extremely effective use of curves, was complemented by small areas of pink and pale green. Unfortunately, at the beginning, Mackintosh was not able to plan and finish the other rooms with their furnishings as complete units, as the owner wanted to keep some of his own furniture. But, over the years, Mackintosh designed more single pieces for Hill House. Like the artists of the Vienna Workshop, Mackintosh could only put his ideas into practice in a few houses, as they required considerable financial investment.

Whereas Mackintosh only worked in Glasgow – apart from a few small commissions – designers on the continent were more mobile. It was typical of the new artistic movement – and the international orientation of the clientele which provided it with financial support – that the Belgian, Henry van de Velde, had better opportunities in Germany than he did in Brussels. Yet the main works of Josef Hoffmann and the Viennese Workshop were created in the Belgian capital: the Palais Stoclet. To a large extent, this building fulfilled the ideal of the total integration of architecture, interior design and furnishings. Thanks to its relatively late date – 1905 to 1911 – it has none of the tentativeness of the initial stages. By this time, Josef Hoffmann had reached his peak as a designer in various spheres. The house clearly bears his mark. There were apparently no financial limitations, and the banker Adolphe Stoclet does not seem to have

Josef Hoffmann, side view of the Palais Stoclet in Brussels, 1905–11.

tried to influence the work as it progressed. As the family had previously lived in Vienna for a few years, a relationship was formed which resulted in one of the best works of the era. The building site was on the Avenue de Trevueren, a good area near the town. The cubic-shaped house had an exterior of Norwegian marble, bordered with strips of bronze. Inside, the elegant furniture was effectively complemented by objects from the owner's East Asian collection and – in the dining room – by mosaic friezes by Gustav Klimt. Everyday life in such a thoroughly planned and homogeneously designed house must have required a high degree of discipline. Many of the private rooms provide a better idea of the owners' lifestyle than the well-known official rooms – for instance, the lady's dressing room, completely designed in grey and white. It provides an ideal environment for every sort of clothes.

In spite of several major orders, such as the sanatorium in Purkersdorf or the Palais Stoclet, the Vienna Workshop was not economically successful. Materials and tools for the various crafts – it offered gold and silver utensils, book binding and leatherwork as well as furniture – were extremely expensive. Considerable sums were invested in "pet projects", which did not make any profit. The advance paid by Adolphe Stoclet for his villa in Brussels was used to finance a small nightclub, the "Fledermaus" or "Bat" cabaret, an investment doomed to failure from the start because of the limited amount of space in the small cellar where it was set up. But the main problem was that the artists failed to build up the broad spectrum of middle-class customers Hoffmann and Moser had explicitly aimed at in their original manifesto and called upon to become "leaders in the artistic sphere".

Yet in spite of its difficult financial position, the workshop's programme was repeatedly extended – for instance by a fashion section in 1910 – influenced by the idea of the integration of all the arts and made possible thanks to generous support from Fritz Wärndorfer, the son of a rich family in the textiles industry. Josef Hoffmann often reacted extremely indignantly if a customer dared to

Josef Hoffmann, dining room, Palais Stoclet, 1911. It is one of the richest and most successful interiors of the luxury villa, which was built for the Belgian banker, Adolphe Stoclet. Only the most exquisite materials were used: marble, silver, selected luxury wood. The room was given a distinctive note by the coloured mosaics of marble, glass and semi-precious stones, by Gustav Klimt, which can be seen in the background and above the two sideboards.

Josef Hoffmann, lady's dressing room in the Palais Stoclet, 1911. The wardrobes are all inbuilt, the dressing table is provided with natural and artificial sources of light.

Josef Hoffmann, kitchen in the Palais Stoclet, 1911. The auxiliary rooms were planned and designed with just as much care as the splendid public rooms of the villa. An even grid of square tiles covers the walls and ceiling. Typical characteristics of the Vienna school are to be seen in the oval insets on the covers and the exquisite lights.

make changes to an interior which he had designed, or to add things which he had not approved. He expected the lady of the house to adapt her wardrobe to suit the rooms. Until the fashion department was founded, this meant, ideally, buying clothes from Emilie Flöge, Gustav Klimt's Lady friend. In her fashion salon – which, of course, was also designed and created by the Vienna Workshop – she offered "rational clothes", without constricting whalebone corsets or bustles, but at the same time avoiding the ungainliness of other "alternative" clothes. The fashions designed by Eduard Josef Wimmer-Wisgrill continued in this direction with international success.

Adolf Loos, an architect like Josef Hoffmann, but at the same time a keen journalist and sworn opponent of the Vienna Workshop, expressed his criticism of the total stylisation of life in the famous satire *The Poor Rich Man,* which, of course, also applied to the rich woman: "I want to tell you the story of a poor rich man. He had money and property, a faithful wife, who kissed his business worries from his forehead, children that were the envy of all his workers..." What he did not have was "art". But he was "a powerful man... and so that same day he went to a famous architect and said to him: bring me art, inside my own four walls. Never mind the price." The architect threw out all the furniture and left an army of craftsmen in the house. When everything was ready, the rich man went through all the rooms and was overjoyed: "Everywhere he looked, he saw art". Everybody praised him, everybody envied him, the artistic journals exalted him as a distinguished patron. "From now on, he dedicated a lot of his time to studying his home. After all, that was something he had to learn, as he soon realised." Deep in thought, he pushed a book onto a shelf designed for newspapers. Sometimes the architect had to get out the detailed plans to rediscover the place designed for a matchbox. "Yet, it must be admitted that he chose to spend as little time as possible at home... Well, could you live in an art gallery? Or go to 'Tristan and Isolde' night after night for months? Well then!"

Dagobert Peche, "Spider" design for a textile pattern, Vienna, around 1912.
Österreichisches Museum für angewandte Kunst, Vienna

Carl Krenek, design for a textile pattern called "Grenades", Vienna, around 1912.
Österreichisches Museum für angewandte Kunst, Vienna

Marcel Kammerer, lady's desk, painted soft wood with granite top, Vienna, 1909, made by Franz X. Schenzel, Vienna.
Galerie Metropol, Vienna, New York

His dear friends showered him with gifts on his birthday and he summoned the architect to give him good advice on how to display them." The architect's expression darkened considerably. Then he burst out: 'How dare you let people give you presents? Did I not design everything for you? You don't need anything else. Your household is complete!' ... The master of the house was crushed ... He had the feeling the only thing left was to learn how to live with his own corpse."

The high standards which the Vienna Workshop kept up at the beginning disappeared over the years, as routine set in. Dagobert Peche was the only one who succeeded in making a name for himself as an interior designer. But he represented the late period of the Vienna Workshop, when it had drifted away from its original uncompromising ideals. For an exhibition organised by the Cologne "Werkbund" in 1914, he created a room, which was actually just meant for showing paintings. But, using the leitmotif "Ladies in the centre of society", Peche designed a boudoir which negated Josef Hoffmann's strict ideas on architecture. The walls and floor were dominated by the patterns of the wallpaper and carpet. There was no longer any scope for subtle architectonic structuring.

J. Schwarz, sketch for a bathroom, from the magazine "Das Interieur" III, 1902.

Hans Stubner, two sketches for a hairdressing salon from the magazine "Das Interieur" III, 1902 (overleaf).

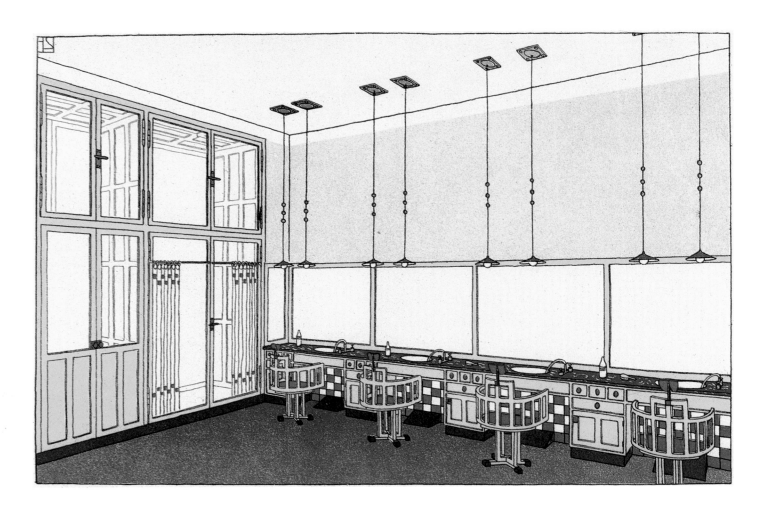

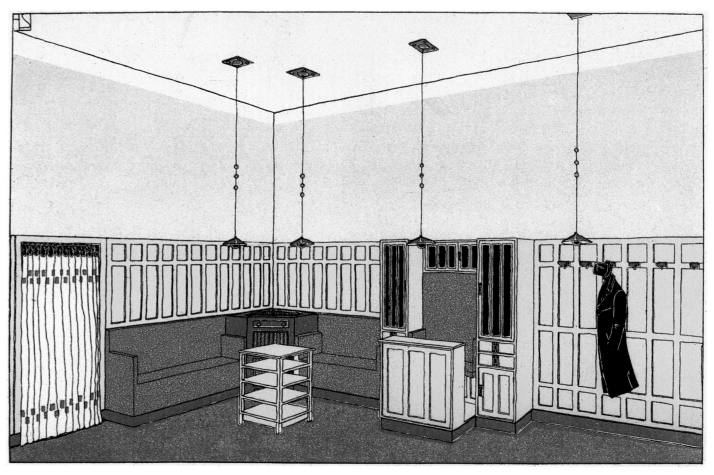

SCENE THREE
THE GENTLEMAN'S ROOM

THE CAST:

PETER BEHRENS
AUGUST ENDELL
WALTER GROPIUS
JOSEF HOFFMANN
ADOLF LOOS
CHARLES RENNIE MACKINTOSH
GEORG METZENDORF
BRUNO PAUL
RICHARD RIEMERSCHMID
GUSTAV STICKLEY
HENRY VAN DE VELDE
OTTO WAGNER
KARL WITZMANN
FRANK LLOYD WRIGHT

Otto Wagner, display room in the Telegram Office of the daily newspaper, "Die Zeit", Vienna, 1902, illustrated in "Deutsche Kunst und Dekoration" XI, 1902/03.

the requirements of fast, high-pressure city life, will soon seem an indispensable means of communication. After all, it forms a necessary complement to today's inventions in the field of communications, as it is designed to provide the public with the latest information even faster than a newspaper can." Contemporary critics on the whole agreed that Otto Wagner had excelled himself in his task of providing a suitable design for the new service. The narrow façade and the entrance were made entirely of aluminium sheets and glass. In an article for the magazine *Deutsche Kunst und Dekoration,* Joseph August Lux wrote: "The silvery sheen of the portal made of the 'newest material', with its 'brand new aesthetic style', reflects the modern nature of the service".

The interior rooms were as modern in their design as the façade: white plaster ceilings and wall surfaces inset with small aluminium squares, wall coverings of grey-painted linoleum, and marble skirtings. The tables with tubular metal frames which Otto Wagner set up in the telegram office are reminiscent of the occasional tables in the bedroom and bathroom of his own flat. He had previously exhibited these two rooms at the Emperor's Jubilee Trade Exhibition in the Prater Rotunda in 1898, with resounding success. People were especially impressed by his glass baths.

Otto Wagner, who taught Joseph Maria Olbrich, Josef Hoffmann, Leopold Bauer and Marcel Kammerer, to name but a few, is regarded as the Nestor of the Viennese modern period. If he had been able to carry out all his designs, he would have become the most famous architect for monumental structures of the century, including especially the Viennese Ringstrasse. But instead of him it was Gottfried Semper and Karl Hasenauer who built the Neue Hofburg, the stock exchange and the Burgtheater. Josef Hoffmann wrote in retrospect: "He was only actually able to complete a few of his works, after arduous and unpleasant struggles. These successes include the buildings for the city rail network – the only one of its kind that does not disfigure a town, but actually creates a series of the most charming views –, the buildings for the Danube canal, the Nussdorfer Nadelwehr – including the necessary buildings – the church 'Am Steinhof' and the post-office savings bank, which was the first real office building." The colour scheme in the counter hall in this "first real office building" is the same as in the telegram office: white, grey, greyish brown; the metal is again aluminium.

Otto Wagner, modern reconstruction of the façade to the telegram office of the daily newspaper "Die Zeit". The original was built in Vienna in 1902. Otto Wagner used fine brushed aluminium sheets, mounted on an iron structure. Natural oxidation provided them with a protective anti-corrosive layer. The nine frames in the windows on either side were used to display the telegrams which came in.
Historisches Museum der Stadt Wien, Vienna

Otto Wagner, side-table from the bedroom of Wagner's own flat in the "Köstlergasse", Vienna, 1898/99. Its construction is related to that of the tables in the telegram office. Note the emphasis on the joints.
Privately owned

Josef Hoffmann (?), dining room, around 1903

Josef Hoffmann, small bureau-type desk, black-stained polished oak, Vienna 1905. Chalk was rubbed into the pores. This was one of the most successful models Hoffmann designed for the Vienna Workshops, one model was in the salon of Dr. Hermann Wittgenstein in Vienna. Österreichisches Museum für angewandte Kunst, Vienna

Josef Hoffmann, hall in the villa of Dr. F. V. Spitzer, "Hohe Warte", Vienna, 1902. The walls were of roughcast white plaster, the furniture of black-stained wood. There was a copper and lead fireplace, the lights were of tin-plated metal. The dark grey oak floorboards had a yellow and grey covering. Illustrated in "Dekorative Kunst", XII, 1903.

Josef Hoffmann, armchair, black-stained oak, rubbed with chalk and polished, Vienna, 1904. It was in Dr. Wittgenstein's flat and was also used with the desk illustrated. On a contemporary photo it has a cushion.
Galerie Metropol, Vienna, New York

Charles Rennie Mackintosh, modern replicas of a
stained ash table with foldaway leaves, and a
stained ash armchair with a seat of plaited cord.
Mackintosh probably designed this furniture in
1918 for the dining room at W. J. Basset-Lowke's
Candida Cottage in Roade near Northampton. It
was not manufactured during his lifetime.
Cassina's replica is based on Mackintosh's
painstaking drawings.
Cassina, Meda/Milan

that, depending on scale, had the ability to give small forms monumentality and
major constructions an almost precious lightness. The absolutes of geometry
could give brute, cubic authority to a chair's form, and at the same time –
repeated as pattern on the surface – dissolve its bulk into rich graphic planes. A
metal plant stand could have both the look of a visionary skyscraper and a
gauze-like airiness. The dominant form was the impersonal and scaleless
square, and the most pervasive motifs were the grid and checkerboard – as
basic as the graph paper on which Hoffmann sketched out his floor plans,
façades, and furniture."

Many authors believe Mackintosh had a considerable influence on the Viennese designers, especially Josef Hoffmann and his pupils. It is not possible to
provide conclusive evidence of this – at least not within the present framework. It
is certainly true that Mackintosh's work was well known, thanks to the periodicals and the 1900 Secession exhibition, but the pieces presented there can
hardly be seen as models for the increasing geometricality of the Viennese
furniture. But individual elements typical of Mackintosh's designs can be traced,
for instance the motif formed from a group of several small squares. The other
clear similarity is to be found in the super-slim pillars, directly in front of a wall
or next to the side surfaces of a piece of furniture. They were used to structure
Mackintosh's room at the Secession exhibition and later appeared in interiors
designed by Hoffmann and armchairs by Koloman Moser and other Viennese
designers. But this design feature was also used in a lot of furniture by Ashbee,
who was probably known both to Mackintosh and to the Viennese designers.

The entrance hall designed by Hoffmann for Spitzer's house displays obvious differences to the entrance hall at Hill House created by Mackintosh. Some people also argue that Mackintosh's white-painted furniture inspired the Viennese artists to similar experiments. But, at the same time, apart from white furniture, Mackintosh only used dark-stained wooden furniture. Other colours like red and blue, which the Viennese liked to use, do not occur at all in Mackintosh's work.

It would be wrong to suggest that the Viennese designers were the only ones with an understanding of tectonics. When describing developments in the history of art, there is a tendency to highlight styles developed by groups of designers working together. Other individual, isolated moves in the same direction are often neglected. For instance, August Endell, who is better knows for pieces of furniture with unusual, wildly irregular contours, which appear to derive from the world of mushrooms and algae, was interested at a very early

Charles Rennie Mackintosh, modern replica of an armchair with a rounded back, ash stained ebony black. The 1904 original oak chair stood in the Willow Tea Rooms in Glasgow, and was designed for the attendant who took the orders from the waitresses. The back also served as a divider between a light and a dark area inside the restaurant.
Cassina, Meda/Milan

Charles Rennie Mackintosh, hall in Hill House in Helensburgh, 1903. The furniture was of stained oak, the chairs with rush seats. The hall was not just designed as an entrance, but had seats and a fireplace as well.

71

August Endell, shoe shop for the Salamander company, for whom Endell designed several shops at this time, Berlin, 1910/11.

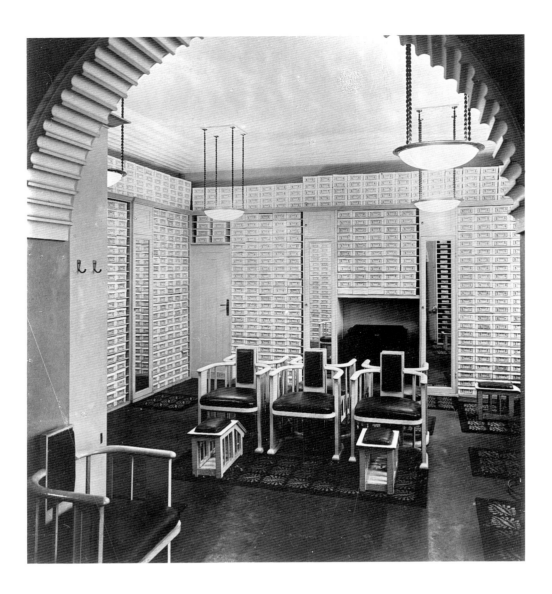

stage in developing shapes for furniture from basic geometric elements. The shoe-shop he designed for the Salamander company represents a high-point of his work in this style. The straightforward shape of the chairs provided for customers trying on shoes featured a tiny, right-angled back. This demonstrates that it is not a chair to rest in and that the focus is on the feet, for which a matching support is provided as part of a small stool. This also functioned as a seat for the shop assistant, while she helped to lace up the shoes.

Another surprising design is a dining room presented by Peter Behrens at the exhibition organised by the Dresden Werkstätten für Handwerkskunst in 1903. The dark-red mahogany furniture was placed in a white room. The chairs were like miniature log cabins, planks put together to form squares, and made the impression of having been assembled from a construction kit. The cupboards were designed in a similar way. The sideboard and the cupboard for the glasses had supports at the side, which fitted into rectangular wooden brackets.

It was not yet time for the next step from a constructional style of furniture to deliberate practical and functional design in Germany. At this time, people in general were too concerned with displaying national greatness to show any real interest in fundamental changes to design criteria. Thus the "modern movement", which was constantly being talked about, remained hidden and was unable to make a breakthrough.

Towards the end of the 19th century there was a series of attempts to make it

Peter Behrens, dining room at the exhibition by the Dresden Werkstätten für Handwerkskunst (Workshops for Artist Craftsmanship), 1903. The ceilings and walls were in white, furniture and door-frame in dark red mahogany, illustrated in "Dekorative Kunst" XII, 1903.

Karl Witzmann, two chairs in red-painted beech, from the loggia of Bergmann's villa in Pressbaum, Austria, 1902.
Galerie Metropol, Vienna, New York

possible for the working class to gain access to practical, hygienic, aesthetically acceptable and useful furniture at a reasonable price. Several competitions were organised to attract the imagination of designers to cheap furniture. In 1892, the König Ludwig Preisstiftung (King Ludwig Prize Foundation) in Nuremberg offered a prize for the manufacture of simple furniture for a middle-class living room. This was repeated at the turn of the century. The design had to include a table, four chairs, a sofa, a cupboard, chest of drawers, a sewing table and a mirror for a living room with an area of approximately 16 square metres. The price was not to exceed 350 Marks. Richard Riemerschmid won the competition with furnishings manufactured by the company Fleischauer's Sons. Industry was also interested in finding solutions to the housing problem, as conditions were intolerable in the overcrowded city centres. One consideration for firms which provided housing for their own employees was how to remove them from the sphere of influence of the politically unstable town centres. For this reason, estates were built up just for the workers of one particular company. An association to promote housing for workers carried out a survey which included the question: how much a worker paid on average for a piece of furniture. This was used as a basis to decide on price limits for a design competition. Kitchen furnishings had to be provided for 125–200 Marks, living room furniture for 230–330 Marks and bedroom furnishings for 160–250 Marks. But hardly any of

Richard Riemerschmid, beechwood cupboard, Munich, 1900. It is part of the same living room suite as the chair on the opposite page. Beginning in 1900, these pieces were produced for a decade. Riemerschmid often used variations of the basic construction of the cupboard, a box inserted in a frame.
Museum Industriekultur, Nuremberg

Hermann Obrist, commented on Riemerschmid's furniture designs: "Clarity, constructive, logical, down-to earth, with a simplicity which occasionally borders on dullness, but never quite goes this far; at the same time, it shows his feeling for a certain cheery sort of comfort."

the designs submitted were able to keep to these market prices, and they all left a lot to be desired. The problem was that many designers tended to look down on "simple people" and felt they had to provide them with furniture in the traditional, rural German style. The result was that all the pieces had a sort of cuckoo-clock air. Of course the designers were genuinely concerned to produce items which would appeal to their future buyers. Richard Riemerschmid also wanted to design unpretentious furniture to be manufactured in large quantities, along the lines of traditional rural styles. His Fleischauer room was the first step in this direction. Riemerschmid, one of the founders of the United Workshops in Munich, had soon turned away from the somewhat luxury-oriented city and then worked for the Dresdener Werkstätten für Handwerkskunst (Dresden Workshops for Artist Craftmanship), which later became the Deutsche Werkstätten Hellerau. He started to design furniture for this concern, managed by Karl Schmidt, in 1903. But it was only in 1906, at the 3rd Arts and Crafts Exhibition in Dresden, that he presented something new, "machine furniture — popular furniture which, although machine-produced, fulfills all the requirements of style and taste". Three complete sets of furnishings were offered, the cheapest one — consisting of living room, bedroom and kitchen — at a price of 570 Marks. It was characterised by the use of simple pine wood, plain fronts and screws at the joints. The furniture could also be bought in pieces to

Richard Riemerschmid, beechwood chair, 1900, made by the company Fleischauer's Sons in Nuremberg.
Museum Industriekultur, Nuremberg

Richard Riemerschmid, living and dining room, red-painted pine, known as furniture suite I in the machine-produced furniture programme, which the Dresden Workshops showed for the first time at the Third German Arts and Crafts Exhibition in Dresden in 1906.

Richard Riemerschmid, "Propeller table", mahogany, 1905. It belonged to the living and reception room of furniture suite III by the Dresden Workshops.
Museum für Kunst und Gewerbe, Hamburg

assemble at home. In 1906, the Dresden Workshops displayed seventeen sets of furnishings and a machine room, where the manufacture of the machine furniture was demonstrated, in a hall of its own. With this wide selection, the company was able to grow fast: in 1910, it already employed 500 workers. In 1908, the United Workshops in Munich followed suit and presented its own machine-produced furniture, known as the "Standard furniture programme", designed by Bruno Paul. From 1912 on, it also manufactured "Furniture for the working man", by Peter Behrens.

Thanks to his connections to the Dresden Workshops, Riemerschmid received the major commission of planning the Hellerau garden city, near Dresden. Karl Schmidt had had the idea of creating a housing estate for employees next to the factory, and the opportunity arose in 1906, when the expansion of the Dresden Workshops made it necessary to build a new factory outside the town. In an advertisement, the programme was described as follows: "No more stylistic nonsense. At least – modern town design without any tasteless features." As well as Riemerschmid, Hermann Muthesius, Heinrich Tessenow and Theodor Fischer were involved in Hellerau. The idea of these garden cities spread rapidly. Many people helped to promote it, for instance the publisher, Eugen Diederichs, who published the important book *Garden Cities in Sight* by the Englishman Ebenezer Howard. From 1909 on, a garden city was built up in Nuremberg, in which Riemerschmid was also involved. In the same year, the Hessian architect, Georg Metzendorf, from the Margarethe-Krupp-Stiftung für Wohnungsfürsorge (Margarethe Krupp Housing Foundation) was persuaded to build a settlement near Essen – not a real garden city in the English sense, which had to have industry and be economically independent, but an estate with shady trees and a pleasant lay-out. Metzendorf also acted as adviser for the furnishings of the houses in the settlement, which soon became known as the "Margarethenhöhe".

Apart from the machine-produced furniture, the 1906 Dresden exhibition created a very poor image of German standards. Evidently, the influence of

Georg Metzendorf, bay window in a house for industrial workers, produced by the Rheinische Werkstätten für Handwerkskunst in Essen and shown at the World Fair in Brussels in 1910. "These simple but beautiful homes will help us to win the respect of nations. A nation whose proletarians are learning to appreciate this sort of style has to become a leader in the industrial world." So ran the wording in the catalogue for the Brussels exhibition, under the heading "Taking stock of German style".

Advertising poster by the publisher Eugen Diederich for the German edition of the book "Garden Cities in Sight", by Ebenezer Howard. The drawing of a man, planting houses like seeds, was often used again by the Garden Cities movement, and even appeared on flags as an emblem.
Bibliothek der Landesgewerbeanstalt, Nuremberg

Leopold and John George Stickley, oak sofa with leather upholstery, Fayetteville, N.Y., 1910. Gustav Stickley, a leading figure in the American Arts and Crafts movement, set up a furniture company in 1898 and established contact to famous designers on a tour of Europe. When his firm became famous, with the aid of his own magazine "Craftsman", it was his own brothers who became his main competitors, by copying his designs.
In the catalogue of the Arts and Crafts Exhibition in Syracuse in 1903, Gustav Stickley listed the principles behind his work: "the supremacy of the constructive idea, by means of which an object openly acknowledges the purpose for which it was designed . . ., the absence of ornamentation, of any decoration whatsoever, which could disguise or detract from the constructional elements" and "the uncompromising adaptation of every work to suit the material in which it is made".
Cathers & Dembrowsky, New York

artists on industrial products had remained very slight. For this reason, new attempts had to be made to "re-educate the classes of today's society towards the old ideas of solidity, honesty and simplicity"; so, at least, said Hermann Muthesius in a speech to the Berlin College of Commerce, where he had taken up a new chair in applied art in spring, 1907. He said industry would "soil the domain of the visible" with its products. Of course statements of this sort provoked a storm of protest. At a meeting of the Association for the Economic Interests of the Commercial Arts, there was a major disagreement, and several firms left the association. After this, twelve artists and twelve manufacturers signed a joint appeal, which resulted in a meeting of about one hundred architects, artist craftsmen, industrialists and art lovers in Munich at the beginning of October. They united to form the Deutscher Werkbund, an association aimed at improving the form and quality of utility goods. To a large extent, it was influenced by the English Arts and Crafts movement, but it was more open to machine production. From the beginning, it displayed a strong missionary attitude. Its openness to the industrial society was one of the mainstays of the association's success.

In the USA, the architect Frank Lloyd Wright had hoped to reform the American Arts and Crafts Society in a way similar to the programme of the Werkbund as early as 1903, but he failed because of resistance from the dogmatic followers of Morris and Ruskin. Developments in Germany were closely observed in England, and after several attempts, the Design and Industries Association was founded in 1915. The most prominent Austrian designers had joined the German association in 1907. At its annual conference in June 1912 in Vienna, a separate Austrian organisation, the Österreichischer Werkbund was formed. 178 members attended the official opening ceremony. As well as the famous artists of the Viennese Secession, there were many young designers, and, above all, influential institutions, associations, and manufacturing companies.

The idea of an association which promoted cooperation between arts, crafts and industry spread quickly and was undoubtedly a major advantage. But the move from the luxury item to the mass-produced object reached its limits when even the simplest designs became too expensive for less well-off customers. A major exhibition organised by the Deutscher Werkbund in Cologne in 1914 demonstrated just how little of the initial élan had survived. Instead of new ideas, there was a lot of repetition. Everyone involved was aware of this problem. While the Austrians secured their traditional reputation by demonstrating classical craftmanship, the Germans left themselves open to criticism with their struggle to implement the new, industrial form. The famous debate on standardisation, which took place at this time, demonstrates the division of opinions. Hermann Muthesuis believed the solution lay in cooperation with industry and in the introduction of standardised industrial designs: "Architecture and all those involved in arts and crafts and industry are just crying out for standardisation, and can only regain the general significance they used to have when our culture was more harmonious, by means of standardisation..." The most important spokesman for the other point of view was Henry van de Velde, who protested strongly: "The artist is an ardent individualist in his innermost being, a free, spontaneous creator." Both these artists were putting forward opinions which could not be recognised explicitly in their own work.

Karl Weissbach, whose opinion on ladies' rooms was quoted above, also provides some comments on gentlemen's rooms. The author of the handbook

Henry van de Velde, mahogany rocking-chair with leather cushions, 1904. Museum für Kunsthandwerk, Frankfurt am Main

Bruno Paul, corner seating arrangement in the "gentleman's room" in Count Alexander von Faber-Castell's Schloss Stein, near Nuremberg, 1906.

Bruno Paul, "gentleman's room" in Schloss Stein, 1906, carried out by the United Workshops in Munich. Bruno Paul had designed an almost identical room for the official residence of the regions's chief administrator in Bayreuth and had exhibited it at the 1904 World Fair in St. Louis – with great success. It won a gold medal. The furnishings were then shown again at the Third German Arts nd rafts Exhibition in Dresden in 1906, as a successful, up-to-date version of a gentleman's room.

Design, Layout and Furnishing writes: "This room allows the gentleman either to enjoy peace and quiet or to live for his career ... A room of the first type – which only rarely serves the other function as well – also provides a meeting place for male guests on social occasions. After the meal, they settle down here with their host for some time. The gentleman's room then becomes a smoking room and a games room at the same time." Whereas Weissbach provided a very detailed list of furnishings for a lady's room, down to the pictures, small statues, vases, even the books the lady of the house should have in her library, and presented very detailed ideas, he is much more reticent about the gentleman's retreat. "It is not really possible to give a more detailed description of the interior, as the room can be furnished in numerous different ways, depending on the owner's needs and inclinations, or even on his own particular hobby-horse. The room of a hunter will be different from that of an academic." But he did make some stipulations: "The walls and curtains should be in rich, deep colours, the furniture should be in matching colours and should be firmly put together with a simple, powerful structure. Woodwork can be used to decorate the walls and the ceiling."

The gentleman's room designed by Bruno Paul for Count Alexander von Faber-Castell corresponds perfectly to these recommendations. The walls and ceiling are panelled in dark-stained oak and maple and, like the artfully integrated cupboards, sparingly decorated with geometric inlays. The rounded desk makes an aristocratic, distinguished impression, but without appearing too bulky. The matching chair is also elegantly shaped. From the coupé-like window recess, the master of the house could survey his large factory complex. A rich but unpretentious ambience for wealthy clients provided Bruno Paul with the territory where he moved with the greatest of ease. Via the managing director of the North-German Lloyd company, he also gained the opportunity to prove his talent in the sector of ship's furnishing. In 1907 and 1908, he created well-balanced, exclusive public rooms and luxury cabins for the steamers

Henry van de Velde, dining room in House Esche
in Lauterbach, Thuringia, 1908. Narrow strips of
wood were used to fasten the red textile wall-
covering and to structure the room, the furniture
surfaces were painted with flatting varnish.

"Kronprinzessin Cäcilie", "Derfflinger", "Prinz Friedrich Wilhelm" and
"George Washington". Their quality was such that they could "carry the reputation of German art across the sea". Bruno Paul wrote: "Nowhere did the
contrast between the high standard of technical development and the decline
and inadequacy of the productions of decorative art become as obvious as in
the interiors of ships at the beginning of the century... Yet there were worthwhile
and extremely attractive challenges to be taken up. The old narrow, stuffy rooms
had turned into large dining rooms, spacious salons. Suites of four or five rooms
were used to accommodate wealthy passengers. There were no longer any
ships without cafes, restaurants, tearooms and bars... Features were taken
from all the different stylistic eras, and all this resulted in sights worth seeing,
although they were mostly of a dubious sort of beauty..."

By about 1908, Art Nouveau had finally become outdated. German designers
had lapsed into a strictly developed line, which often made a somewhat heavy-
handed impression. But some of the interiors designed by Henry van de Velde at
this time show that disciplined design does not have to be boring. The demon-
strative features he had favoured in the early stages had developed into truly
functional features, without losing any of their power and conviction. Rooms
and furniture were dominated by precise concepts of order. The varying size of
the wall sections in the dining room he designed for the Esche manor-house in

Henry van de Velde, dining room in Villa Hohenhof in Hagen, 1908.
Karl Ernst Osthaus, a wealthy man of independent means, became one of the first Germans to commission work from Henry van de Velde, when he charged him with the interior design of the Folkwang Museum in Hagen, which he was financing. He continued to support him and became his first biographer in 1920. Villa Hohenhof is an example of van de Velde's mature work, between 1904 and 1910, which was marked by functionality clothed in a strict but rich form. Unlike his artistic contemporaries, he did not borrow classicistic or Biedermeier elements.

Henry van de Velde, bedroom in the Villa Hohenhof in Hagen, 1908.

Peter Behrens, living room in House Schede, Wetter an der Ruhr, 1904. The room and a round bay window were built into an old house in an extremely individualistic fashion.

Peter Behrens, corner cupboard from the living room in House Schede, 1904.

Walter Gropius, seating arrangement in a house near Hannover, 1913.

Lauterbach also demonstrates that van de Velde did not proceed mechanically, but had a highly developed feeling for rhythm and proportion.

Peter Behrens's style tended to move more and more in the direction of neo-classicism. The basic geometric shapes – the circle and the square – dominated his designs, and he tried to transfer the proportional rules of his classical models to all areas of design. The serious overtones of his furniture corresponded to an age which was looking for a characteristic, national form of expression in art and architecture. This was already to be seen in contemporary criticism of his Hamburger Vorhalle der Macht und Schönheit (Hamburg Hall of Power and Beauty), which he had presented in Turin in 1902, and reached its climax in monumental constructions like the German embassy in Saint Petersburg or the villa for the famous archaeologist, Theodor Wiegand, in Berlin in 1912.

His corner-room in Haus Schede in Wetter an der Ruhr shows how many individual details which appear to be extremely modern combine to form a rather inflexible overall impression. The polished surfaces of the cupboards with their round port-holes and the deliberate geometry in the structure of the chairs reflect a sort of compulsion which was bound to have an effect on the user.

The development of furniture design at the turn of the century in the United States was completely independent of that in Europe. There were major achievements in the engineering sector, but apart from that there was little which

Frank Lloyd Wright, living room in the country
house of Francis W. Little in Wayzata, Minnesota,
1912/14. It was removed in 1972 and
reconstructed in the Metropolitan Museum
of Art in New York.

could be compared to developments in Europe. Tiffany glass, which was amaz-
ingly successful, was the only area which differed from the widespread his-
toricising products. The American arts and crafts scene remained relatively
limited and there was no major breakthrough either within an industrial
framework or in the area of high-quality, individual craftmanship.

The only area where a new emphasis appeared was architecture, especially
in the construction of buildings for business. Here, Chicago was the main centre
of development, where architects like Daniel Burnham, John W. Root and Louis
H. Sullivan were already developing a very functional style of multi-storey
architecture by about 1890. Although Frank Lloyd Wright had not studied
architecture, he was given the opportunity to supervise small projects like
houses and weekend houses while working as a draughtsman in Sullivan's
office. After a short time, he opened his own successful business. Even his first
houses showed the characteristic features of his style, which he explained
programmatically in an article in 1900, entitled "A Home in a Prairie Town".

The Prairie House represented a move away from the traditional idea of
closed, compact construction. The rooms, which were often arranged in the
shape of a cross on the plan, were grouped around a central large fireplace.
Wright emphasised the horizontal line with low, flat, roofs and long extended
windows. He was very careful in his choice of materials and often left brickwork
visible, both outside and in. The architectural tectonics also determined the

Frank Lloyd Wright, living room in Avery Coonley's house in Riverside, Illinois, 1907/08. The fireplace formed the focal point of the room. It is the centre of the whole house and reminiscent of a campfire. In accordance with the overall architectonic principles, the room continues up to the roof, in a manner not unlike a tent.

Frank Lloyd Wright, modern replica of a chair which can be traced back to a 1937 version. But it was already in place in 1905 in the house of Darwin D. Martin in Buffalo, N.Y., but with differences in some minor details. The most notable was that the point where the arm joins the front support was made more striking by a slight widening of the arm and a rounder corner. The cushion was also flatter and less pillshaped. Cassina, Meda/Milan

interior. The coloured glass windows were the only element which provided a playfully ornamental note. The furniture which Wright designed made an almost architectural, constructed impression. In Frank Lloyd Wright's first office building, designed in 1903 for the Larkin Company, he reversed the principle of his prairie houses, which was to open the rooms to the outside and so to relate Life to Nature. The exterior of his five-storey office block gave it the impression of being hermetically sealed off. But inside, he used large, open-plan offices to suggest a more democratically-oriented office landscape.

The first concentrated summary of his work and his ideas, which Frank Lloyd Wright himself put together for the Berlin publisher Wasmuth, became little short of a bible for young students of architecture. Many of them were inspired by the houses illustrated in it. They developed his ideas further and then, after the First World War, created the modern style which would have been virtually impossible during the reign of the German emperor.

Frank Lloyd Wright, office swivel chair, painted steel, 1904, from the administrative building of the Larkin Company in Buffalo, N.Y. Metropolitan Museum of Art, New York

Frank Lloyd Wright, An exhibition entitled "Frank Lloyd Wright's Work" in the Art Institute of Chicago, 1907. The situation is obviously modelled on his work-room, the desk is surrounded by drawings and models. In the foreground on the left is a plaster model of the Larkin Building in Chicago and one of the typical glass windows which Wright always used when he wanted to restore a degree of intimacy to his open rooms with their rows of windows. Decorative details of the glass pattern re-appear in the lamps and vases on the table. The method of hanging up pictures by means of taut wires is admirably clever. Necessity is here turned into a principle of design, the layout of the whole room is determined by practical considerations. At the same time they also remind the observer that Frank Lloyd Wright was an expert in Japanese architecture. The lighting rail on the ceiling and the metal furniture are obviously new, and visibly determined by technical factors. A particularly sophisticated element is the chair, which is attached to the desk and can be moved. Whether it was actually comfortable is another matter. Frank Lloyd Wright admitted: "Somehow, I've had bruises all my life from too much close contact with my own furniture."

Central room in the Pavillon de L'Esprit Nouveau, Le Corbusier, 1925

ACT II

SCENE ONE
THE KEEP-FIT ROOM

THE CAST:

ALVAR AALTO
MARCEL BREUER
LE CORBUSIER
ERICH DIECKMANN
WALTER GROPIUS
RENE HERBST
FERDINAND KRAMER
HANS AND WASSILY LUCKHARDT
LUDWIG MIES VAN DER ROHE
GABRIELE MUCCHI
CHARLOTTE PERRIAND
GERRIT RIETVELD
GRETE SCHÜTTE-LIHOTZKY
MART STAM
GIUSEPPE TERRAGNI

The numerous shocks caused by the First World War on the one hand strengthened reactionary tendencies, which opposed change in any form, and on the other unleashed hitherto undreamt-of powers. The era that followed was pervaded by this contrast, which had positive and negative effects. The change from a well-off era to a poor age – at least in Germany, defeated in war and rocked by inflation – created a new consciousness, which first emerged as late expressionist emotionalism, but soon turned into formal asceticism. This was the age of "Bauhaus" in Germany, of "Esprit Nouveau" in France and of "De Stijl" in Holland, all movements which were reactions to social changes and which aspired to social as well as aesthetic relevance. An active, athletic attitude, which paid equal regard to mind and body and included both in its aesthetic image of the "New Man", became the ideal, an isolated ideal at first, but much more widespread later. The purism of the early stages, with its emphasis on straight edges, soon gave way to smooth, slim, taut, sinewy shapes or soft, flowing forms, combined with bright, dazzling colours. The rooms were sparsely furnished, but filled with a hygienic freshness. Superfluous features

Gerrit Rietveld, modern replica of a side table, painted wood, designed 1922/23 for Truus Schröder's house in Utrecht.
Cassina, Meda/Milan

Gerrit Rietveld, the "Red-and-Blue" chair, painted beech, 1918. Rietveld was convinced that chairs, tables and cupboards of the type he built would be "abstract-real sculptures in the interiors of the future".
Stedelijk Museum, Amsterdam

Gerrit Rietveld, 1951 reconstruction of a sideboard designed in 1919. This piece of furniture, which makes the impression of being somehow transparent, consists of a structure of horizontal and vertical bars and surfaces. Many of Rietveld's contemporaries may have regarded it as a bulky dust collector, but for others, it was a manifesto.
Stedelijk Museum, Amsterdam

were taboo. No wonder shining tubular steel was discovered as a material for furniture at this time. The most courageous new start had already been made in Holland during the war. In 1917, the periodical "De Stijl" was set up. The main force behind it was the architect and painter Theo van Doesburg. One of its prominent supporters was the painter Piet Mondrian, who wrote a programmatic article on "Abstraction as representation of the pure spirit" for the first issue. And it was not only in the visual arts that people were seeking new avenues by means of this sort of idealistic concept. The same was also happening in architecture and interior design. The cabinet-maker Gerrit Rietveld soon joined the group. A new type of chair on which he was working seemed to provide one option in the search for new solutions. The first prototype in 1917 still had boards below the armrests. It also lacked the characteristic colour scheme. The painter Bart van der Leck, who was working in the same architect's office as Rietveld at the time, suggested making a brightly coloured model of the chair. And so, a new coloured version was created, with thinner pieces of wood. Doesburg was delighted and surrounded the piece with an aura of solemnity, speaking of its "dumb eloquence, like that of a machine".

Gerrit Rietveld, exterior of the house commissioned by Truus Schröder in Utrecht, 1924, illustration from: Walter Gropius, *Internationale Architektur*, 1925. The plasterwork is painted grey and white, the visible supporting steel structure and the window frames stand out in yellow, red, blue and black.

A striking feature of Rietveld's chair are the joints. The wooden components are not joined together in the conventional way, but fixed on top of or beside each other by means of small dowels. This goes against any sense of durability. The colour scheme – especially the use of a contrasting colour for the end pieces – shows an obvious relation to Mondrian's pictures. Like his orthogonally crossing lines, the supporting bars seem to be sections of imagined lines which continue beyond the physical outline of the actual chair. The simplicity of the construction suggested the possibility of multiple production and Rietveld had probably already considered using standardised single components to make cheap machine production possible. But, for the time being, the chair remained an individual piece. It was only in 1924 that Gerrit Rietveld got the opportunity to transfer his ideas to a whole building. The location was Utrecht. He worked in close cooperation with Mrs. Truus Schröder, who commissioned the building, and who had also worked with him on other projects. The construction consisted of wall sections of plaster-covered brickwork, concrete balcony floors and visible steel girders.

And so, important steps were taken in Holland towards a new design concept,

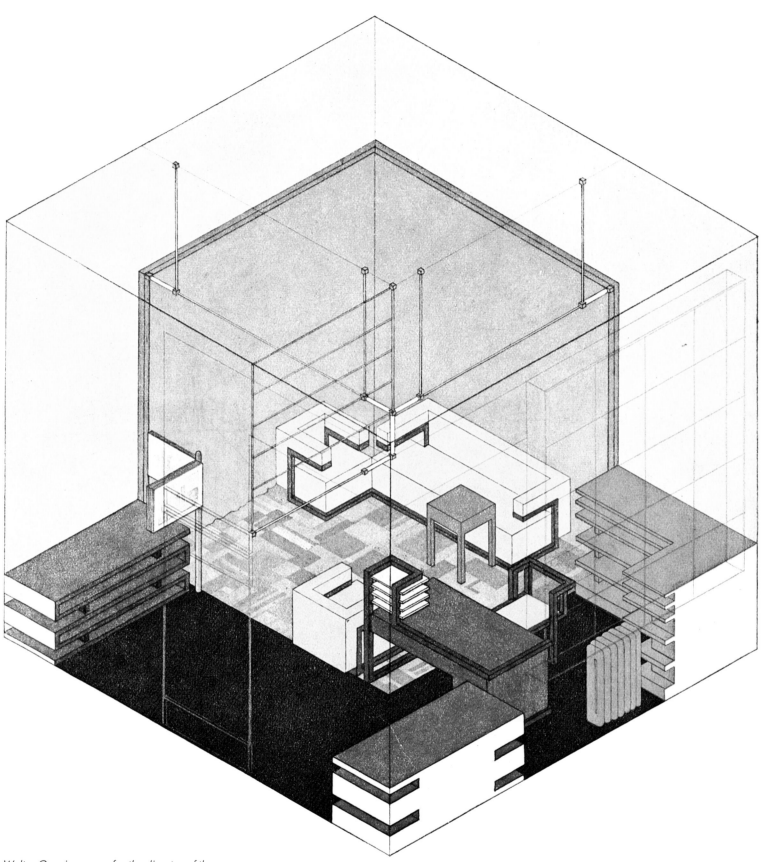

Walter Gropius, room for the director of the
Bauhaus in Weimar, 1923; isometric drawing by
Herbert Bayer, a graphics teacher at the Bauhaus.
The basic shape of the room is the square, which
develops into a cube in the armchairs, table etc.
The furniture – including the carpets – was
manufactured by students in the Bauhaus
workshops.

but it was in Germany that the new, experimental artistic work was given an institutional framework.

In Weimar, under the direction of Walter Gropius, the "Bauhaus" state school of architecture and design developed in 1919 from the Grand Duchy of Saxony's colleges for the visual arts and for arts and crafts – the latter was set up by Henry van de Velde in 1906. In 1925, Gropius described its principles: "Bauhaus aims to serve the development of contemporary housing, from the most basic household equipment to the complete house. Bauhaus is convinced that houses and their furnishings must have a meaningful relation to each other, and aims to derive the form of every object from its natural functions and limitations, by means of systematic experimentation – formal, technical and economic – in theory and practice... An object is determined by its essence. In order to design it in such a way that it will function adequately – whether it be a container, a chair, a house – we must first research into its essence. ... The result of this research is that when all modern production methods, constructions and materials are taken into consideration, unconventional forms are created, which often appear unusual and surprising."

For Gropius, changing the design of a product also meant re-formulating the aim of the designer: "Bauhaus wants to educate a new type of worker in industry and craftwork, who has never existed before, one who will be equally skilled in form and technics... in the future, there will be a new integrated craftmanship, which will also take on the task of preparatory experimental work for industrial production. Speculative experiments in laboratory workshops will provide models – types – for manufacture in factories." In accordance with this doctrine, the "Bauhaus" curriculum combined theoretical teaching (preparatory course

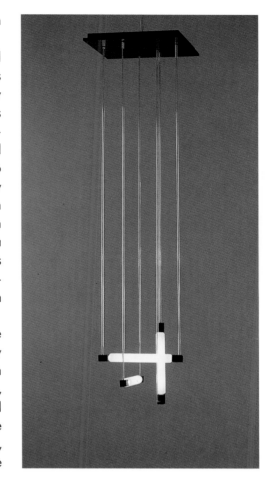

Gerrit Rietveld, modern replica of a pendant lamp, designed in 1920. The lighting system in the director's (Walter Gropius's) room at the Bauhaus academy showed clear similarities to the Rietveld model.
Tecta, Lauenförde; License Cassina

Walter Gropius, modern replica of an armchair designed in the early twenties. Two of these chairs and a matching couch were placed in the director's room in the Bauhaus in Weimar. They had lemon-coloured wool covers, the frames were of solid cherry wood.
Tecta, Lauenförde

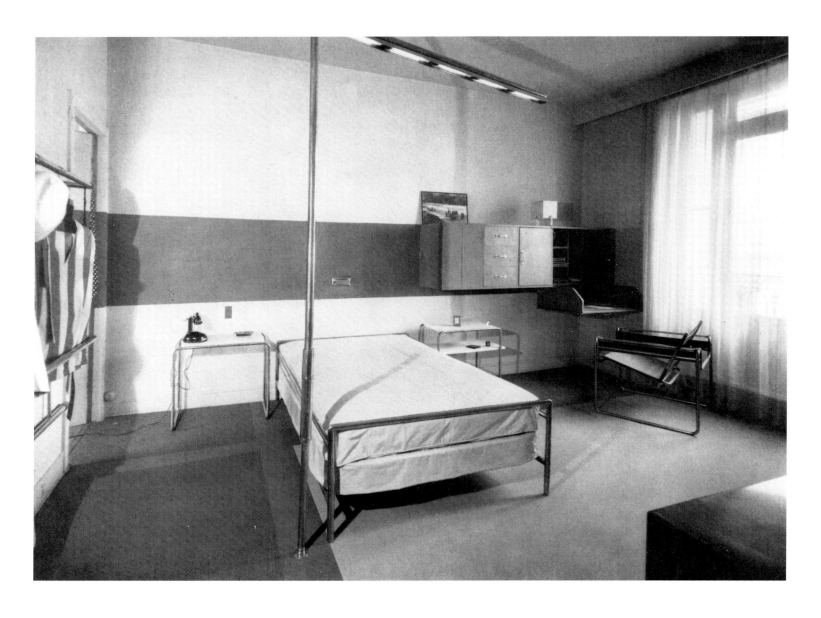

Bedroom of J. C. d'Ahetze, a Paris tailor, which he designed himself and furnished with models from Thonet's tubular steel collection; illustration from "Innen-Dekoration", 1930. The room was completely in blue and yellow. The large standard lamp with tube lighting at the bottom of the bed could be turned around, at the head of the bed, light was provided by a small lamp. An interior which matches the "light, sparse, unassuming manner in which modern man wishes to live out his existence". (Alexander Koch)

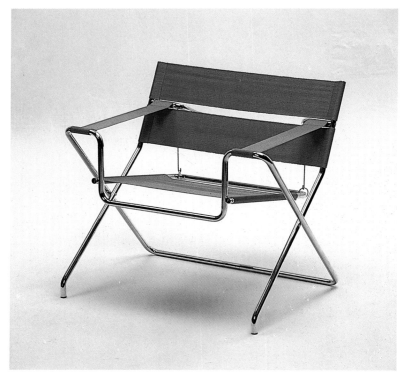

Marcel Breuer, modern replica of a tubular steel folding chair, a further development of his "Wassily", designed in 1926 and first shown to the wider public at the Weißenhof exhibition in Stuttgart in 1927, in Gropius' house. The material is made of extra-strong yarn.
Tecta, Lauenförde

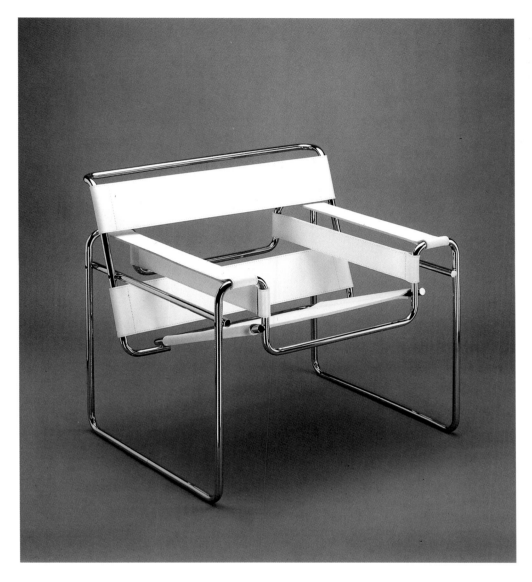

Marcel Breuer, modern replica of a tubular steel chair called "Wassily", with leather covering, designed in 1925. Originally, "Wassily" – like much early tubular steel furniture – was made of seamless drawn nickel-plated tube, but it was soon also offered with chromium plating, to achieve "pure, dazzling lines in the room". Marcel Breuer declared: "I regarded these shining, sweeping lines not only as symbols of technology but as technology itself." The Italian Dino Gavina succeeded in acquiring the rights to reproduce the chair from Marcel Breuer in the early sixties. In Italy, it is traditional to give furniture names. B3, as this chair was described in catalogues in the late twenties, was given the name "Wassily", after the Bauhaus master Wassily Kandinsky, for whose home in Dessau the chair was initially designed.
Knoll International, Murr/Murr

and theory of design) with practical training in the workshops. As teachers, or "Bauhausmeister", as they were called, Gropius was able to engage Lyonel Feininger, Wassily Kandinsky, Paul Klee, Johannes Itten, Oskar Schlemmer and Laszlo Moholy-Nagy.

One of the first students was the Hungarian Marcel Breuer. In 1925 he became a "Bauhausmeister", in charge of the carpentry workshop. Yet it was not the wood he had worked with during this studies but metal that became the material with which he revolutionised the image of furniture. In 1925, he created "Wassily", the first tubular steel armchair. The bent metal tubing seemed to continue in a never-ending curve to form the silhouette of the chair. The seat and back were of light fabric.

But the prototype was not created in the Bauhaus workshops, as one might have expected, but by a metalworker outside. Marcel Breuer is said to have got his inspiration for this model from a bicycle, and he wanted a bicycle factory to mass-produce it on the assembly line. However, the industrialists he approached were not keen to become furniture producers. Thus it was the small Berlin company Standard-Möbel, which Marcel Breuer had set up with fellow Hungarian Kalman Lengyel, an architect, which first produced the chair, in nickel or chromium-plated tubular steel, with covers made from extra-strong yarn.

"The characteristic, ideal posture of any era can best be seen in how people sit. Whereas once it was the saddle or later the imposing attitude of the ruler that affected everyday life, nowadays it is the casual but tense position of a car driver, leaning back, with his legs stretched out, which unconsciously influences our imagination. The tubular steel chair, with its elegant, sweeping lines, is the best match for a body steeled by sport and physical exercise. It allows the contours to be displayed to their best advantage and promotes a relaxed, but also a disciplined posture. Thus, this confident way of sitting furthers awareness of one's physical appearance and also, ultimately, – like light sportswear or short skirts – helps to improve the body." (Walter Müller-Wulckow in: "Die deutsche Wohnung der Gegenwart", 1932)

Le Corbusier, Pavillon de L'Esprit Nouveau at the Exposition Internationale des Arts Décoratifs et Industriels Modernes in Paris, 1925. In the foreground, a sculpture by Jacques Lipchitz. At the time, the exhibition organisers found the design provocative and allotted the construction an out-of-the-way location on the "Rive droite". It is reported to have been hidden behind a wooden fence at the opening.

"The new furniture" was the catch-phrase which Breuer's company advertised its programme. Their advertisements tried to counter people's reservations: "Tubular steel and fabric furniture is as comfortable as good upholstered furniture, but it is lighter, cheaper, less bulky and more hygienic." Obviously this sort of publicity work was necessary. "Bauhausmeister" Josef Albers, a painter and furniture designer, described his first impression as follows: "People are usually taken aback when they first see the chair. They usually doubt whether it is really comfortable to sit on. But when they try it out, it becomes clear that it was not the chair that provoked the original reaction, but just the fact that they looked at it with very conventional eyes."

Another irritatingly new and unusual piece was the one presented by the architect Le Corbusier – his real name was Charles-Edouard Jeanneret-Gris – at the Exposition Internationale des Arts Décoratifs et Industriels Modernes in Paris in 1925. The design of the Pavillon de L'Esprit Nouveau, which he showed there, was in accordance with his maxim that one should establish the typical requirements for a flat and design suitable pieces in the same way as one does for a railway carriage or tools. Of course a rigorous stance such as this provoked contradiction from his more conservative colleagues. Paul Follot, for example – an acknowledged and popular master of luxurious and aristocratic furniture – missed no opportunity to take up the opposite attitude: "We know that man is not content with just 'the necessary', that he cannot do without the superfluous, otherwise we could do away with music, flowers, perfume or the smile of a woman! The theory of this school insists that our art must be inspired by the essential characteristics of our time. This means the home it creates is directly inspired by laboratories and factories; as well as inadequate fittings, we find nothing but metal furniture, glass tables, cold lighting, pink and other pale colours, only geometrical shapes, and no decoration whatsoever." This sort of criticism was not only aimed at Le Corbusier. It could equally well have been directed at Louis Sognot, André Lurçat and René Herbst. As Louis Cheronnet wrote: "They only think that this century, which has a new type of beauty that is gradually unfolding in photographs and films, a century of precision tools and speed, a century of aeroplanes, electricity and steel, has to develop expressive analogies in design to harmonize better with its resources and outer appearances."

The most important forum where representatives of modern architecture and new design could present their ideas and their work was set up in Stuttgart in 1927. The Deutscher Werkbund set up a large exhibition, "Die Wohnung" (The Home), where new constructional materials and building styles, furniture and new concepts of home design were presented. It included a model estate or colony, "Auf dem Weissenhof". The Berlin architect Ludwig Mies van der Rohe, who was initially the adviser, and from October 1925 on the artistic director of

Le Corbusier, Louis Sognot, André Lurçat, Francis Jourdain, Pierre Chareau, Robert Mallet-Stevens and René Herbst were amongst the loose grouping of avant-garde artists who wanted to form an association. This only happened at a very late stage, in 1930, with the Union des Artistes Modernes, by which time the members had already put forward the joint aims set out by the association. By the time the manifesto of the U. A. M. was published in 1934, the struggle it propagated against the "goût antiquaire", by which they meant the presentation of the old and traditional, had already been won.

René Herbst, modern replica of a chair designed in 1930. Herbst was one of the first designers in France to work with the new furniture material, metal. This earned him a nickname which also had a martial ring to it, "L'homme d'acier". From 1926 on, he began to replace wooden parts of his furniture with metal, glass and mirror glass. In 1929, for the first time he presented models with spring elements like strong elastic bands for the seat and back.
Formes Nouvelles/Habit, Leverkusen

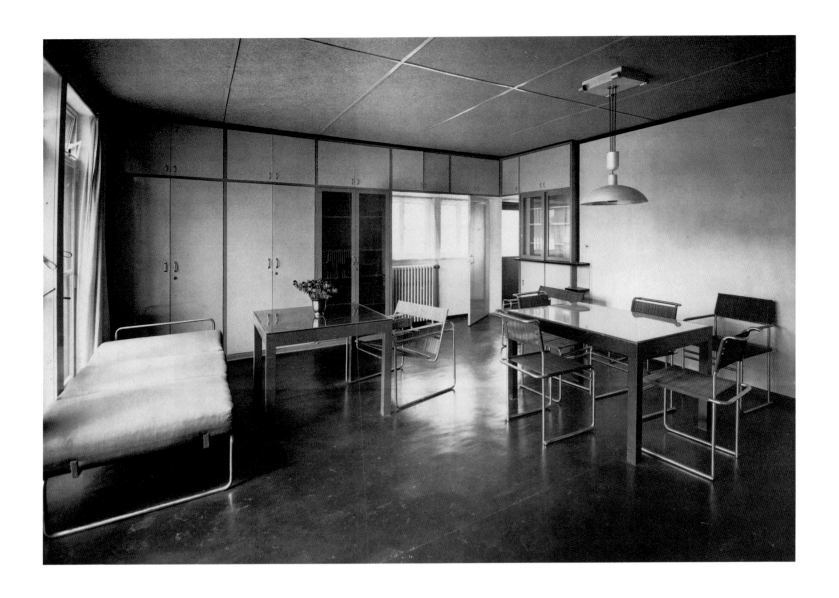

Walter Gropius, living room in House 16 of the Weißenhof estate in Stuttgart, 1927; provided with tubular steel furniture by Marcel Breuer. Above the dining table, an adjustable pendant lamp, which Marianne Brandt developed at the Bauhaus around 1925. Today, a replica of the lamp is manufactured by the company Tecnolumen in Bremen.

Erich Dieckmann, cherry-wood chair with wickerwork seat, around 1925. It was placed in House 2 of the Weissenhof estate, in Mies van der Rohe's block. Dieckmann had developed the furniture used there at the State College for Crafts and Architecture in Weimar. These pieces were suggested as possible standard designs for the industrial production of furniture for small flats.

the exhibition, drew up the building plan, which envisaged a loose grouping of various buildings, which were to be built by an international selection of architects. In the end, there were 21 houses on display, designed by 17 different architects – including the Swiss-French Le Corbusier, the Austrian Josef Frank, two Dutchmen, Jacobus Johannes Pieter Oud and Mart Stam, and the Germans Ludwig Mies van der Rohe, Walter Gropius and Hans Scharoun – and mostly containing newly designed furniture.

Although the financing for the estate had been provided within the framework of a social housing programme, the homes presented were designed for the new "city-dweller". Mies van der Rohe had planned not for people with a minimum living standard, but for well-off modern city society. But other designers, like Erich Dieckmann and Ferdinand Kramer, did take up the challenge of furnishing a "home for people on the breadline". The flat furnished by Mies himself contained his "Freischwinger", a type of tubular steel chair. It demonstrated harmony between industrial production and convincing design better than any other piece of furniture.

The principle of this new chair, which had two legs instead of the usual four, was developed in 1926 by the architect Mart Stam in Rotterdam. He built the first model from ordinary gas pipes and right-angled joints. At the "Werkbund" exhibition in Stuttgart in 1927, this "self-supporting" or "cantilever" chair, which had no back legs, was first presented by Mart Stam to the wider public. It

Le Corbusier and Pierre Jeanneret, living room in House 13 of the Weissenhof estate in Stuttgart, 1927. On the left one can see the open gallery, above the table the "Wall picture with stripes II", by Willi Baumeister, 1920. Bentwood armchairs by Thonet, Model No. 9, were used all over the house, as they had been in the Pavillon de L'Esprit Nouveau in 1925. Le Corbusier explained his preference for this simple and reasonable priced piece of furniture by saying he believed "that this chair, millions of which are in use in Europe and the Americas, possesses a nobility of its own."

Ludwig Mies van der Rohe, modern replica of a springy, cantilever chair, Model D42, designed in 1927. The covering was made by Mies van der Rohe's partner Lilly Reich, who learned her craft in the Vienna Workshop. The chair, like all the MR models, was first produced in Joseph Müller's metal workshop in Berlin, known as the Bamberg Metallwerkstätten from 1930/31 on. MR 10 was without, MR 20 with armrests. For the cover, there was a choice of steel thread textiles, leather or wickerwork.
Tecta, Lauenförde

had been manufactured by the L. & C. Arnold company, the largest manufacturer of iron furniture in Europe at the time. Of course it was no longer put together from gas pipes like the prototype, but was made of a single long piece of tubular iron, bent to the necessary shape. Since the chair threatened to break during tests, the tube was reinforced with iron inside. This construction made it impossible to achieve a springy effect, but that was not the intention.

During the preparations for the Weissenhof exhibition, Mart Stam probably discussed the new type of chair with his fellow architects. Perhaps he even drew sketches or showed them early models. It is not possible to say whether he actually inspired Mies van der Rohe directly to design something similar or whether the idea of a chair without back legs was just "in the air", as Sigfried Giedion suggests. At any rate, with his model "MR 10", as it was called, in 1927, Mies developed the first springy, self-supporting tubular steel chair, which was superior to Stam's chair, firstly from a technical point of view – since it was made of seamless drawn steel tubing, which stood up to pressure without hidden reinforcement – and secondly, aesthetically, with its powerful, sweeping lines. A few days before the opening of the Weissenhof exhibition, where it was first displayed, Mies took out a patent for his model. What he wanted to protect was not the style, but the springy construction. In a series of court cases between 1928 and 1944, he defended his claim against manufacturers whose models were nothing like his elegant designs, but who, in his opinion, were exploiting the elasticity of tubular steel.

The versions which Marcel Breuer presented after 1927 had the same basic shape as Mart Stam's cantilever chair and were the continuation of his own tubular steel experiments in the mid-twenties. His models turned out to be the most popular, even to the present day. He made them particularly attractive by combining the new material with classical bentwood and cane-work.

Unlike Mies van der Rohe's models, Breuer's designs were not legally protected or patented. Anton Lorenz, the director of the Standard Möbel company which produced Marcel Breuer's designs at that time, had bought the rights for the use of Mart Stam's chair; this seemed to be enough for him. When the Thonet company bought up Standard Möbel in 1929, it thought it had automatically acquired the rights for the tubular steel chair. But the courts did not agree. Lorenz kept the monopoly. All the chair models taken over by Thonet which had straight front legs and no support at the back had to be marked Mart Stam or Lorenz/Stam, according to copyright law. At this time, Mart Stam was already in Russia working on town planning, while Lorenz extended his patenting strategy and established himself in the thirties as a key figure in the European tubular

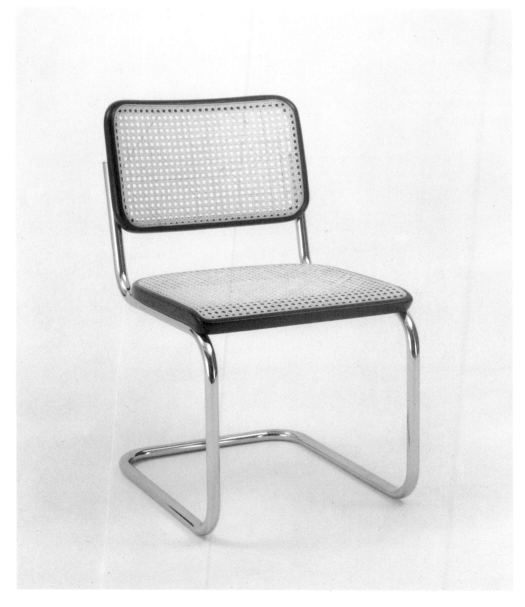

Marcel Breuer, copyright requires Mart Stam to be named, modern reconstruction of a cantilever chair, model S32, tubular steel and wickerwork on a beechwood frame, designed in 1929. Gebrüder Thonet, Frankenberg

Otto Bartning, interior of a prefabricated house, 1932. The central core was approximately 25 square metres in area and could be extended as much as desired without changing the supporting structure. The supporting skeleton and the wall panels were manufactured in a shipyard.

Ludwig Mies van der Rohe, modern replica of a couch table, tubular steel and glass, designed in 1927 and first shown at the Werkbund Exhibition in Stuttgart.
Knoll International, Murr/Murr

steel furniture business. But in many countries, even minor variations sufficed to get round copyright law and avoid the long, expensive court cases, which industry dreaded. The example of these chairs had a stimulating effect. Now tables, beds and even cupboards were made of tubular steel, although the latter were less successful. The manufacturers tried to transfer the attraction of the cool, durable material to as many pieces of furniture as possible. The idea behind this was to create a complete programme of related single pieces which could be combined in any way desired. For instance, a department store called "Feder" offered a whole series of unit furniture for living room, bedroom and study as well as office furnishings, developed by Walter Gropius's office. At the time, the furniture was shown at numerous exhibitions, including the one in Berlin in 1929, with the theme "cheap and beautiful homes". But people often criticised it for being too expensive for the working class.

A visible expression of wholehearted confidence in the social and humane potential of technology as a guarantee of social progress was to be seen especially in the architecture of the twenties and early thirties. Between 1925 and 1933, Frankfurt am Main – like Berlin, Vienna and Rotterdam – was one of the towns which provided a successful example of this social aspect of the new building trends with an extensive flat-building programme. Praunheim, Römerstadt, Hellerhof and Westhausen were the most important housing colonies to be completed. The periodical *Das Neue Frankfurt*, which appeared monthly

Walter Gropius, add-on unit furniture with tubular steel frames and a wood veneer on the doors, designed 1929/30 for "Feder", a cheap department store in Moabit, a working-class area of Berlin. It was also shown at the Exhibition by the German Werkbund in Paris in 1930 and elsewhere.

*Grete Schütte-Lihotzky, the "Frankfurt Kitchen",
as it was called, 1926. On the left of the picture, a
gas cooker with an extractor, pot-rest, hay-box
and, underneath, a drawer for flour; oak was
used to prevent mealworms. On the window side,
a working surface with a swivel stool, left of it, a
food cupboard and foldaway ironing board,
fixed to the wall. On the right, a crockery
cupboard, sink and series of aluminium drawer-
type containers. The cupboards reached up to the
ceiling so that there was no surface to collect dust.
Initially, the units were painted green, but this was
changed when it was discovered "that flies tend
to avoid blue". The floor and walls were tiled, the
walls in grey. The light could be moved along a
rail on the ceiling. Although the kitchen was
thoroughly planned and designed to suit the lack
of space in the development houses, it still
provided enough material for sarcastic
commentaries. For instance, in the "Frankfurter
General-Anzeiger" in December 1926, an ironic
report said: after the housewife came into the
kitchen, she would have to sit on the cooker to
make room for other people. Then she could
impressively explain and demonstrate the
advantages of her new kitchen. She wouldn't
need to bring any of her own furniture, as
everything was already fitted, for instance the
pantry, contained in a drawer. And she wouldn't
have any difficulties covering the remaining
wallspace. The one wall could be covered by a
kitchen clock, the other one wallpapered with a
calender.*

until 1931, also shows that the Frankfurt avant-garde did not understand architecture in isolation, but as part of a comprehensive process of cultural
change. The topics of the articles ranged from the reform of schools, new
photography, Sergej Eisenstein's revolutionary Russian film and the theatre of
Erwin Piscator to mass participation in sport. As a supplement, the *Frankfurter
Register* appeared, which presented "practical and beautiful" utility goods,
which were available as "factory-made" and mass-produced items, and which
did without "any trace of luxury". As a partner in a non-profitmaking household
goods company, the town also directly supported efforts to "provide the less
well-off classes of the population with quality household goods which could be
paid for in instalments". Ernst May, the head of the town surveyor's office,
explained this initiative: "Housing policy used to be more or less limited to

handing over the unfurnished flat to the tenant. But it is becoming clearer all the time that there is something lacking in this process. No matter how well the layout of a flat is designed, it is impossible to put the space to good use if the furniture brought in is old and not the right size or type." An attempt was made to convince the future tenants "that an interior did not have to become completely desolate if one stopped sticking wood carvings on furniture or using imitations and expensive veneers", by opening ready-furnished show-flats. The architect Ferdinand Kramer used similar arguments: there was a need for new, utility furniture to be manufactured, since the traditional furniture on the market – "complete suites for whole rooms", as a status symbol – did not match the new flats with their fewer and smaller rooms, either in size or in style and purpose. The town administration set up a centre for the unemployed in a disused barracks. There, unemployed joiners produced furniture designed by Franz Schuster and Ferdinand Kramer, particularly simple, combinable free-standing furniture, using plywood, a material developed to a high quality during the war in the construction of aircraft. The resulting products were simple, but not shabby.

The architect Margarete Schütte-Lihotzky designed the "Frankfurt kitchen" for the town's council houses. All the usual equipment necessary for a family household was fitted into an area of 3.5 by 1.9 metres. This closely integrated kitchen was influenced by a publication by an American housewife, Christine Frederick, which appeared in Germany in 1922 and outlined methods of better household organisation, based on motion studies.

The isolation into which Germany had slipped after the First World War could only be overcome step by step. Little of the exemplary development of architecture and design in this country had become known abroad by the end of the twenties. In 1929, the first official invitation to an exhibition by the Société des Artistes Décorateurs was issued. The Foreign Ministry entrusted the Deutscher Werkbund with the preparation of the German contribution, and they in turn

Unknown designer, modern replica of a pendant lamp with an opal sphere, probably first manufactured around 1920. The cap which holds the sphere has two layers and the glass is inserted between them. In the twenties and thirties, lamps of this sort were produced in large numbers, especially for schools and offices; in the private sphere, they were often used for staircases, corridors and kitchens.
Tecnolumen, Bremen

Ferdinand Kramer, kitchen table with stool, 1925. Both pieces were part of the standard furniture programme designed by Kramer for Hausrat GmbH in Frankfurt am Main. They were manufactured in the town's centre for the unemployed.

107

German section of the spring exhibition of the Societé des Artistes Décorateurs, Paris, 1930. On the right, the poster for the Section allemande by Herbert Bayer; behind the glass partition, the swimming pool of Walter Gropius's recreation room for a block of flats, in the background, the lampshade exhibition by Laslo Moholy-Nagy.

Marcel Breuer, modern replica of a tubular steel armchair, Model S35R, designed in 1929. This club armchair was first shown in 1930 in the Paris Grand Palais as part of the display by the German Werkbund. At the time, a leather version was shown.
Gebrüder Thonet, Frankenberg

commissioned Walter Gropius to run the project. In 1925, Gropius had presented one of the most resolute constructional modern designs with his new Bauhaus building. The associated houses for the "Bauhausmeister" had been extremely generously designed as objects to demonstrate a new style of life and housing, to match the machine age. But these successful, frequently praised buildings were only suitable as models for similar projects to a limited extent, as the manufacturing costs were well above the official limits for staff accommodation. Oskar Schlemmer wrote to his wife: "I got a shock when I saw the houses. I had the feeling, someday the homeless will be standing here while our great artists are sunbathing on the roofs of their villas."

It is certainly true that the designs being drawn up in the Bauhaus from the early 1920s on for "economic housing" and "small and economical flats" for the homeless were not entirely convincing. The house created by Gropius for the Weissenhof exhibition, made of industrially produced ready-made components set up on a sheet of concrete, also met with harsh criticism. The Reichsforschungsgesellschaft für Wirtschaftlichkeit im Bau und Wohnungswesen (Imperial Research Institute for Economy in Building and Housing), which provided financial

Walter Gropius, Hall I at the 1930 exhibition in Paris by the German Werkbund. Gropius presented recreation rooms for a block of flats in the extensive hall: a library with reading alcoves, seating arrangements, sports and rest areas; the picture shows the "Cafébar", which had an adjoining dance floor.

Walter Gropius, sports room at the Building Exhibition in Berlin, 1931. The loungers in the foreground are by Breuer's colleague, Kalman Lengyel. A brochure by the company Standard-Möbel, which manufactured this Spartan design until 1929, says: "We introduce the furniture of the new age, of modern man, who does not clutter up his surroundings with unnecessary junk, but moves freely and with a clear mind in sunny rooms. Our material is tubular steel. We create furniture in the simplest way, with the simplest materials, to suit the requirements of cultured modern man. Our furniture satisfies the sense of beauty of modern man, who is firmly rooted in the tempo of the 20th century in everything he thinks and does."

support for the Weissenhof project, came to a conclusion in its final report that was anything but flattering: the layout was systematic, but not innovative, the construction was amongst the most expensive of the whole estate, although it had serious faults. The general verdict was: "the constructivist doctrinarism of the 'Bauhaus' gives the houses a characteristically dry, pedantic air, and at the same time something provisional and barrack-like." Many Bauhaus students, who preferred Le Corbusier's design, expressed similar views.

In the late 1920s, Gropius turned intensively to multi-storey housing blocks. In his opinion, the "large house" was "not a necessary evil, but a healthy form of city housing which fits the times ... Only the large multi-storey house – with open green play and rest areas – can make life easier and pleasant for people by means of central house facilities and common recreation rooms."

Gropius had the chance to show just what these common rooms could be like in Paris in 1930. The German contribution to this otherwise insignificant exhibition was enormously successful. It included a large swimming and bathing room with gymnastic equipment and loungers, a "cafe-bar" with a dance-floor and alcoves for reading, games, and listening to the radio or gramophone, with a library on a gallery above. French critics were more than keen on the German designers' presentation, and referred to successful combinations of space and light, the "magic of precision" and the "mysterious beauty of the exact forms". In 1931, the Paris constructions were again presented at the German Construction Exhibition in Berlin, as the contribution of the Baugewerbebund (Building Trade Association). Again, the sports room was particularly elegant and well-designed, with wallbars, weights, a punch-ball, a wooden sparring partner and other equipment. The ideal person of the age had to be fit and active. Apparently, an up-to-date flat was incomplete if it did not have a room for physical training. There are sketches for a "Salle de culture physique" by Charlotte Perriand, drawings for a "Salle d'exercises et de massage" by Gabriel Guevrekian, a Persian living in Paris, and a series of designs for a "salle de gymnastique" by Robert Mallet-Stevens. A much-publicised villa built by Mallet-Stevens in the south of France in 1926 had its own sports tract with a swimming pool. Marcel Breuer created a "House for a Sportsman" at the Berlin building exhibition, which consisted mainly of a large training room, with cabins for sleeping, bathing, changing, eating and work separated off by cupboards and folding partitions.

Unlike the architects Ludwig Mies van der Rohe, Walter Gropius or Marcel Breuer, who also designed and provided furniture to match their buildings, Le Corbusier used items on the normal market for his until the late twenties. On the terraces he placed mass-produced light, ornate iron furniture, for the interiors he took heavy, conventional armchairs and the common Thonet chairs, especially model No. 9, which he made particularly frequent use of.

The first building for which he provided at least some of his own furniture was the controversial Pavillon de L'Esprit Nouveau, his contribution to the Exposition Internationale des Arts Décoratifs et Industriels Modernes in Paris in 1925 (page

Ludwig Mies van der Rohe, modern replica of a lounger in tubular steel with leather upholstery, Model 242, designed 1931/32. Initially, it was offered by the Bamberg Metallwerkstätten in Berlin in a less luxurious version, with rubber or linen covers.
Knoll International, Murr/Murr

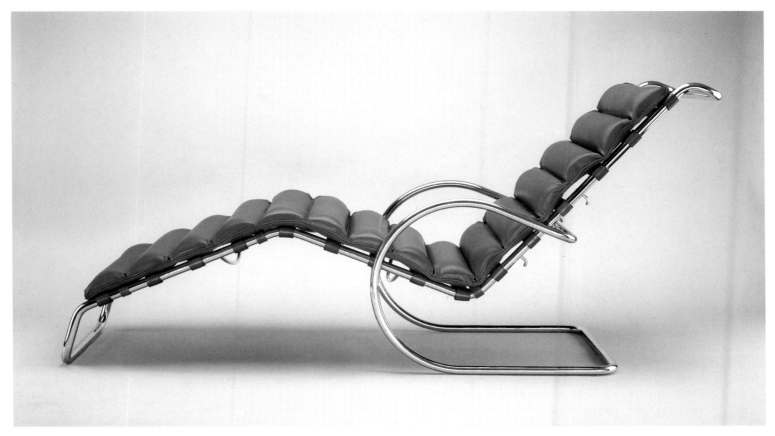

Le Corbusier, Pierre Jeanneret, Charlotte Perriand, "one-room-flat" at the Salon d'Automne, Paris, 1929. The team of designers here for the first time exhibited an interior completely furnished with their own designs; illustration from "Innen-Dekoration" XLI, 1930.

98). Le Corbusier exhibited a house, which he understood as part of a "machine à habiter": from the outside, it was a strict cube, with large, geometrically structured glass surfaces and a terrace cut in to it, inside, an open living hall with a sleeping gallery (page 90). The living room was structured only by freestanding box elements, the "casiers standards", developed by Le Corbusier.

Le Corbusier believed the term "furnishings" was somewhat "loose and vague", and so, at this time, he preferred to refer to *equipement*. "Equipment means ordering the various elements necessary to meet household requirements by means of a clear analysis of their function. Boxes replace the numerous pieces of furniture with all their different names . . . Boxes for clothes, all sorts of textiles, crockery, glasses, artistic objects, books. They are no longer manufactured in wood, but in metal, and in those factories which used to produce only office furniture. The boxes form the complete equipment for a house and leave a maximum of space free in the rooms. Chairs and tables are the only other pieces which remain." Trunks, the shelf systems in shops and metal office cupboards were probably the models for these "casiers".

At the Paris autumn "Salon" in 1929, Le Corbusier presented a "Single-Room Flat", for the first time completely with his own furniture. Two thirds of the total ninety square metres were furnished as a large living area, with the rest for cooking, sleeping and bathing. The only partitions were formed by box combinations, open to both sides, only half the height of the room, apart from the kitchen, where they reached up to the ceiling. The floor was covered in robust, greenish glass tiles, and the tables also had glass tops with a green shimmer.

These and the chairs had chromium-plated or painted steel frames. The covers were of yellowish brown leather, calfskin and a linen-type fabric. The ceilings and walls were in smooth, ivory-coloured plaster. The "casiers" had glass shelves, wooden or metal compartments or other components to suit a particular purpose – for instance in the kitchen, wooden racks for fruit and vegetables. The boxes were closed off with sheet steel doors, sometimes painted, or noulded glass sliding doors.

If contemporary reports are to be believed, public reaction to this new "Single-Room Flat" was reticent rather than approving. Of course widely differing explanations were offered for this. Alfred Wenzel, an author for the periodical *Innendekoration*, tried a psychological approach. He argued that it was caused by "fear of the emptiness of the external environment", by the *horror vacui*, which he said was symptomatic of a lack of inner fulfilment. "Things which are not useful, which people collect and place or hang around them, are just aids, which represent attempts to provide content: a short of self-defence against the huge yawning emptiness, which emerges from inside the self." He believed that the fact that houses have become a little emptier was a point in favour of modern man. "There seems to be a need inside us for light, free spaces, areas onto which we can project a new, richer feeling for life . . . that is why an 'empty' wall no longer seems to be gaping at us. It seems we don't have the same need to focus our vision. Everything suggests that we no longer need the "many" things which people used to need to protect them from being alone with themselves."

All the Corbusier furniture pieces, which are produced today as modern classics, were designed in 1928, apart from the "casier standard" cupboards system: the "Fauteuil à dossier basculant", a small armchair with a flexible back, the "Fauteuil grand confort" as a "petit" and a "grand modèle"; the

Le Corbusier, Pierre Jeanneret, Charlotte Perriand, modern replica of a table, Model LC6, designed in 1928 as a "Table tube d'avion". For the frame, Le Corbusier intended to use prefabricated, aerodynamically shaped steel sections produced for the aviation industry. The tubes used in the replica have an elliptic cross-section instead of the drop-shape used at that time.
Cassina, Meda/Milan
Le Corbusier believed that the materials and products used in industry were ideally suited for the "equipement" of contemporary homes; they were functional, practical and had no unnecessary decoration. For instance, he used flasks and beakers from chemical accessories dealers as vases.

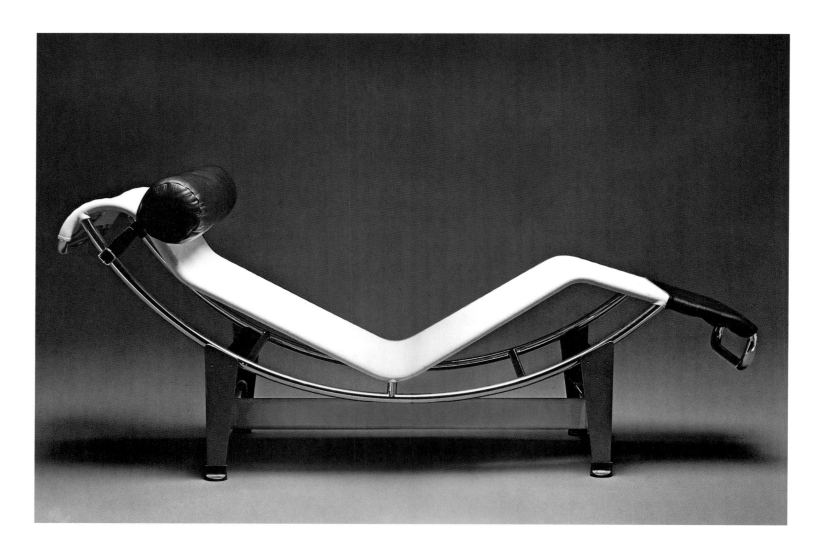

Le Corbusier, Pierre Jeanneret, Charlotte Perriand, modern replica of a chaise-longue, Model LC4, designed in 1928; the lower steel frame is painted in two colours, the steel upper frame is chromium-plated. The cover is of white fabric with a pillow and footrest of black leather. The angle of the bed can be adjusted. Cassina, Meda/Milan

"Chaise longue à réglage continu", a "rest machine", as Corbusier called it; the large glass-topped table "Table tube d'avion, section ovoïde"; the "Siège tournant, fauteuil", a swivel chair with armrests and the "Siège tournant, tabouret", a matching swivel stool. Le Corbusier is named as the designer of these models, along with his cousin Pierre Jeanneret and Charlotte Perriand, who joined the office of the other two in 1927. Pierre Jeanneret probably concerned himself mostly with business affairs. Charlotte Perriand's share in the design work is now thought to have been more important than it was a few years ago. Le Corbusier was already working on the lounger in the early 1920s. The first sketches are reminiscent of traditional wooden loungers, the final form is like the "Surrepos" of the Paris doctor Pascaud: an upholstered seat shaped like the human body, mounted on a steel frame and with a hand-wheel to adjust it to the required position. Le Corbusier did not keep to this mechanism. The user of his chaise longue had to get up to adjust the position. The "Basculant" is a successful adaptation of the colonial or safari chair. And Le Corbusier did not deny this relationship; on the contrary, in the Swiss students' house for the university in Paris, for example, he blatantly displayed his shining chrome "Basculant" together with the original wooden model. Tubular steel furniture was not expensive in the late twenties and early thirties, although it was only produced in relatively small quantities. Yet it was bought mostly by fairly well-off customers, who were open-minded enough to appreciate it. The intellectual élite that opted for these obviously technically orientated objects, thus demonstrated its aesthetic awareness. The architect Hans Luckardt wrote: "The in-

Le Corbusier, Pierre Jeanneret, Charlotte Perriand, combined bath and bedroom of a "one-room-flat", presented at the 1929 Autumn Salon in Paris. In the foreground, a stool with a towelling seat, in the background a "Fauteuil à dossier basculant"; both pieces are offered by the Cassina company in replica today.

Le Corbusier, Pierre Jeanneret, Charlotte Perriand, modern replica of an armchair, Model LC3, as "Fauteuil grand confort, grand modèle", designed in 1928; chromium-plated steel frame, black leather. The cushions are loose; on old pictures, they appear to be softer, more flexible and casual. This makes the chair less plain and stiff than today's version. The join between the L-shaped components and the tubular elements of the frame, which consists of one welded seam, turned out to be a weak point in the construction. Cassina, Meda/Milan

creased use of steel in the manufacture of furniture is beginning to have a significant influence on the development of a new furniture style in the same way as the use of steel structures in building construction did on modern architecture. The formal transformation of chairs and sofas by the use of a framework of resilient metal is a clearly visible characteristic. The seat is held by elastic supports, which has led to completely new and unusual forms. Everything is dominated by smooth, elegant lines; from this point of view, the steel armchair is unsurpassed. Steel has a natural elasticity, which can be exploited to a high degree in the interests of comfort. And steel had the added advantage of a certain uniformity, from a psychological and an aesthetic point of view, it makes the impression of being 'pure'. This leads to new relations between man and material, house occupant and house furnishings, when it is used in the home."

While utopian ideas were beginning to be put into practice in Germany and France as numerous projects and designs were carried out in a technical, functional style, in Austria, the country which had shown such promising signs of modern development around 1900, some subtle and refined pieces emerged, but there were no signs of anything avant-garde. There was a different emphasis there. The major community housing construction projects, which were created in Vienna in the course of the 1920s, proved that there were people in the Austrian capital who were conscious of the need for social projects. The

Marcel Breuer, library in the house of the banker Eduard von der Heydt, around 1930. Breuer's prominent clientele in Berlin at this time included the theatre producer Erwin Piscator and the psychology professor Kurt Lewin, who, as Breuer himself put it, allowed him to furnish their homes with complete disregard for tradition and what was usual.

Wassily and Hans Luckhardt, dining room, 1930; manufactured by the Deutsche Stahlmöbel Company, Berlin. At the table, chair Model SS32 by the Luckhardt brothers. For the surfaces of the cabinets in the background, a new material was used – pressed, high-gloss synthetic resin. Illustrated in "Innen-Dekoration" XLII, 1931.

Wassily and Hans Luckhardt, copyright Lorenz/ Luckhardt, modern replica of a tubular steel chair, Model S36, designed in 1930. Gebr. Thonet, Frankenberg

Hans Luckhardt wrote in the magazine "Innen-Dekoration" in 1931: "With its clear and attractive appearance, steel furniture is a living expression of our striving for rhythm, functionality, hygiene, cleanliness, lightness, simplicity of form. Steel is the material that is hard, resistant, durable, but which, at the same, flexibly responds to the free creative urge. A well-formed piece of steel furniture possesses an exclusive, independent aesthetic value of its own."

Adolf Loos, Parts of glass set No. 248, 1931. Loos
wrote confidently in a letter to the manufacturer,
J & L. Lobmeyr in Vienna: "I have given you the
measurements and cutting instructions for a new
glass set, and it must be manufactured without
any changes. Changes should be left to time. The
designs for this set did not stem from the whim of
a dessinateur . . ., they represent an attempt to
express a new philosophy in these glasses."

Viennese architect Franz Schuster, who also worked for Das Neue Frankfurt,
was the one who developed the most consistent ideas here. His unit assembly
furniture was designed to make it possible for people to furnish their homes
individually from a programme of separate units. But the "official" style, represented by the Austrian Werkbund, avoided this sort of experimentation. It
was only towards the end of the twenties that change set in, when various
quarrelling groups within the association were united, and progressive forces
gained influence. This was also the signal to start a project comparable to the
Weissendorf estate project. This resulted in new contacts between Austria and
the German Werkbund. Austria was re-connected with the outside world. But
the 1930 exhibition by the Austrian Werkbund was still very conservative. It did
not propagate the idea of a "New Vienna", but was dominated by the old
favourite themes: fashion and the coffee house. Josef Frank, for instance,
showed a tea salon, Oswald Haerdt built a room for the Austrian government-
owned tobacco trade, Eduard Josef Wimmer-Wisgrill designed a beauty parlour and Oskar Strnad a bar. The transparency of Ernst Lichtblau's tourism
pavilion and the bright, automated elegance of Felix Augenfeld's espresso bar
were, however, convincingly modern. These contributions created the impression that nothing had seen left to chance. In contrast to some of the objects shown
at exhibitions at this time, they really appeared to be designed for use.

At this time, Josef Frank was in charge of planning a model estate based on
the Stuttgart one. Since the community house building aid programme was
financing the Vienna project, the initial idea of houses with flats on several
floors had to be abandoned in favour of small single houses, mostly terraced
houses. In spite of the economic crisis, the Hagenau estate was completed in
1932, and contained seventy houses. Josef Frank had made a point of inviting
important architects who had not been considered in Stuttgart, including Gerrit
Rietveld, Hugo Häring and André Lurçat. He found the line taken by Gropius
and Le Corbusier too formalistic. But as far as interior decoration was con-

*Café terrace with yellow and red painted tubular
steel furniture at the exhibition by the Austrian
Werkbund, 1930. Behind the pool is Ernst
Lichtblau's tourism pavilion.*

Felix Augenfeld, Karl Hofmann, interior of an espresso bar at the exhibition by the Austrian Werkbund, 1930.

cerned, nothing new was forthcoming in Vienna. The construction method also remained to a large extent traditional. Whereas the Weissendorf estate had been extended by an experimental area for new building methods, Frank's estate was limited to houses which could actually go on sale. But although the price was lowered several times, only fifteen houses could actually be sold. The rest became the property of the town and were let out.

In Italy, which was under fascist rule from 1923 onwards, promoting progressive development was an important part of official government policy. This gave a chance to other modern tendencies which were rejected in Germany as "cultural bolshevism". It was not necessarily odd to be a representative of the avant-garde and a fascist at the same time. One famous example is Giuseppe Terragni, whose Casa del Fascio in Como is a classic example of modern building. The undisturbed relationship also became clear from the Milan Triennials, the large-scale, three-yearly forum for new Italian design. From 1933 on, the official title was "Triennale internazionale delle arti decorative e industriali moderne e dell'architettura moderna". This was clearly reminiscent of the Paris exhibition in 1925, but the programme placed a greater emphasis on taking account of new technical developments. The "Casa elettrica" in 1930 – an elegant building full of electrical appliances –, Luciano Baldessari's press pavilion in 1933 and Franco Albini's graceful exhibition room for antique goldsmiths' work showed a high architectural standard. Apart from the designers

Enrico Prampolini, the hall of an airport building, displayed at the 5th Triennial in Milan, 1933. Prampolini was one of the outstanding futurists. In Paris in 1925, he showed a "magnetic theatre", in which actors were replaced by lighting effects.

"Modern life knows two apparently opposed phenomena: the loud call of the masses for collective gatherings – especially sports events – and an increasingly lively interest in the house, its architecture, management and comfort ... and so architecture today has experienced the growth not only of stadiums and public gym halls, but also of domestic facilities for exercise and sport." Quoted from the magazine "Domus", 1936.

mentioned already, Gio Ponti and Gabriele Mucchi were also important. They both worked a lot for industry, Ponti for Fontana arte, Mucchi for Emilio Pino's furniture factory.

Unlike in Germany and Austria, Italian designers in the thirties were particularly engaged in converting the interiors of old buildings. The few designers who were interested in creating new furniture were confronted with a specifically Italian problem: a shortage of wood. The country's autarkic policy made imports difficult. And so, other materials, such as iron and steel, which had been neglected in Italy, came to the forefront. Italian visitors to the Weissenhof exhibition in Stuttgart had seen that these materials were well-suited to the construction of modern furniture. These objects exerted a certain fascination, and aroused the desire to produce similar designs in this field. Numerous calls for the development of a typically Italian modern style unleashed a feverish search for original tubular steel designs. In 1936, Gabriele Mucchi, dissatisfied with achievements in Italy to date, wrote in an essay for the magazine *Domus*: "Let's create an authentic object rather than a copy." Nine years after the Weissenhof exhibition, it looked as if the Italians were still worried by the lack of originality in their furniture designs. They also got little support from manufacturers. For instance in 1929, a two-legged tubular steel chair designed by Piero Bottoni was rejected by all the furniture companies. It was only finally produced by Thonet in 1930. Of course, at the Triennial Exhibitions, model flats also played a role. In 1936, Franco Albini exhibited an innovative solution for a small flat. Underneath a high-rise bed, he stored sports equipment, and the ladder also functioned as wallbars. The same year, the architects Banfi, Belgioioso, Peressutti and Rogers presented a room for two sporty young men – an allusion to Marcel Breuer's design. The room was divided into sleeping, sports and bathroom areas by translucent ceiling-to-floor curtains. The Triennial Exhibition increasingly became an international event. The discovery of 1936 was the Finnish architect Alvar Aalto, with his light, elegantly bent plywood furniture.

The Italians had evidently been quick to realise that the Scandinavian was introducing a completely new aesthetic. The construction principles were the same as with tubular steel furniture, but the warmth of the blonde wood seemed more friendly than cool metal. All Alvar Aalto's furniture designs originated in connection with his buildings. He regarded furniture as "accessories to architecture". For the town library in Viipuri, he developed a whole family of chairs and stools. The common feature was the design of the legs. In order to be able to shape the solid birchwood, slits were sawn into it, which made it flexible. Veneer strips were glued in to reinforce it.

For the sanatorium in Paimio, Aalto at first experimented with tubular steel frames, in the shape of Mart Stam's cantilever chair. But, he wrote later, "we soon changed over to wood, because a lot of this nickel or chromium-plated steel furniture seems too harsh, psychologically, for the environment of sick people. And so we began to work with wood, using this warmer and more pliant material as a basis to construct a functional style of furniture for patients. From these beginnings, we gradually went into furniture construction, not just for the sanatorium, but for general purposes as well." In the mid-thirties, Alvar Aalto founded his own furniture factory, Artek, as a Centre for Contemporary Furniture, Interiors, Art and Industrial Design, an enterprise which is still active today. From playful experiments with birchwood, which is extremely elastic, and was used in Finnish industry exclusively for skis at this time, Aalto developed a new

Giuseppe Terragni, modern replica of a tubular steel chair with seat and back of beech plywood, Model "Lariana", designed in 1936. Zanotta, Nova Milanese

Gabriele Mucchi, modern replica of an adjustable reclining chair of tubular steel, Model "Genni", leather upholstery, designed in 1934. Zanotta, Nova Milanese

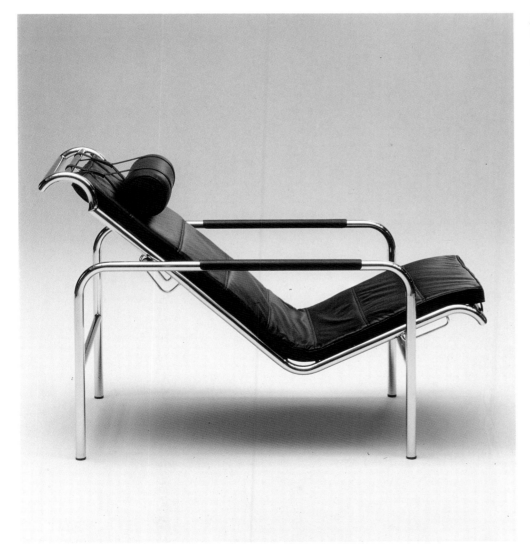

Alvar Aalto, stool, Model 60, birchwood,
linoleum-covered seat, 1930–33.
Artek, Helsinki

Alvar Aalto, chair, Model 69, seat and frame of
birchwood, 1930–33.
Artek, Helsinki

process for the manufacture of solid frame constructions: plywood sheets glued in layers on top of each other were bent and pressed using steam, and then cut into strips of the required width. Thanks to improved glues, such as those developed by Otto Korhonen – a furniture manufacturer and friend of Aalto's – for the aviation industry, production could be simplified and the dry wood bent in hydraulic presses. The early 1930s armchair called "Paimio", after the sanatorium, stood on wooden runners. All that was missing was the springy, self-supporting chair. Aalto created it in the mid-thirties, exploiting the elasticity of birchwood glued together in layers.

A flat in a house in Doldertal, near Zürich, gave the impression of being a resumé of all the trends in design during the twenties and thirties. It represented in miniature the "International Style" described and celebrated in a 1932 New York Exhibition by the American Philip Johnson. In the room, which has clear contours, broad openings and pleasingly exact details, Marcel Breuer's tubular steel furniture encounter Alvar Aalto's plywood furniture. A serving trolley was designed by the Swiss Alfred Roth, who worked with Le Corbusier for some time. On the terrace there are aluminium loungers, which Breuer designed in 1933 for the Embru company.

The house was designed by the architects Marcel Breuer and Alfred and Emil Roth in 1936/37 for the engineer and modernist propagandist Sigfried Giedion. For many years, Giedion was secretary general of the International Congress of Modern Architecture (CIAM), and one of the initiators of the model estate Neubühl, which the Swiss Werkbund had built in 1931 as a counterpart to the Stuttgart project. The furniture for this "experimental area for a liberated lifestyle" could be acquired from the Wohnbedarf AG company in Zürich, a concern founded by Sigfried Giedion along with Werner Moser and Rudolf Graber. Their modern furniture, which included the "Volksmodell", an armchair without back legs, shared the fate of that in other countries. It did not become commercially successful. In Switzerland too, the modern style remained "for the time being, a matter for the élite".

Alvar Aalto, armchair, Model 41, laminated, bent birchwood frame, seat of shaped, varnished plywood, 1930–33. Aalto designed it with his wife Aino for the Paimio sanatorium in western Finland, which they built together.

Alvar Aalto, armchair, Model 406, bent birchwood with interwoven straps, 1935–39. This use of jute or fabric for the seat and back was typical of Scandinavian furniture design and was probably used most consistently by the Swede, Bruno Mathsson.
Artek, Helsinki

Jules Leleu, dining room, shown at the Exposition Internationale des Arts Décoratifs et Industriels Modernes in Paris, 1925. The suite of furniture was complemented by carpets by Bruno da Silva Bruhns.

In France, the Establishment had survived the First World War virtually intact, and continued with its earlier lifestyle. Paris remained the starting point for artists' careers – whether they were French or foreign. It was fashionable to have tea, arrange meetings or even live as long-term guests in the large hotels. Biographical reports by Serge Diaghilev, Misia Sert and Coco Chanel, his two rivalling patronesses, provide a detailed picture of this. Although Berlin was increasingly becoming the meeting place for the avant-garde, Paris remained the centre for international society. It continuously drew attention to this with spectacular events, for instance the four major "Salons", which took place annually. The spring and autumn "Salons" were an important forum for applied art.

All this was overshadowed in 1925 by the Exposition Internationale des Arts Décoratifs et Industriels Modernes. It turned into an encounter between asceticism and luxury, but they were not evenly natched. The one side was probably most convincingly represented by Konstantin Melnikov's Russian pavilion, in the contructivist tradition of Vladimir Tatlin; by the Austrian "Raumstadt" contribution by Friedrich Kiesler, the model of a metropolis off the ground, or the Pavillon de L'Esprit Nouveau by Le Corbusier. But important representatives were not present: the De Stijl artists had been rejected and Germany was not

Dining room in the Pavillon de Sèvres at the Exposition Internationale, Paris, 1925. The architect was Marc Ducluzeau, the furniture was by Bernel, all the glass elements in the room were designed by René Lalique. Glass was used in various differing ways: it filled the panels of the coffered ceiling and formed the round inserts on the floor. There were also candlesticks, candelabra and table glasses.

Pierre Chareau, desk of palm wood, shown at the Exposition Internationale in 1925. It was part of the contribution by the Societé des Artistes Décorateurs, who presented interiors for the residence of a French diplomat in their pavilion. Musée des Arts Décoratifs, Paris

Emile-Jacques Ruhlmann's pavilion at the 1925
Exposition Internationale in Paris, called "L'Hotel
d'un Collectionneur". The architect was Pierre
Patout. Inside, Ruhlmann – his name can be seen
on the roof – displayed suites for whole rooms in
the "Home of a wealthy art collector". His
furniture was complemented by works by famous
artists, such as Edgar Brandt and Jean Dupas.

Emile-Jacques Ruhlmann, "Table lambiotte a
plateau pivotant", a table with a movable top of
amboyna root with ivory inlay, 1925.
Galerie Vallois, Paris

Emile-Jacques Ruhlmann, amboyna root
"chiffonier" with inlaid ivory, 1922/23. Ruhlmann
frequently used variations of this basic form.
Typical features are the slim, almost pointed legs
and the sparse, but effective decoration.
Alain Lesieutre, Paris

invited at all. For the other side, French designers exhibited "in extravagant profusion" what Alastair Duncan described as the "last of the great culinary styles", "Art Déco", as it was later called, an allusion to the title of the exhibition at the time.

In 1912, the French parliament had already approved the project of an "Exposition Internationale" in Paris, to restore the prestige of French arts and crafts, halt the influx of foreign products and promote French articles. Only works in the "new style" were to be allowed, copies of historic designs were to be excluded. The event was envisaged as a reaction to the activities of the German Werkbund, especially to its vehemently self-confident appearance at the World Fair in Brussels in 1910. The opening was originally planned for 1915, but was postponed several times because of the war and only actually took place in 1925. The leading manufacturers and designers were grouped together on the "Rive Gauche". The best places were allotted to the large Paris department stores, Au Bon Marché, Le Louvre, Au Printemps and Les Galeries Lafayette. Their art studios, for instance Printemps' Primavera, enjoyed an excellent reputation, and their designs were considered to be trendsetters. But the pavilions of the individual exhibitors could compare favourably with them, although some of them looked like oversized chocolate boxes set out in the grass.

Emile-Jacques Ruhlmann, "cabinet du travail" for
an art collector, shown at the Salon des Artistes
Décorateurs in Paris in 1926. The desk and the
bookcase in front of Jean Dupas' monumental
wall painting were solid Macassar ebony with
metal frames. The voluminous armchair in the
background, known as the "Elephant chair", was
one of the exhibition's much-admired attractions.

The exhibition was an enormous success and a triumph for the French art of
furniture making. One favourite with the public – and with French critics – was
the "Ambassade Française" in the pavilion of the Société des Artistes Décorateurs, which was given generous financial support from the Ministry of the
Arts. The designs for this residence for a French diplomat came from excellent
designers like Francis Jourdain, the old master of the straight line and strict
form, Jean Dunand, Pierre Chareau, Jean Lurçat, Robert Mallet-Stevens, André
Groult and the new star, Emile-Jacques Ruhlmann.

Recognition of the exhibition was, of course, balm to France's self-confidence
and justified in retrospect the considerable expense of the presentation. The
effort paid off. Leleu, for instance, who also had some individual pieces in the
"Ambassade" mentioned above, received orders for interiors of ministries and
embassies, and even provided a dining room for the Elysée palace.

The "Hotel d'un Collectionneur", by Emile-Jacques Ruhlmann, was unanim-
ously declared to be the high-point of the exhibition. In this pavilion, he displayed a complete set of furniture for the "residence of a rich art collector". His
furniture suites were complemented by exceptional pieces by other artists.
Contemporary critics showered him with praise and drew extremely flattering
comparisons. He was described as the only true artistic cabinet maker of the
20th century, worthy of comparison with the great artist craftsmen of the 18th
century. It must be added that Ruhlmann himself was not a cabinet maker, but he

was able to acquire excellent advisers and to select good craftsmen, who could still be found in the Faubourg St. Antoine just as they could in 18th century Paris. Ruhlmann drew small-scale sketches of his pieces from various perspectives, which were then turned into working plans under strict control in a special drawing office. He selected rare and expensive materials: as well as the traditional ebony, he used extremely rare materials such as Amboyna wood, combined with parchment or Galuchat, the skin of the cat shark; for the inlay work he used ivory, tortoise-shell or horn. His furniture was characterised by a certain tension between the relatively simple basic form, the delightful decor and the extravagant material. It surprises us today to hear that Ruhlmann said he was concerned to create "pure forms, determined by reason". But we can follow him when he says he wanted to achieve "a beautiful relation between the various elements as well as elegant and direct lines".

The manufacture of his pieces was time-consuming. Jules Deroubaix, one of Ruhlmann's most faithful and conscientious workers, worked for two to five months on one single piece. Of course, this had its price. Some critics attacked Ruhlmann's extraordinary exclusiveness, which only a few people could afford. His response was: "The development of a contemporary style for interior decoration will only really succeed properly when people in the middle income bracket begin to become interested in it. But since expensive experiments with luxury furniture are necessary as a first step in this Renaissance of interior

Eugène Printz, "commode à tiroirs", of Brasilian jacaranda wood, known as Rio polisander, and patinated, gold-plated copper, 1933. Musée d'Art Moderne de la Ville de Paris

Emile-Jacques Ruhlmann, desk from the study of the Maharajah of Indore, Macassar ebony and chrome, 1932. Originally, Ruhlmann had designed a black lacquered version for the French politician André Tardieu.
Sotheby's, London

design, art of this sort must first be developed with the patronage of the rich, just as art in earlier eras developed with the patronage of the court." The prices for Ruhlmann's furniture were really exorbitant and could only be paid by a handful of chosen customers: industrial magnates, bankers, stars on the artistic scene or well-to-do aristocrats. He also had public orders, for instance for the new interior of the conference room and the ballroom for the Chambre de Commerce or orders from large companies, like the New York City Bank, which commissioned him to design its Paris branch.

Even if "Les Etablissements Ruhlmann et Laurent" – the expert on paintings, Pierre Laurent, was a friend and companion – were amongst the most exclusive which Paris had to offer at the time, the order books of other Art Déco tists were also filled with prominent names. For instance the Princess de la Tour d'Auvergne, Vicomte de Richmont or the famous fashion designer Jeanne Lanvin were amongst the famous customers of Eugène Printz. Whereas it was the dignified elegance and the excellent working of luxurious materials that attracted people to Ruhlmann's work, Printz's strong-point was the eccentricity of his designs and the imaginative combination of materials. Eugène Printz had contributed to the 1925 exhibition, but he had not attracted a lot of attention. His real debut was at the 1926 autumn "Salon", where he successfully exhibited a rosewood bedroom suite. A series of his most notable designs originated in the 1930s. These are pieces with a contrasting combination of metal and wood.

One cupboard, which he designed in 1933, has a long polisander unit of drawers resting on a massive cabinet with clearly defined inlay work, of Gabon ebony – one of Printz's favourite materials – which appeared to be suspended above the ground by an ornate filigree pedestal. Apart from this, sophisticated folding furniture and mobile elements were characteristic of Printz, for instance small, compact sets of occasional tables which could be unfolded. He introduced "portes d'accordéon" for cupboards, doors which could be opened and shut like an accordeon.

One fertile and prestigeous area of activity was the furnishing of the large French luxury liners, which were being produced one after the other in the twenties and early thirties: the "Paris", the "Ile de France", the "Lafayette", the "Atlantique" and, the final crowning glory, the "Normandie", which the newspapers described as the "most luxurious ship ever". For the leading designers responsible for the interiors, Lalique, Leleu, Follot, Dufrene, Dunand and Ruhlmann himself – he designed the First Class lounge on the "Ile de France" for instance – they were floating international shop windows. Critics praised them enthusiastically as "museums of interior decoration" and compared a stroll through the public rooms and luxury cabins of these ocean-going liners with a visit to the furniture sections of the "Salon d'Automne" or the "Salon des Artistes Décorateurs". But in some cases the magnificence of these "palaces of the seven seas" was short-lived. The "Atlantique", for example, was burnt out completely after just fifteen months. The "Normandie", which was anchored in New York harbour when the Second World War broke out, was requisitioned by the U.S. government and turned into a troop transporter.

The different schools and styles encountered each other in an unexpected location, far from Europe. The Maharajah Yeshwant Rao Holkar wanted to turn his new palace in Indore into a temple of the *goût moderniste*. The young prince had studied in Oxford in the late twenties, where he met the German architect Eckart Muthesius and commissioned him to build his palace. It was to contain

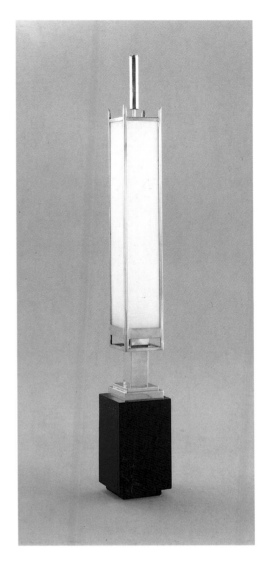

Eckart Muthesius, standard lamp, one of two designed for the palace of the Maharajah of Indore, nickel silver and glass, 1930/33. The lamp, two metres high overall, stands on a wooden base.
Sotheby's, London

The Maharajah of Indore's study, 1933. The furniture was supplied by the "Etablissements Ruhlmann et Laurent", the carpet was by Bruno da Silva Bruhns, and the wall decoration behind the bookcase was by Eckart Muthesius.

133

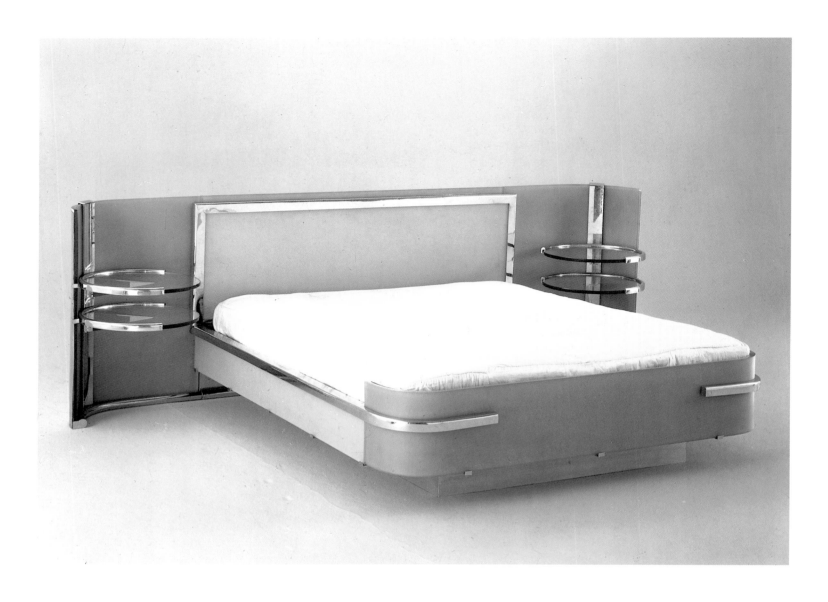

Louis Sognot, chrome and glass bed from the Maharani's bedroom in the Indore palace, 1930/33.
Sotheby's, London

private chambers, large public rooms – for instance a ballroom and banquet hall – and numerous guest rooms. Eckart Muthesius was also responsible for all the interiors. For the walls, he devised a mixture of gold, silver and glass dust, which shimmered golden yellow in the indirect lighting – also designed by Muthesius. A well-proportioned seating arrangement, combining black synthetic material with red paintwork, which he complemented with medium-high black cupboards, was one of his most successful pieces. For the library, he designed a particularly original piece: a deep armchair of bright red synthetic material with an inbuilt cigarette case, lighter and ashtray, and lamps integrated into each side of the back.

The palace was a dream commission for the architect, who had just turned twenty-five. His home city, Berlin, also benefitted: apart from the stonework of the walls, everything – from the floors to the window-frames – was made by German companies and then shipped to India. A series of furniture was bought in Paris and London, in Paris, predominately models by the designers in the Union des Artistes Modernes.

This group, U.A.M. for short, was brought together in 1930 by its joint rejection of the *goût antiquaire* and sought new forms of contemporary furniture by experimenting with metal, glass and synthetics. For the bedrooms of the Indore palace, aluminium and chrome beds by Louis Sognot and Charlotte Alix were chosen, and a dressing table and additional pieces made of the same materials;

complemented by leather armchairs with frames of chrome-plated band iron. Only some of these were actually new models. They were often variations on already existing designs. The glass and aluminium bed for the Maharani's bedroom, for instance, was based on a bed for first-class cabins on the "Atlantique". The chaise longue by Le Corbusier was given an exotic air by leopardskin covering, loungers by René Herbst and the "Transat" armchair by Eileen Gray were used without any changes. The commission for the maharajah's impressive study was given to the "Etablissements Ruhlmann et Laurent": a large, stately desk, bookcases of single cubic elements which could be combined in different ways and closed by glass doors, chairs and a suite of armchairs and settee. The clear styling, in expensive Macassar wood with chrome and glass, showed that Ruhlmann was able to adapt to the new trends of the early thirties, but there was still a disturbing lack of experience in dealing with technical details. For instance, the small hand-wheel to adjust the height of the desk is reminiscent of a common plumbing appliance. And the wastepaper basket attached to the desk looks cheap and is unsatisfactory. The tubular steel furniture in the less prestige-orientated rooms was provided by the English firm P.E.L. (Practical Equipment Limited); self-supporting chairs designed by the Luckhardt brothers were bought for the music room.

Another major order placed with a young architect at the same time was the Maison de Verre in Paris. The architect, Pierre Chareau, had made a successful debut at the 1925 Paris exhibition. His best piece at that time was an angular desk of palm wood. Chareau later continued to use this type of wood, but he combined it with metal to create exciting new furniture designs. For the less pretentious furniture which he designed around 1927, he combined wood with wrought iron. Here, he anticipated constructive features of his most famous work, completed a short time later. A suitable site for the Maison de Verre in Paris, a town villa for the wealthy gynaecologist, Dr. Jean Dalsace, was initially to be gained by demolishing a house at the back of it in the Rue St. Guillaume.

Eckart Muthesius, "coiffeuse roulante" of German silver and tinted mirror glass, designed for the Indore palace, 1930/33. Sotheby's, London

Eckart Muthesius, library in the Indore place, 1933. The table and bookshelves are of mahogany with a striking grain, glass and metal. The shelves in the background are like those of a glass cabinet, the shape is repeated in the wall-lamp. In the foreground is one of the most original models designed by Muthesius for the Maharajah: a deep armchair with inbuilt reading lamps.

Pierre Chareau, living hall in the villa of Dr. Jean Dalsace, Paris, 1932. Chareau was not only the architect, he also designed the furnishings.

However, since it could only be partially demolished, Chareau had to slot his new building underneath the remaining storeys of the old building. He solved the problem using a steel supporting construction, into which he inserted façades of glass bricks. The practice was on the ground floor, the private rooms above it, including an extensive hall over two storeys, used as a living room, the heart of the house. The massive metal supports stand undisguised in the room, which is evenly and gently lit through the opaque glass bricks. The floor covering is anti-slip rubber of the sort often used today in airports or schools. There is a remarkable discrepancy between the furniture, in the best Art Déco style, and the Corbusier-type fitted units, for instance the metal shelves for books at the back of the hall and along the banisters. The two floors, which are open to each other, are joined by gangway-like stairs. It is reminiscent of the interior of a ship, except for the abundance of light. There are only a few hatch-like windows allowing a view of the outside.

From 1930 on, Pierre Chareau regularly contributed to the U.A.M. exhibitions, especially developed versions of his early metal models, which he now used for offices. He did not use tubular steel – often the favourite material with the avant-garde – at all. One striking feature which relates him to other members of the U.A.M., such as Robert Mallet-Stevens or René Herbst, was his completely unconventional combination of materials, cheap elements with expensive ones, new technical features with traditional ones.

The architectonic principle of a large, fluctuating room, a house more or less without doors, which was used to such effect in the Maison de Verres, was developed to a particularly pure form in the work of the architect Ludwig Mies van der Rohe. The German pavilion at the International Exhibition in Barcelona in 1929 gave him the opportunity to put his idea into practice without any faults or limitations. He combined spatial freedom with a very consistent constructional principle. Elegant supports held all the weight, while the wall partitions only served the purpose of dividing the room. Large areas of glass formed the outer shell.

Ludwig Mies van der Rohe had moved in cosmopolitan circles in Berlin in the early twenties, including artists like Theo van Doesburg, El Lissitzky, Hans Arp, Tristan Tzara, Naum Gabo, Man Ray and Walter Benjamin. Thanks to the exhibitions by the group known as the Novembergruppe, he got the opportunity to display his visionary architectural projects – such as glass multi-storeys, or a reinforced concrete office block. Although the buildings were not constructed at the time, they made his name known.

As director of the Weissenhof exhibition in Stuttgart, he attained that international attention and recognition which made him a suitable designer for the German contribution to the International Exhibition in Barcelona in 1929. As well as the actual exhibition halls, a building was required, solely for reasons of prestige. It was also to house the official opening ceremony by the Spanish King Alfonso XIII and Queen Victoria Eugenia.

Ludwig Mies van der Rohe created a bright and spacious elegant pavilion. In front of the long, flat-roofed building was a broad travertine terrace with a shallow pool, which cleverly separated the building from the street. The interior was dominated by an extensive onyx doré wall partition, an exquisite golden brown shimmering marble with striking markings. For the surrounding walls, Mies used green Tinos marble and sheets of white, grey and green tinted glass with metal frames. The various areas flowed into each other. This made the

Eugène Printz, hexagonal side table, which can be unfolded to give a chain of three similar elements, around 1930.
Galerie L'Arc en Seine, Paris

Pierre Chareau, armchair, around 1928. Chareau liked to use wood with warm tones, like polisander and walnut, which were polished to give a high shine.
Sonnabend Gallery, New York

Ludwig Mies van der Rohe, reconstruction of the German pavilion at the International Exhibition in Barcelona in 1929. In the foreground, modern replicas of the Barcelona chair and matching stool. The foam cushions have leather covers and rest on leather straps. The frame of special chromium-plated spring steel has to be welded by hand even today, because of the difficult cross join.

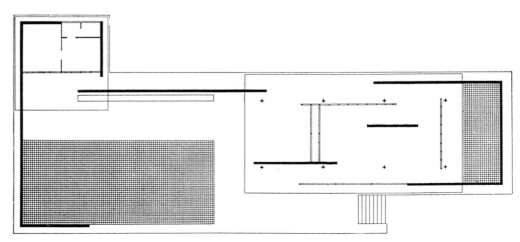

Ludwig Mies van der Rohe, ground plan for the Barcelona pavilion, 1929.

whole interior into a sort of continuum, an uninterrupted series of rooms, which made the impression of being extremely extensive, thanks to the clever opening up to the outside, which could be seen especially in the optical link to an attached courtyard, where the female nude statue "Morgen" by Georg Kolbe appeared to rise up out of a pool lined with a black glass. On a black carpet, Mies van der Rohe placed two chairs especially designed for the pavilion, and matching stools. During the opening ceremony they were to serve more or less as substitute thrones. The frames were of chromium-plated flat steel, the cushions, with white kid leather covers, rested on leather straps. The chairs were heavy, and they were meant to be. Unlike Breuer, who wanted mobility, Mies envisaged set positions for his furniture, from which they were not to be moved.

The report on the exhibition by the American critic Helen Appleton Read was very clear-sighted, and seems to be confirmed by the fame attained by the pavilion. At that time, she wrote: "Germany was the only one of the nations represented to symbolically express its modern industrial and cultural status... The austere elegance of the pavilion by Mies van der Rohe, a pioneer of modern architecture, is a symbol of the country's post-war culture, a convincing representation of the aesthetics of modern architecture... He is a radical rationalist, and his designs are determined by a passion for beautiful architecture. Mies is one of the few modern architects who goes beyond sterile functional formulas and turns his theory into artistic design. The means he uses to achieve the

René Herbst, Lady's desk, shown at the Exposition de Bureaux des Dames, Paris, 1928. Galerie Maria de Beyrie, Paris

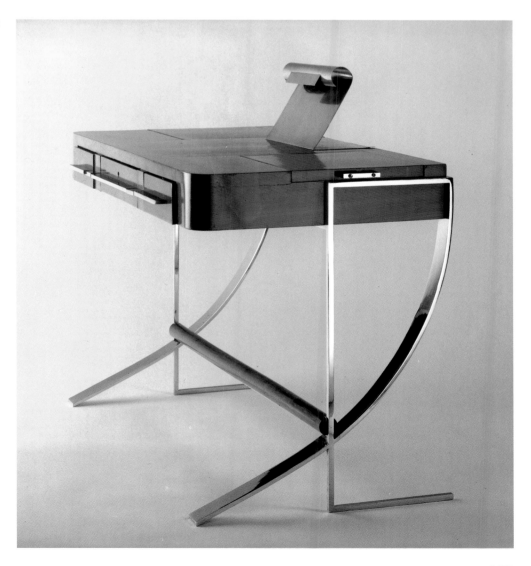

Ludwig Mies van der Rohe, living room in the Tugendhat villa in Brünn, 1931. The dining area is separated off from the other areas by a semi-circular partition.

Ludwig Mies van der Rohe, modern replica of a tubular steel armchair, Model "Brno", designed 1929/30 for the Tugendhat villa. For the original model, which was produced in Joseph Müller's metal workshop in Berlin, Mies used chromium-plated tubular steel and white calfskin upholstery. This re-edition pictured here is based on a later version in flat steel.
Knoll International, Murr/Murr

impression of elegant serenity are his materials and his concept of space."

The architectural concept behind the Barcelona pavilion was first used for a house in the Villa Tugendhat. The living area, 250 square metres, was divided up solely by means of a semi-circular wooden partition of Macassar ebony with a striking grain, and a wall of onyx doré, similar to the one used in Barcelona. The room opened out onto the garden to the south and east through wide, continuous glass sheets. Some of these windows could be lowered. The carefully placed Barcelona chairs were covered with emerald green leather, the covers for the Tugendhat chairs, specially designed for the house, were of silver-grey fabric, and those of the chairs which became famous as "Brno" were of ruby red velvet or white kid leather. Unfortunately, surviving photographs are in black-and-white. The curtains, which could be closed to hide the glass wall, were in silver-grey shantung silk, the floor covered with white linoleum. The eye was caught by the shining metal of the tables and chairs and of the supports and curtain rails.

The house was sharply attacked by contemporary critics, using trivial, niggling arguments. The Tugendhats defended their domicile and its architect in readers' letters: "This discipline makes it impossible to just pass the time resting and letting oneself go. And this compulsion to be active is just what people today need, tired out after work, feeling drained. We feel it to be a form of liberation." But it had taken quite some time before the master of the house came to accept

Ludwig Mies van der Rohe, group of chairs in the Tugendhat villa in Brünn, 1931. Opposite the Barcelona chairs are cantilever armchairs, designed by Mies van der Rohe especially for this house. In the background on the right, the library can be seen.

Salon with glass floor in the Paris flat of the milliner Suzanne Talbot, designed by Paul Ruaud with furniture designed by Eileen Gray in the early and late twenties; illustration from "L'Illustration", 1933.

Mies van der Rohe's designs. Mies commented: "Herr Tugendhat came to me. He received this house as a wedding present... He had seen a house I built when I was very young, and he liked it. He expected something similar... I went and had a look at the situation. I designed the house. I remember he saw the design on Christmas Eve. He almost collapsed! But his wife was interested in art; she had several van Gogh pictures. She said: 'Let's think about it.' Tugendhat would have liked to throw her out."

After the solitary task of the Barcelona pavilion, in the Villa Tugendhat Mies van der Rohe succeeded in establishing avant-garde design at a high social level and formulating it in an extremely elegant fashion. The artistic Art Déco movement, which based itself on tradition, with Ruhlmann and others, was followed in France by another experimental attitude. An impression of spaciousness was achieved not so much by stringent coolness as by the sovereign mixture of different cultures. Individualistic options were clearly given preference over architectural consistency. For instance, in a Paris interior, archaic African elements were combined with tubular steel and subtle Far-Eastern components on a glass floor.

This is the setting in which we meet the Irish designer Eileen Gray. In 1920, she had already designed luxurious, exotic pieces for the well-known milliner, Suzanne Talbot: armchairs covered in salmon-pink and orange-coloured silk, with carved snakes as armrests, a gondola-shaped chaise longue, reminiscent of a dugout canoe, zebra and leopard skins, and objects from Madame Talbot's African art collection. The walls and floors were in dark, warm colours. The picture was completed by black painted fitted cupboards. Interiors of this sort were en vogue when "La Revue Nègre" on the Champs Elysées was considered to be a chic night-time meeting place, and Josephine Baker was becoming the new Déesse of Paris society.

Eileen Gray, who had come to Paris at the beginning of the century, had made a name for herself with her lacquerwork, influenced by East Asian models. The fashion designer and patron Jacques Doucet, whose protéges at that time included a series of young cubist painters and furniture designers, such as Pierre Legrain and Paul Iribe, had also become an important supporter of Eileen Gray. As well as the artful creation of high-quality lacquered furniture – her paravents were amongst her best pieces – she began to experiment with new materials: aluminium, glass, celluloid and steel. In retrospect, she commented: "I wanted to make objects for our age – something that was possible, but had never been done by anyone. At that time, we were living in a terribly out-of-date world." But response to her unusual, progressive works was not very encouraging. Her small gallery in Faubourg St. Antoine went badly. Only her carpets, with their large geometric patterns, sold reasonably well. Her exhibition contribution for the Salon des Artistes Décorateurs in 1923 – a "Boudoir for Monte Carlo" – was sharply criticised and ridiculed as a "suitable room for Dr. Caligari's daughter". It was only appreciated by colleagues who were seeking solutions along similar lines: Le Corbusier, Walter Gropius and the Dutch De Stijl architects.

The extent to which new furniture design had become established by 1930 can be judged from the transformation of Madame Talbot's home. Instead of a sultry boudoir, there was a lucid and elegant atmosphere, with a mildly colonial touch. The salon was given a glass floor, the walls were painted white. Parts of the exotic furnishings were retained and combined with comfortable leather armchairs, designed by Eileen Gray in 1929.

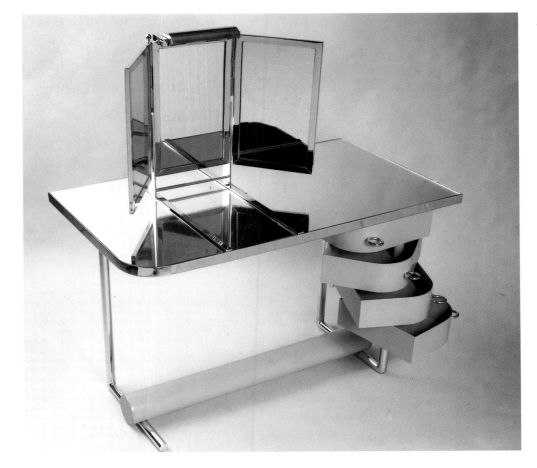

René Herbst, dressing table, chromium-plated and painted steel, designed for the Princess Aga Khan, 1930.
Galerie Maria de Beyrie, Paris

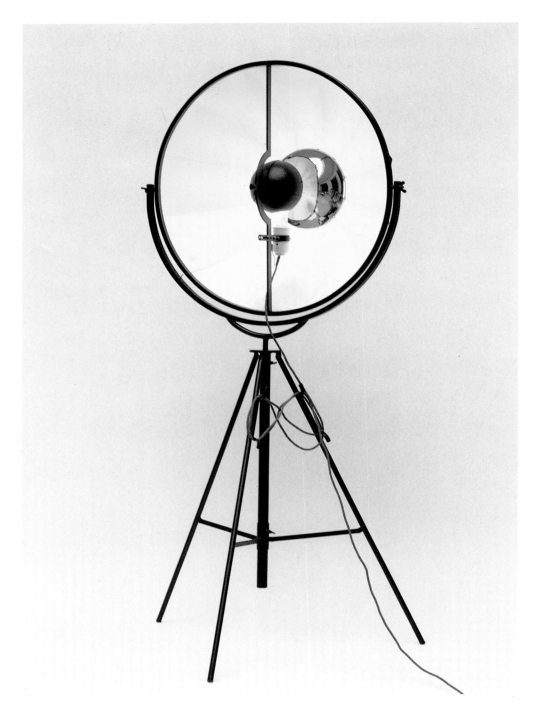

<u>Mariano Fortuny</u>, modern replica of a lamp,
reminiscent of a studio spotlight; painted and
nickel-plated metal, stretched fabric reflector.
Fortuny, who made a name for himself
particularly as a creator of fashion and designer
of stage costumes, had also developed new
electrical lighting systems for the theatre at the
beginning of the century.
Ecart International, Paris

A similar luxurious, cosmopolitan style was to be found in the latest mode of transport: the fast airships, which were now in competition with the large ocean-going liners. In 1935, the Graf Zeppelin made regular trips to South America. The new LZ 129 Hindenburg was to be filled with non-combustible helium, for safety reasons, and was designed especially for the North-Atlantic route between Europe and the USA. It was 245 metres long, almost the length of the Queen Mary, the largest ocean-going steamer at the time. The interior was planned by the architect Fritz August Breuhaus de Groot. Breuhaus had become famous with several luxury villas and the interiors of ships and aircraft. Unlike its predecessor, the Graf Zeppelin, the Hindenburg had several public rooms as well as the 25 double cabins. The two-storey passenger area was down in the belly of the giant airship. On the top deck, as well as the cabins there was a dining room, a sort of and a writing room, at the lower deck a smoking room, the

Eileen Gray, modern replica of the "Siège transat", lacquered wood, nickel-plated metal and leather, designed in 1927 for a villa in Roquebrune on the Côte d'Azur.
Ecart International, Paris

Jean Prouvé, modern replica of an adjustable chair, Model D80, designed in 1930. Two tension springs ensure that the seat element, which runs on ball bearings on the inner side of the supporting elements at the side, can easily be moved from a sitting to a reclining position.
Tecta, Lauenförde

"The construction of a piece of furniture is an important, even a very important thing, especially when it is a matter of creating models to be reproduced in large numbers. Furniture has to face a lot of wear and must be able to stand up to it. The problems which have to be solved here are as complex as with large building constructions. For me, furniture is comparable to the frames for machines which have to take a lot of stress, and that is what brought me to design it with the same care, and even according to the same laws of statics, and even using the same materials. I was not content with bent tubular steel. I was inspired by sheet steel, with finished edges, perforated, corrugated, then welded. This resulted in sections of the same robust quality and strong components, which stood out thanks to sophisticated details and good manufacture... In my opinion, furniture design requires the same procedure as any other building construction." (Jean Prouvé)

145

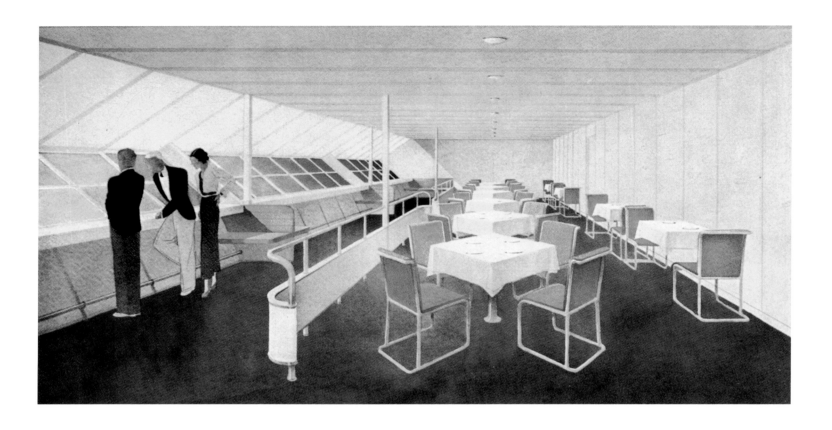

Fritz August Breuhaus, view of the dining room with cushioned aluminium chairs in the Hindenburg, 1935.

kitchen, the washrooms and the rooms for the crew. Whereas the cabins were only one and a half metres by two and had no windows, the public rooms provided quite a lot of room for movement and wide views. To save weight, all the furniture was made of aluminium, including the piano in the largest public room. Its light metal structure was covered with yellow leather.

When the airship made its first journey in March 1936, its gas compartments were filled with explosive hydrogen instead of helium, as the United States had refused to allow the export of the necessary helium. That year, more than a thousand passengers crossed the Atlantic in the airship, which was regularly booked out. But on the first trip of 1937, catastrophe struck at Lakehurst airport in the USA. Shortly before landing, the airship burst into flames. What caused the fire was never discovered. But this marked the end of the zeppelin era; uncomfortable and noisy aeroplanes succeeded them in intercontinental travel.

Progress in the United States was always open to European influences, but generally succeeded in finding paths of its own. The artistic battles of principle in the "Old World" must have been difficult to comprehend from the point of view of the deliberately pragmatic lifestyle of the USA. Apart from Tiffany, there was no strongly developed American Art Nouveau, and the influence of Art Déco only made an impact on the architecture of skyscrapers, hardly at all on furniture design. The Bauhaus and related styles really remained outsiders in the initial stages. But one area of extremely imaginative innovation was design for revues, musicals and especially films. Right down to the present day, people have never really appreciated the influence of Hollywood on American taste. Once films developed beyond the initial stages, the major production companies competed to outdo each other, and became extremely ambitious with regard to fashion and set design. Modern tendencies were accepted here far more readily than elsewhere. But the models which were presented could not easily find acceptance in everyday life. The American trade ministry noted that manufacturers lacked the readiness to design their products in a way which

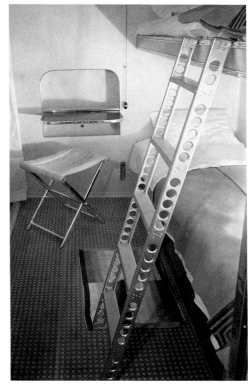

Fritz August Breuhaus, smoking room in the Hindenburg, 1936. The room was just eighteen square metres in size. The pressure inside was increased slightly and the door was constructed as an air-lock, to stop any hydrogen from getting in. This was the only place where smoking or fire was allowed, under the strict supervision of a steward. On the right, behind the railing are the windows, through which passengers could look down, vertically (top left).

Fritz August Breuhaus, cabin in the Hindenburg, 1936. Every cabin had a wardrobe, a folding stool and a foldaway wash basin with warm and cold water, and a foldaway writing top. During the day, the top bunk disappeared into the ceiling, the lower one was used as a couch (top right).

Fritz August Breuhaus, lounge in the Hindenburg, 1936. The light-metal furniture was manufactured by Neue Kühler- und Flugzeugteile GmbH in Berlin. The large world map shows the routes of the zeppelins and the routes of Columbus, Vasco da Gama, Magellan and Cook.

Entrance hall to The Beverly Theater, a cinema in Chicago, Illinois, photographed in 1935; the architect is not known.

would promote sales. In 1926, an exhibition was organised which travelled through all the larger towns in the USA and showed four hundred exhibits from the 1925 Paris exhibition. But the Americans did not like to merely copy other designs. The Great Depression in 1929 was what really set off the development of a typically American style. The main determining factor was the feeling that it was possible to overcome the economic crisis and its effects by giving the nation a new, progressive image of itself. It would perhaps be an exaggeration to apply the word "streamlined" to the design of this area in general. But certain objects took on a key function, for instance turbine-shaped vacuum cleaners or shiny electric toasters. These objects also showed just how the new style made its way into people's homes: via the garage through the backdoor into the kitchen. It began with new, streamlined aeroplanes, locomotives and cars. The 1930 Lockheed Orion was already significantly different from the portly Dornier or Junkers corrugated iron planes. Famous trains like the Zephyr, a diesel train of the Chicago, Burlington and Quincy Railroad, and vehicles like the Chrysler Airflow and the famous Cord 810 by the Auburn Automobile Corporation, a wonderfully elegant car without the usual monstrous radiator grille, founded the "streamline" myth. The aerodynamic form, which was certainly justified in the construction of vehicles, was soon transferred to household goods and office machines, a growth area of production, thanks to increasing electrification. The organisation of American kitchens was the topic of much discussion around

Abel Faidy, reception room at the Hedrich-Blessing photo studios in Chicago, 1935/36. The photos on the right-hand wall show buildings by Walter Dorwin Teague and the Holabird and Root architect team, the Zephyr, a streamlined train on the Burlington Line, a clock by Gilbert Rohde and a scientist using a microscope (left).

Donald Deskey, S. L. Rothafel's apartment on the upper floor of the Radio City Music Hall, New York City, 1933.

1930. The manufacturers propagated their new kitchen furnishings by arguing that if working areas were better organised and numerous electrical appliances installed, the workload could be a lot lighter.

A common element of the numerous new designs for household goods was the introduction of metal exteriors, which were supposed to give the equipment a uniform appearance. Normally, it took the form of a clearly structured main body, with rounded corners, decorated with narrow parallel strips of chrome or aluminium. But more important than the actual appearance was the principle of having a metal casing at all. Following the example of the car industry, technical details, which did not interest the user, were hidden away under the bodywork. This meant that the external form was independent of the technical parts inside, and could be changed at any time to suit the latest fashion. The new shapes could also be used for furniture. A round armchair, completely covered with fabric or leather, became the symbol of comfortable domesticity.

Around 1930, ambitious furniture designs were provided by architects, including many immigrants from Europe. These designs defined the new look. The first forum at which they were introduced was an exhibition held in 1929 in the New York Metropolitan Museum of Art and entitled "The Architect and Industrial Design". A lot of aluminium furniture was shown, which was quite different from European models. An interior in this style was created in 1933 by Donald Deskey on the upper floor of the New York Radio City Music Hall, for the owner's private suite. Between 1921 and 1923, Deskey had studied in Paris and, before he returned to the USA, he probably saw the 1925 Paris Exhibition and the Bauhaus. The multitude of different impressions which he took back across the Atlantic with him gave this room its distinctive character, with the cinema-like splendour of walls panelled with exotic wood, and shining aluminium furniture. Another important figure was Paul T. Frankl. He was renowned for his furniture, which looked like miniature skyscrapers, and he tried to propagate modern European developments in his writings, *New Dimensions* and *Form and Re-Form*.

The new style was developed to perfection in designs by Norman Bel Geddes, Raymond Loewy and Walter Dorwin Teague. Their offices tackled not only the design of products and their packaging, but also the development of urban perspectives for the future. In accounts written by Loewy, it becomes clear that everyday life in America had taken on a completely new look. In events such as the great Century of Progress Exhibition in Chicago in 1933, and finally in the New York World Fair in 1939, designers' ambition culminated in the professed

Walter Dorwin Teague, interior room in the Ford pavilion at the New York World Fair, 1939. The wall behind the sofa was covered with tan-coloured leather divided into squares by fine golden strips. The white leather armchairs stood on a moss-green carpet. The rounded alcoves were lit from inside the golden pillars.

Hermann Gretsch, music room suite, polished cherry wood, displayed at the Triennial in Milan in 1940, manufactured by several small firms in the Stuttgart area.

People in Clean Factories" were introduced to promote the redesign of out-dated plants. Out of the necessity to gain credibility by means of remedying grievances, campaigns were born, for instance to improve lighting at the work-place, re-furbish offices, canteens and washrooms, which sometimes actually directly took up models from the Bauhaus movement. This apparently contradictory trend can best be seen in architecture. The architect Otto Ernst Schweitzer, who had been ostracized, and whose planetarium in Nuremberg was demolished in 1934 as an example of the building style of the "Systems Era", was mentioned in 1936 in the official publication *Schönheit der Arbeit* (Beauty of Work) by the party organ of the same name. The central dairy he had designed in Nuremberg in 1930 was presented as a model for architecture. The reason for this becomes clear if one looks behind the scenes. Many members of the Werkbund had become involved in the "Beauty of Work" organisation. For instance, the editor of the periodical *Die Form*, which had closed down, found a new position there. It is not really surprising that such people became involved in this way. After all, the motto: "the beauty of work is socialism in practice" was not so far away from slogans of the preceding age.

But in the new model office, metal surfaces and tubular steel constructions were not used at all. The progress of the debate can be gathered from an article by the head of the department, Hans Stolper: "In those circles which used to see their life's aim in inventing keywords like 'die Neue Sachlichkeit' (function-alism), 'constructivism' etc., making a show of chatting wittily and writing about them to show their own importance, even today it is the done thing to remark that nowadays, there is still enough nonsense being carried out in these areas, and claiming that there has been absolutely no improvement". Stolper presented his department's model furniture, which was to set an example for furnishing places of work, as the functional product of ideologically influenced design work: "We really do not want to force everything into one system. It is not the individual form that is important, but the attitude . . . It is not a matter of taste but, ultimately, of meeting the requirements for 'Beauty of Work', that is, a question of philosophy."

The furniture created in this way was made of wood – either for philosophical reasons or because of the lack of raw materials – and it was basically boring, but practical. But in the proposals for the interiors of the corresponding rooms, the narrow-minded attitude of the planners came to the fore. The "party-supporters' room" was allotted particular significance. In works, it served as a canteen and assembly room. Wrought-iron lamps, wall-paintings depicting traditional rural scenes combined with loudspeakers and slogans on the wall formed the backdrop for the uniform, party followers, seated in orderly rows. In contrast to the efforts of the Beauty of Work department, the official Chancellery of the German Reich style was nothing other than a clumsy attempt at classicism. The common factors were the lack of experimentation, the limitation to traditional material and the overall clumsy, provincial impression. It made a pretence of appealing to the bourgeois fetish for "cosiness" and was a success with a public that lacked stylistic confidence. On several occasions, model houses were put on show, which clearly demonstrated the unusual, ambivalent style. One occasion was the 1940 Milan "Triennial". Hermann Gretsch, a Stuttgart architect and student of the traditionalists Bonatz and Schmitthenner, had designed a music room, in which he had succeeded in lending a cultured air to the traditional image of a parlour. The affected style of the furniture still made a

Hermann Gretsch, bedroom wardrobe, maple wood, shown at the 1940 Milan Triennial, manufactured in the Werkstätten für deutsche Wertmöbel Richard Münch in Fürth, Bavaria.

157

Model home in a "settler's house" in Dorf im Warndt in the Saarland, 1936. The manufacturer of the furniture is not known.

dignified impression, and possessed enough intimacy to appeal to the soft-hearted.

Gretsch himself had calculated this very carefully. In an article for *Innendekoration* in 1942, he explained his rejection of technical innovation: "The decisive factor for cultural achievement is not whether a utensil or a piece of furniture is a technical or economic miracle, but whether it is suitable to turn a house into a home where people feel safe and contented. This means cultural value is determined not by technical or materialistic factors, but by spiritual criteria." And so, his music room is more than just a music room. The piano, the print of a romantic painting on the wall, the music stand, all express a certain attitude. The character of the room is determined not by its purpose, but by the cultural tradition it wants to convey. As well as this version for the middle classes, Gretsch also had a second method of creating "homeliness" in his proposals for furniture for municipal housing: the use of wood as the exclusive material was to meet the town-dweller's longing for the countryside and to cultivate the desire for what was "natural, plain and simple". That was why, in another of his furniture pieces, the early, mass-produced radio set disappeared behind the doors of a small wooden cabinet. Whereas Gretsch still aimed at solid craftmanship, many other interior designers embarked on the course of imitating regional art, and filled flats with coarse, carved wooden rural furniture. Expensive products of craftmanship were certainly ideologically acceptable, but official party organs felt that only industrial mass production was suitable to equip the towns already being planned for post-war Germany.

Within the framework of the National Socialist housing programme, the housing office set up several exhibitions, which presented furnishings for standardised flats. Since the Nazi Party's criticism of the principles of "New Architecture" had been reduced to absurdum by standardising housing types, and the insistence on an indigenous character was only to be seen in variations of the façades to suit "regional styles", differences from the ostracized "Neue Sachlichkeit" can be seen most clearly in the furniture exhibited.

The basis for the exhibition programme was either a small, privately owned house "as a healthy form of four-roomed home for the complete German family" – the version with a garden and room for keeping animals was described as the "settler's version" – or a rented flat. By varying the basic lay-out, especially by doing away with long, dark central corridors, they were to meet higher "requirements for cultivated living". Rationalisation by means of standardisation was the first commandment of the wartime economy. Under the key concept of "total planning and design", housing and everything related to it were to be standardised.

The few projects which were actually completed during the war were so insignificant that even the organisers began to doubt the usefulness of centralised architectural design. But the estate projects, with small houses, gardens and the related possibility of partial self-sufficiency, did meet with positive response. Perhaps it was because people were forced to do a lot of the building work themselves, and also the fact that the estates were often isolated, outside of the large conurbations, which promoted solidarity amongst the "estate communities". It is not possible to say whether people accepted the furnishings of the model homes. But it is clear that the style developed here – half functional, half romantic – did leave its mark on typical German interior design. Many furniture programmes in the post-war period took up exactly where these models left off.

Dining area in the model home, Dorf im Warndt, 1936. Furniture of this sort was not only offered by large firms like the Deutsche Werkstätten, it was also produced from patterns by small workshops.

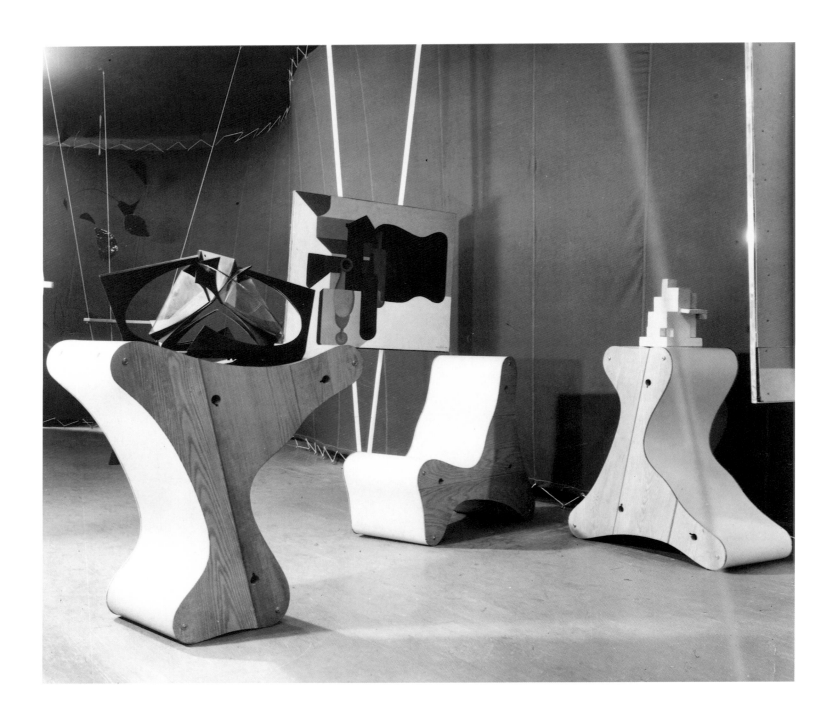

Peggy Guggenheim's Gallery in New York, designed by Friedrich Kiesler, 1942

ACT III

SCENE ONE
VERNISSAGE

THE CAST:

HARRY BERTOIA
OSVALDO BORSANI
CHARLES EAMES
CARLO GRAFFI
FRIEDRICH KIESLER
CARLO MOLLINO
ICO PARISI
WARREN PLATNER
GIO PONTI
EERO SAARINEN

Charles Eames and Eero Saarinen, cabinet units, armchairs, chairs and tables, designed for the *Organic Design in Home Furnishings* competition, 1941. The competition was organised by the Museum of Modern Art in New York and the results shown at an exhibition.

Eero Saarinen, three models from a 1948 collection. The "Womb Chair" in the foreground is a more highly developed version of the model with which he and Charles Eames jointly won the first prize in the Museum of Modern Art competition in 1941. But in the early forties, industry still lacked the technical know-how to mass produce it.
Knoll International, Murr/Murr

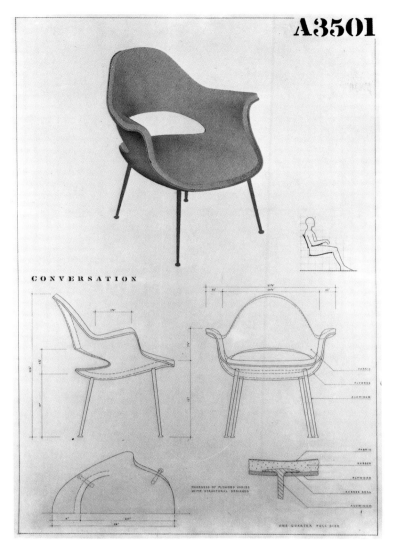

CONVERSATION

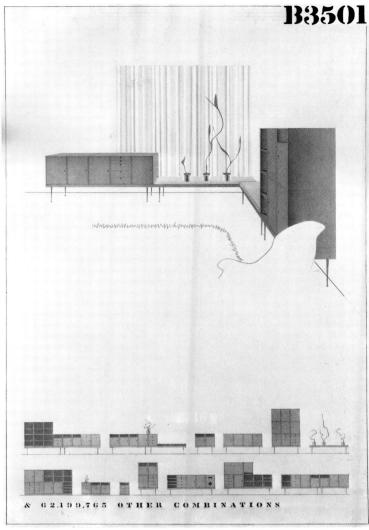

& 62.199.765 OTHER COMBINATIONS

By 1930, designers had succeeded in creating furniture whose construction and material no longer merely imitated traditional shapes with variations, and tried to adapt them to the new age. Solutions to many problems had actually already been found – if only there had not been emotional and nationalistic opposition, which repeatedly found the modern style politically suspicious. It was only after the Second World War that the moment arrived to trust in the power of innovation. The USA, the victor in moral as well as military terms, took on the leading role. By this time, a series of architects were now working there who had belonged to the German avant-garde around 1930 – Ludwig Mies van der Rohe, Walter Gropius and Marcel Breuer – and they were putting up buildings of a size and importance Europe could never have offered.

Unlike in Europe, people in America found modern design exciting, stimulating and original. The Americans wanted a degree of wit and unconventionality. People were prepared to show their astonishment and unprejudiced appreciation. Once the phase of having to gain recognition for style had been overcome, people expected furniture to distinguish itself with originality and changing ideas. Organic forms, which, compared with the clearly contoured styles of around 1930, could be viewed as "free", were a convincing illustration of the new attitude and gave a fresh appearance to everything.

The degree of freedom which was already possible in the USA by 1942 was demonstrated in the "Art of this Century" gallery, which was set up in New York

Charles Eames and Eero Saarinen, drawings for the Organic Design in Home Furnishings competition, organised by the Museum of Modern Art in New York in 1940.

163

Charles Eames, "La Chaise", prototype, compression-moulded hard rubber between two layers of plastic, lower frame of wood and metal, 1948. Eames submitted the model for an international competition by the Museum of Art with the theme "Low-Cost Furniture Design", but it was never produced.

Charles Eames, rocking chair, polyester seat on a metal base with wooden rockers, 1950. Galerie Rotor, Amsterdam

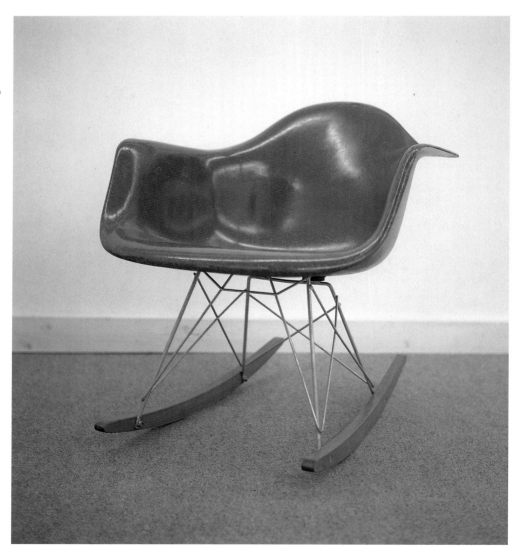

by Peggy Guggenheim. It was a lively meeting place for art and design. Friedrich Kiesler, an Austrian, had provided it with curiously shaped multifunctional furniture and irritating lighting tricks, which did not exactly help the appreciation of the works of art, but which did show a carefree attitude towards them. America taught the Europeans that, in the New World, art was a source of acknowledgement for progress. A central institution here was the Museum of Modern Art in New York, which was backed by some of the wealthiest Americans. It propagated the European avant-garde at a very early stage. Its programme of exhibitions ranged from art to architecture and design: "Cubism and Abstract Art" (1936), "The International Style" (1932) and "Bauhaus 1919–1928" (1938). An American competition entitled "Organic Design in Home Furnishings", organised by the Department of Industrial Design of the Museum for Modern Art in 1940, airned to find new, up-to-date furnishings, including lamps and textiles. The idea came from the leading New York department store, Bloomingdale's. Other important concerns – furniture factories and dealers – were persuaded to sponsor it. This meant the winners would get not only attractive diplomas and money prizes, but also contracts with important manufacturers.

The first prize went to Eero Saarinen and Charles Eames, who jointly submitted not only tables and a system of cupboard units, but also designs for gently curved moulded seats. But, at that time, there was no company with the techno-

Charles Eames, room as part of the exhibition "New Furniture Designed by Charles Eames" in the Museum of Modern Art in New York, 1946. As well as wooden models of varying height and with different seat tops, there is a chair with a metal base behind the table. Like most of the three-legged models designed up to this date, it tended to tip over. For that reason, it never went into production.

165

Charles Eames, wire chair with removable upholstered elements, frame of metal rods, designed in 1951. From a historical perspective, it can be seen as the forerunner of plastic chairs. First, Eames built bowl-shaped constructions from spot-welded wire. These experiments led to a plastic moulded seat reinforced with fibreglass. But the wire model also led on to the "Wire Chair". It was reminiscent of a sculpture, a three-dimensional object, light and transparent. Vitra, Weil am Rhein

Charles Eames, table and chair from the "Plywood Group", black-stained ash with chromium-plated steel frames, designed 1944/46. The final shaping of the moulded elements was the result of long experimentation. To join the components to each other, Eames used techniques from the car industry. Vitra, Weil am Rhein

Charles Eames, his own house in Santa Monica, California, 1949. It was constructed mostly from ordinary elements sold for industrial buildings.

"Charles Eames was a technician, an engineer. He thought in terms of industrial production and, working from this perspective, created real furniture for our century. It goes without saying that without the Bauhaus, there wouldn't have been the same scope for new design, but Eames' chairs, armchairs and tables as well as his architecture, which is now again getting the respect it deserves, resulted from machine technology, not just from craftsmanship using prefabricated technical components."
(Otl Aicher)

logy to mass-produce the necessary three-dimensional, prefabricated plywood components. Eames found a solution in dividing the components into simpler parts and then joining the curved seat to the back with metal components. The idea is reminiscent of the sculptures created by Alexander Calder at this time: freely shaped surfaces were to be joined to each other using light constructional elements. In order to have an elastic mounting for the plywood components, Eames used sheets of flexible rubber. He was convinced that ultimately details of this sort would determine the quality of the product. All the separate parts were originally made of wood. But when a long series of experiments showed that the base always required thicker plywood than the seat and the back, Eames turned to steel for the supporting elements. In his opinion, these designs looked more attractive, and they were also cheaper. He decided he had found the final version when he felt he could recognise living creatures in the chairs. In 1946, he first presented what he called his "Plywood Group" in a very successful exhibition of his own in the Museum of Modern Art.

He tried to carry out his original idea of a chair with the shell moulded in one

Harry Bertoia, armchair, Model "421",
*chromium-plated round bar steel, fabric-covered
cushion, designed in 1952. It is one of a series of
seats, which – as Bertoia put it – "are made mostly
of air, the room just goes straight through them".
Knoll International, Murr/Murr*

piece by using aluminium, which was then sprayed with neopren, a synthetic
rubber. Once more his model was awarded a prize by the Museum of Modern
Art, but it was not suitable for mass production because of the high costs of tools
and material. Initial experiments with synthetic materials then led to models
which were manufactured in series. The moulded main component was made of
heat-treated polyester resin, reinforced with a dense glassfibre structure. This
visible reinforcement also created a fine, warm structuring of the surface.
Eames always used metal for the lower frames.

The Eames models were manufactured by Herman Miller, who had supported
his experiments for a long time. They achieved a distribution of millions, and the
company – previously insignificant – grew rapidly. Herman Miller again demonstrated his feeling for the modern trend when he accepted the famous table
by the sculptor Isamu Noguchi into his programme. It consisted of a sculptured
wooden base in two parts, and a glass plate placed loosely on top (pages 238
and 244).

Eero Saarinen and Charles Eames had developed their early models in the
workshops of Cranbrook University in Birmingham/Michigan, which were directed by Eero's father, the Finnish architect Eliel Saarinen. They worked there in
a small, intimate circle of young architects and artists, who were to have a
decisive influence on American design in the years that followed. As well as
Eames and Saarinen, it included the sculptor Harry Bertoia, Ray Kaiser, who

Richard Neutra, house for Warren Tremaine, 1947. Neutra, an Austrian who went to America at an early stage, continued and updated the idea of a fanned-out lay-out, first formulated by Frank Lloyd Wright. He built numerous villas in California, in which architecture and landscape came into contact with each other.

Jorge Ferrari-Hardoy, _Antonio Bonet_, _Juan Kurchan_, the "Hardoy Chair", round bar steel frame, linen cover. The model can be traced back to a design for which Joseph Barly Fenby had already applied for a patent in 1877. It was first built at the beginning of this century – still in wood at that time – and presented at the 1904 World Fair in St. Louis. Around 1940, the Argentinian architect and designer Ferrari-Hardoy and some of his colleagues developed the metal version known today. After the Second World War, the chair was one of the first successful models for the Knoll company.
Die Neue Sammlung, Munich

Warren Platner, wire armchair and stool with upholstery from a 1966 collection.
Knoll International, Murr/Murr

Warren Platner, variant of the model shown above, 1966.
Knoll International, Murr/Murr

With Charles Pollock, Platner was one of the most important Knoll designers in the sixties. His chairs, armchairs, stools and tables made of numerous fine metal rods are similar to Bertoia's in terms of material, but aim at a different effect. The moiré effect of the rod construction is designed to have a deliberately decorative effect.

later became the wife and partner of Charles Eames, and Florence Schust, who built up an international furniture company with her husband Hans Knoll, after the Second World War. They successfully started off with furniture designed by their former colleagues at Cranbrook and designs of their own for the central administration offices of large companies. Eero Saarinen, who worked primarily as an architect (the shell-shaped terminal for Trans World Airlines in New York was one of his designs), took up the old idea of the moulded seat in his own way in the 1940s. In contrast to Eames, he was not particularly interested in the technical problems. In his early models, the supporting structure remained hidden underneath closed upholstery. His designs aimed at casual shapes, in which people could let themselves go. The basic idea was, as he put it, "a basket full of cushions". In the mid-fifties, Saarinen developed a series of chairs, tables and stools which only had one central base, to do away with the usual "jumble of legs". He placed thin, white moulded seats or table-tops on slim, trumpet-shaped bases. Although it was not his intention, he was forced to use metal for the pedestals at this time. A synthetic coating made this invisible. The sculptor Harry Bertoia, who had become famous for his filigree metal sculptures, created the first armchairs made from metal latticework. Here, Bertoia transferred experiences he made in his artistic work to furniture design: "Certainly, with chairs, functional problems have to be solved first... but, if you look at it carefully, chairs, too, are studies in space, form and metal".

In Europe after the Second World War, the Milan Triennial Exhibitions emerged as trend-setting, international design shows. In 1951, the motto of the exhibition was "The Unity of the Arts". In Luciano Baldessari's entrance hall, a neon sculpture, created by Lucio Fontana, combined surprisingly well with three

Eero Saarinen, chairs known as Tulip-Chairs, with and without armrests, base of coated light metal, moulded seat of polyester with loose cushions, designed in 1956.
Knoll International, Murr/Murr

Foyer at the 1951 Milan Triennial, designed by
Luciano Baldessari, with a neon sculpture by
Lucio Fontana.

soft sofas. They introduced the novelty of the exhibition: Italian foam furniture.
Marco Zanuso was awarded a gold medal for his contribution, a somewhat
helpless-looking armchair with the name "Lady". The Pirelli company had
given him samples of their material and asked him to investigate new ways of
using it. "Numerous experiments showed that there was enormous potential to
use it in upholstered furniture. It made it possible to revolutionize not only the
upholstery itself, but also the structure, shapes and manufacturing techniques" –
as Zanuso later explained. The next Triennial in 1954 already took the connection between artistic design and the industrial product for granted: "The theme
of the main section of the tenth Triennial is industrial aesthetics, which is now
commonly referred to as 'Industrial Design', the American expression".

Along with the prototypes, new companies appeared, such as Arflex, which
manufactured the "Lady" chair, an immediate sales hit, or the Tecno company,
founded by the architect Osvaldo Borsani, to manufacture his technically
sophisticated products.

The necessary propaganda was taken care of by the established Italian
design magazines, *Domus* and *Casabella*, whose chief editors were not the
usual journalists, but architects – for instance, Gio Ponti for *Domus*. To provide
an additional incentive to national competition, the department store La Rinas-
cente donated the "Compasso d'Oro" in 1954, a coveted award for high-
quality Italian design.

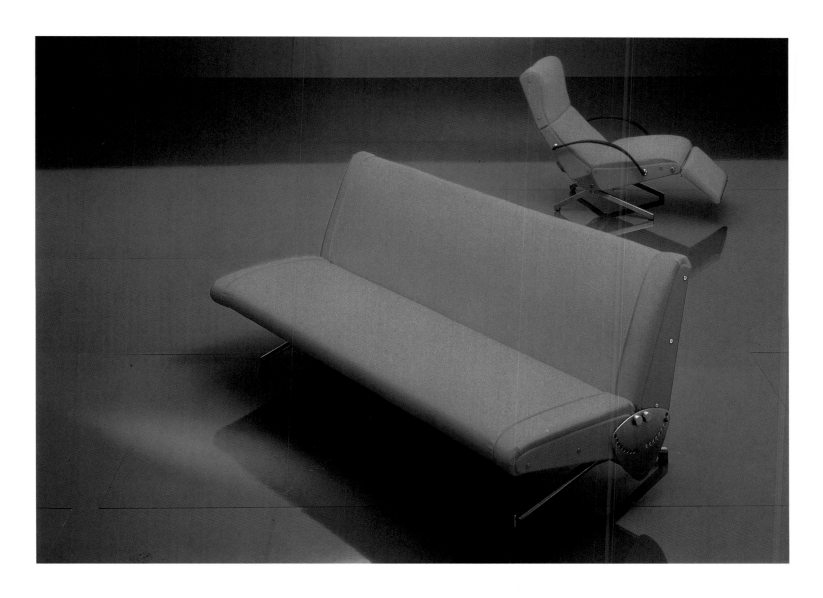

Osvaldo Borsani, in the foreground, replica of a bed settee, Model "D70", the upholstered sections can be turned 90 degrees, designed in 1953. In the background, replica of a Lounge Chair, Model P40, metal frame with foam cushions, rubber armrests, adjustable seat and back, designed in 1955.
Tecno, Milan

Ico Parisi, walnut bookshelves, exhibited at the IXth Triennial, Milan, 1951.
Paolo Curti, Brescia

Carlo Mollini, living room in the house of Ada and
Cesare Minola in Turin, designed in 1944.

Carlo Mollino, an engineer, architect, inventor, designer, photographer, author, stunt pilot and racing driver, worked in a way that matched the spirit of the
time, although he was extremely individualistic. One of his former fellow students described him as an eccentric loner, who went against social conventions
in every possible way: "Carlo Mollino: a diabolical character. When he speaks,
there is a spray of Gillette razor blades, scimitars, splinters of glass, enchanted
gardens and monstrous blossoms, in colours never seen before. He insists he
was born in Turin, but rumour has it that he is really a Saracen. His life constantly
oscillates between brooding and hectic action... Like a sloth, he can sleep for
months; then, when he wakes up, he immediately slips into a condition of
mentally disturbed hectic activity. No matter what outlandish projects he under-
takes, he always sees them through with dead seriousness and wild determina-
tion."

Nevertheless, this d'Annunzio of Italian furniture design was in a position to
undertake major projects, such as the construction of the Turin opera house or
the interior of the auditorium of RAI, the Italian radio station. An impassioned
Alpinist, he built cable-car terminals in the Italian Alps, and he created all the
interior furnishings for the publishing house Einaudi.

In the early forties, he designed opulent interiors for a small circle of friends,
which show his obsessions particularly clearly. Almost all his furniture was
erotically stimulated, "lecherous", as he himself described it. George Nelson,

174

Carlo Mollino, the living room in the Casa Minola in Turin from another angle. Beside the fireplace is a radio-record-player designed by Mollino, above, the adjustable lamps for indirect lighting.

Carlo Mollino, "arabesque" table, bent plywood with a safety glass top, designed in 1949 for the Casa Orengo in Turin. Mollino made several variations of this table, including one for the house of Lisa and Giò Ponti.
Sammlung Christina und Bruno Bischofberger, Zürich

an American, was more restrained when he defined these sensually curved pieces as belonging in the tradition of the Piedmont Baroque.

Carlo Mollino withdrew to get his inspiration to his "Garconnières", batchelor flats, which he furnished for himself. It was here that he kept his extensive collection of Paris sexy underwear catalogues and designed clothes which consisted of little more than a daring decolleté. It was here, too, that he took his nude photographs and wrote his essays.

His imagination covered a very wide range. It went from voluptuous armchairs to skeleton-like table frames, on which he placed naked sheets of glass. These bare pieces were a late return to Art Nouveau à la Gaudí, whom Mollino greatly admired. But unlike the Spaniard's carved structures, Mollino's shaped wooden furniture was ideally suited to industrial mass production, in spite of its artistic character.

Carlo Mollino, desk of bent plywood with wooden compartments and safety glass top, designed in 1950 for Singer's offices in Turin. Sammlung Christina und Bruno Bischofberger, Zürich

Carlo Mollino preferred to work on his own. He only collaborated with colleagues – for instance Pellegrini or Roggero – if the size of a project made it impossible to do otherwise. But these associations – in which he always claimed the leading position – often resulted in quarrels or court cases. The only artist with whom he repeatedly worked on buildings or for competitions for many years was the architect Carlo Graffi, who also designed furniture in a style related to Mollino's.

Carlo Graffi, games table, plywood and glass, designed in 1952.
Galerie Yves Gastou, Paris

Carlo Graffi, armchair, consisting of wooden components screwed together with cushions on top, designed around 1950.
Galerie Yves Gastou, Paris

177

Dining area in a holiday home designed by the architect Anders Grum in Humleboek, Denmark. The "Y-Chair", made of beechwood treated with oil, was manufactured using the bentwood method.

After the end of the Second World War, the political situation in central Europe stabilised more quickly than after Versailles. It was dominated by the Cold War atmosphere and a general tendency to value economic productivity. There were hardly any new artistic debates; pragmatic considerations were now in the foreground. New ideas for design tended to come from the requirements of manufacturing techniques or packaging methods. Standard design, especially that adhered to by German furniture manufacturers, kept for the most part to already existing, proven traditional forms. There was certainly plenty of designing going on, and by 1948 people were already thinking hard about exports, but furniture often still bore the rustical or pseudo-classical features of the fascist years. New ideas could only come to the weakened German design scene from the outside. As well as the North American style, Scandinavian housing and furniture design became models which were to have a lasting effect even into the fifties. And America and northern Europe were not as different from each other as their geographical locations would suggest. Armchairs by Aalto or Mathsson were also to be found in the sitting rooms of many American houses, which looked out through huge windows onto breathtaking countryside. It was not the American furniture manufacturers who conquered the German market, but the Scandinavians. In Germany, as the economy grew stronger, the public was looking for a modern style in a solid form, which was just what the plain, craftsman's furniture from the Scandinavian countries offered. The furniture and

interior design which had developed there, probably influenced to a large extent by the harsher climate, had its own particular attraction, as it appeared modern but homely at the same time.

Another factor was that markets – at least within the western hemisphere – were more open than before. The increasingly international orientation of the economic sphere and a general cosmopolitan attitude now set the standards. But this also resulted in swiftly changing fashions. Many producers reacted to current trends and tried to imitate exemplary objects. It is not surprising that the ideas behind particular designs were mutilated in this way. But it is astonishing that fashion furniture such as flower stands and the kidney-shaped tables with the thin legs and Formica tops actually achieved a widespread distribution. This shows not only that the public was willing to buy up-to-date and somewhat daring furniture, but also that it was very insecure.

The new ground-plans of houses contributed to bringing about changes in the lay-out and style of the interiors. The classical central hallway became a much smaller entrance hall, and a new multi-purpose room became the new centre: a living room with a dining area and serving hatch. This was basically a very practical idea, but, in most small flats with low ceilings, the dining area was very cramped. Of course this led to an increase in the demand for practical, light-weight furniture and the decline of the traditional German dining room, which had a sideboard, a heavy table and six chairs. The big family table disappeared

Living room in a Danish house by the architects Knud Friis and Elmar Moltke Nielsen, 1958. In front of the low table are two "Safari-Chairs", which Kaare Klint had designed back in 1933 – a fine example of a sensible new version of a traditional design.

and the new gathering point was the living-room suite, arranged around the television set. As Günther Anders put it in 1956: "Decades ago, one could already observe that the typical family piece of furniture, the big living-room table in the middle of the room, where the whole family gathered together, was beginning to lose importance and become obsolete. It was even completely absent in some new interiors. But it is only now that its true successor has been found: the television set." The piece of furniture designed to suit this new situation was the coffee table, which was always too low and too far away, the mutilated remains of "the table" as the central pice of furniture. As mentioned above, Scandinavian furniture was more permanent, timeless by comparison with the short-lived kidney-shaped table fashion. And the Danish economy in particular was strongly export-orientated and interested in increasing the scale of its traditional involvement in the furniture sector. In Denmark, ideas which had been suppressed in Nazi Germany were able to be developed. For all the Scandinavian countries, the major exhibition in Stockholm in 1930 may not have marked the advent, but certainly the decisive breakthrough of functional design. Many articles in the periodical *Kritisk Revy*, which was set up by Danish architects, had already been discussing modern furniture and artist craftsmanship

Mogens Koch, beechwood folding chair with brass elements and canvas seat and back, designed in 1938 and mass produced from 1960 on.
Rudolf Rasmussens Snedkerier, Copenhagen

Hans J. Wegner, teak dining-room chair with wickerwork seat, designed for Johannes Hansen's carpentry workshop in 1949. Unfortunately, it is difficult to make out the exquisite connection between the armrests and the back on the illustration, but the delicate joint between armrests and legs can be clearly seen.
Johannes Hansen, Copenhagen

before this date. The Furniture School founded by the Danish Academy of Art in 1924 and its leading figure, Kaare Klint, also played an important role. Klint had a different view from that of modernist architects. He criticised the Bauhaus rejection of old models and suggested that one should learn from the corpus of existing designs. He turned in particular to the eighteenth-century English art of furniture-making and, in spite of his traditionally-orientated method, he became one of the most creative pioneers of Danish furniture style. He was a model and a teacher for a whole generation of designers.

In the late twenties, the carpenters' guild in Copenhagen noted with anxiety that the growing competition between furniture factories was threatening the jobs of small workshops and creating an employment crisis. In order to raise the public's opinion of craftsmanship, a series of annual furniture exhibitions was started in 1927, combined with competitions for new models. Thanks to the participation of young architects and students at the Academy, these exhibitions soon became a forum for outstanding design. Bold, innovative construction was combined with careful observation of the social environment. And so, craftsmen turned to presenting unpretentious, practical, simple furniture, while industry continued to reproduce classical designs.

Now, a lamp took on key significance. It had been designed by Paul Henningsen in 1925 and was already known abroad even at that time. For instance, it was used by Mies van der Rohe for the Tugendhat house. The shade was

Hans J. Wegner, smoked oak folding chair, seat and back of Spanish cane, designed in 1949. The notch on the lower cross-bar makes it possible to hang the chair up on the wall upside down when it is folded up.
Johannes Hansen, Copenhagen

constructed of three parts in such a way that people were not blinded by the bulb. Jacob Bang, a glass designer commented: "Somehow this lamp set off something inside us, and the enthusiasm and devotion which it inspired became something of a cult. Hanging up this lamp-shade meant strengthening oneself as an intellectual, and as an avant-gardist." The lamp shared the success of many other Scandinavian pieces, which were produced for a many years time, with slight variations, and finally achieved a wide distribution in the 1950s.

The astonishing continuity throughout the years of war and occupation was made possible especially by an institution in which a permanent group of craftsmen, draughtsmen and architects could dedicate their time to furniture design: the bulk purchasing company of Danish cooperative societies, which had its own design department. The cheap utility furniture – mostly made of light, natural wood – which was sold in the associated shops, was bought mostly by the middle-class circles who lived in the small terraced houses which had actually been built for working-class families.

At the end of the war, a new element went into the development of Danish furniture. The architect Finn Juhl argued that furniture should not only be useful but should also have a sculptural character. He worked wood three-dimensionally and, with his chairs, placed special emphasis on organically shaped transitions and joins. Even a designer like Hans J. Wegner now skilfully changed the traditional structure of his furniture.

Bruno Mathsson, armchair with fabric strapping on a layered beech frame, designed in 1934. This sort of furniture was also on display at the Berlin "Interbau" Fair in 1957.
Dux, Trelleborg

Around 1950, Danish furniture production lost its emphasis on craftsmanship. New manufacturing processes and materials such as steel and synthetics destroyed the supremacy of wood. The architect Arne Jacobsen became particularly famous for his mastery of industrial techniques. He had already been working on furniture design since the thirties. Now he created a lightweight, three-legged chair, with thin tubular steel legs and a moulded plywood seat. This model, which became known as the "Ant", represented the decisive step towards the modernisation of Scandinavian furniture. Jacobsen had obviously been influenced by Eames here. But the private character of the object was purely Scandinavian. Jacobsen went on to develop the chair further. He changed the contours of the back, and eventually returned to the four-legged form. One characteristic of the early model – the thin synthetic covering over the steel frame – disappeared, but it retained its overall lightness. At the end of the process, one of the classic chairs of this century had been created.

Progress in Sweden was similar to the development of Danish artist craftsmanship. At a very early stage, an association stepped into the foreground which had been founded in 1846: the Swedish handicrafts society, Svenska Slöjdföreningen. It had aims similar to those of the German Werkbund, arranged exhibitions of its own, took part in the 1930 exhibition in Stockholm and other displays, and was also invited to the Berlin "Interbau" fair in 1957. In addition, the Association of Swedish Architects went to great lengths to sys-

Bruno Mathsson's own summer house in Frösakull, 1961. Mathsson had previously constructed a large number of similar buildings, with wide glass windows. The leaf pattern on the upholstery is reminiscent of Josef Frank, who went from Vienna to Stockholm in 1934, where he played an influential role in the development of Swedish design.

tematically study living habits and tried to take the phrase "from cutlery to architectural plan" seriously and work from basic measurements, for instance those of cutlery, to ascertain dimensions for all the furniture – not just in the kitchen – and ultimately even for the whole house. One of Sweden's outstanding designers was Bruno Mathsson. From the mid-thirties on, he developed furniture to suit the human body, in which the seat and the supporting structure were constructed separately. The furniture, which made a nervous impression with its unusual lines, was rendered calmer by means of traditional materials: wood and fabric webbing.

The triumph of Scandinavian furniture began with successes at international exhibitions. In 1951, Finnland picked up where Aalto's success had left off in 1936, and received six "Grand Prix" at the Milan Triennial. The magazine *Domus* devoted a detailed article to Finnish artist craftsmanship. But this interest led to a misunderstanding: it was not the subtle design which made a break-through in the rest of Europe, but the use of teak wood, which was very popular in Scandinavia. In the years that followed, it practically became a synonym for pseudo-Scandinavian design.

In 1947, when most things were still in scarce supply in war-damaged Germany, members of the Werkbund got together again. In their "Lützelbacher Manifesto", they wrote: "For housing and for our public buildings, we are searching for what is simple and valid rather than over-specialisation or

Arne Jacobsen, chair with plywood body and chromium-plated tubular steel frame, designed in 1955. It was a follow-up to the three-legged "Ant", designed five years earlier. The "Ant" had a more complex backrest.
Fritz Hansen, Allerød

Poul Kjaerholm, lounger made of stainless steel and rattan cane, neckroll covered with leather, 1965. The flat steel frame – a typical Kjaerholm feature – makes it possible to have a light, floating construction for the lounger. Fritz Hansen, Allerød

emergency solutions. Because only what is simple and valid is versatile." Although the official re-establishment only really took place in 1950, attempts to take up the old ideals were being made much earlier than that. An Exhibition called "Neues Wohnen" in Cologne in 1949 again pursued the idea of using selected products to demonstrate better design to the consumer, and, in one room, it also introduced foreign products. In 1950, Arno Hennig, a Social Democrat Member of Parliament, proposed that a Design Council should be set up. It was founded two years later and, under Mia Seeger, determined the image of German design at home and abroad for many years to come.

In Dessau, immediately after the war, preparations were made for the re-opening of the Bauhaus. Now, the emphasis was not to be on creating "furniture, houses and equipment for a few snobs – which had unintentionally been the case up to 1933 – but to design an environment for everyone". For this reason, the curriculum was to include landscape architecture and town planning – the most urgent need of the day. With the change in cultural policy in the Soviet zone of occupation, the plan to take over public offices and so gain "concrete positions of power" and influence came to nothing. The active group which had worked on the new beginning moved to the west. There, Ulm was the new location for the institute which, seen from our point of view today, tried to continue the ideas of the Bauhaus.

The Ulm Hochschule für Gestaltung (College of Design) was founded by the

Model flat for the Knoll International Company in the house by Alvar Aalto at the International Building Exhibition in Berlin in 1957. In the foreground, an easy chair by Pierre Jeanneret, which appears to be adjustable, but is not. Against the wall, a sofa with straight lines by Florence Knoll. The two chairs in the dining area in front of the hatch are by Harry Bertoia. The movable lamp, balanced by a counterweight, was designed by Rosemarie Baltensweiler from Switzerland. The "Finlandia" crockery on the coffee table is by Tapio Wirkkala.

Geschwister Scholl Foundation and constructed with the support of the American High Commissioner and donations from industry. The first rector was Max Bill from Switzerland, an ex-student of the Bauhaus. There was a basic course along the Bauhaus lines, but the emphasis was placed on concrete design work, aimed at success. An important feature was cooperation with industry. One of the first products was the "Ulm Stool", a small, Spartan object. The "Schneewittchensarg" (Snow White's coffin), a white radio-record player with a perspex lid, was also created in Ulm. It was conceived by the product-designer Hans Gugelot, in cooperation with the Braun company. It came to be a symbol which every member of the ambitious minority who believed in progress had to possess.

In the graphics sector, there were also some important successes, such as Hans G. Conrad's series of advertisements for the Knoll International company, and an advertising campaign for the Herman Miller Collection by Otl Aicher and Tomás Gonda. In an advertisement designed by Aicher for Braun, with the heading "A choice between 10 chairs", the attitude of a fictitious female consumer was described: "She had taken care to furnish her flat in a modern style. If she had been asked what 'modern' meant, she wouldn't have been able to say; but for her, this word had connotations of 'light', 'clean', 'practical', 'comfortable', perhaps even 'dry', 'understated', 'without ornamentation'. She had taste, if taste means the ability to choose things which suit the personal requirements of an individual lifestyle. She had looked at 10 different chairs to find the one that would not just appeal to her on the spur of the moment, but one that could fulfill her expectations and please her for a lifetime." Beside this text there were illustrations of chairs by Charles Eames, Arne Jacobsen, Gio Ponti and Egon Eiermann. Thus, the choice of a piece of furniture demonstrated one's attitude to modern design and so to the modern trend in general. In spite of the fact that the Ulm college closed down because of internal and external conflicts, at least for some time the theory of functional design had been able to hold its own in an age of kitsch.

A survey in the early fifties had shown that there was a group of German consumers which was willing to accept functional design. Although the group was small, it deserved to be taken seriously. Companies like the electrical appliances concern Braun acted accordingly. Under the designers Dieter Rams and Hans Gugelot, radios like the "Schneewittchensarg" mentioned above and a series of furniture for musical appliances were created. Niels Wiese Vitsoe and Otto Zapf set up a company just to produce Dieter Rams's furniture designs.

Egon Eiermann, "SE 18" folding chair, beechwood, seat and back of moulded plywood. There is also a version with a spring which makes the seat fold up automatically when not in use – very practical for rows of seating. Wilde und Spieth, Esslingen

189

Egon Eiermann, foyer on one floor of the multi-storey office block for members of parliament in Bonn, 1968. To sub-divide the large rooms, Eiermann designed different types of partitions. Those illustrated here consist of white plywood surfaces with holes punched into them in a frame of Oregon Pine. In the foreground, the "620" armchair, by Dieter Rams.

Dieter Rams, chairs "601" and "602", 1960. The supports are made of cast aluminium, the body is of polyester, reinforced with fibreglass. The covers are leather or fabric.
Wiese Vitsoe, Frankfurt am Main

They were manufactured without changes for a long time. In 1962, Rams created the "620" programme of cubic armchairs, which were constructed of flat plastic components, into which cushions were fitted for the seat and back. Apart from Mart Stam, Dieter Rams is the only designer who has been granted artistic copyright protection for one of his creations.

Egon Eiermann was one of the few architects who continued to aim at formal discipline in the hectic period of reconstruction in the fifties. This former student of Hans Poelzig had succeeded in working on industrial buildings during Hitler's Third Reich, which did not endanger his reputation. During the war years, he had designed furniture for his own office. Afterwards, he continued to work on interior furnishings. For instance, in 1949, he designed a model home for the "Wie wohnen" ideal homes exhibition. He often designed furniture to suit his architectural projects. His softly curved, cup-shaped basketwork armchairs were particularly popular. Buildings from the immediate post-war period, such as a factory building for the Ciba AG company in Wehr/Baden or a handkerchief weaving mill in Blumberg in the Black Forest, and later the German pavilions at the World Exhibition in Berlin confirmed his reputation as an architect who thought up imaginative variations of buildings for particular purposes. One of Eiermann's most striking pieces of furniture is a folding chair, which is light, cheap and easy to fold. It only needs very little storage space. It was designed in 1952 and displayed at the tenth "Triennial" in Milan and at the Brussels World Fair.

One large-scale attempt to find an acceptable style in Germany was the international building exhibition organised by the Berlin Senate in 1957 for the reconstruction of the Hansa area of the city. Berlin wanted to take up its tradition as a city of modern architecture. But, in contrast to earlier periods, it was foreign architects who now had the greatest influence. Inside the "Interbau" buildings, model homes were also shown. Scandinavian furnishings were particularly popular at this time. Furniture by the Knoll International company was displayed

Foyer in the administrative offices of the Neue Heimat housing concern in Munich. The "Bastiano" suite of sofa and armchairs was designed by Tobia Scarpa in 1961, originally for his own use. The joints and screws are not hidden and the pieces can be dismantled. Nevertheless, the furniture still has the character of a classical sofa. Dino Gavina, who had previously manufactured it, described it as the first upholstered furniture to be produced in series and entirely by machines.

Sep Ruf, Chancellor's bungalow in Bonn, 1963/ 64, furnished with pieces by Charles Eames. The floor surface is Roman travertine, the ceiling Brasilian pine. The room could be divided by means of a partition, which is lowered on the photograph. The building – a glass and steel construction with a flat roof, consists of two square blocks. One contains the Federal Chancellor's private rooms, the other is used for receptions and official functions and has glass walls the height of the room, opening on to a courtyard and park.

Charles Eames, reclining chair "EA 124", designed in 1958, with a chromium-plated aluminium frame. The cover consists of a sandwich construction, a layer of foam rubber between two layers of fabric, synthetic material or leather.
Vitra, Weil am Rhein

Charles Eames, armchair, model "EA 107", designed in 1958. The illustration provides a clear view of the elegantly shaped components which connect the two sides of the seat frame and support it on the central base.
Vitra, Weil am Rhein

in one of the most successful buildings, the large, slightly curved white house by Alvar Aalto. Knoll International was a model company thanks to its well thought-out products. Almost all the items taken over into the programme were later produced for many years. In spring, 1952, the company had opened its first show-room in Germany, designed by the director herself, Florence Knoll. Furniture by Eero Saarinen and lamps by Isamu Noguchi were arranged on sisal carpeting. The collection included armchairs by Pierre Jeanneret, fabric-covered chairs by Jens Risom and the Hardoy chair.

As well as Knoll International, the Herman Miller company also brought modern American furniture design to Europe, with models by Charles Eames. It enjoyed a major triumph when the new bungalow designed for the Chancellor by the Architect Sep Ruf in 1964 was furnished with its products. The architect, who had created the German pavilion for Brussels along with Egon Eiermann in 1958, was greatly admired by the Federal Chancellor, Ludwig Erhard. But Erhard's successor Kurt Georg Kiesinger had the furnishings changed. Walter Gropius openly expressed regret at this threat to the "wonderful unity of the building ... by second-rate interior furnishings".

In the dining room of the Chancellor's bungalow there were chairs from the "Aluminium Group" designed by Charles Eames in 1958. The construction of cast aluminium components with attached seats created technical and visual tension. In order to be able to produce his design, Eames had developed the

193

necessary tools and manufacturing process. The result was a product which combined a reduction in material with a high degree of comfort.

Eames also created the chair which became symbolic of comfortable seating. The "Lounge Chair" is the modern chair of chairs. It was originally a unique piece and designed for the fiftieth birthday of the film director Billy Wilder, just to please a friend. At first glance, the chair looks much more complex than other pieces by Eames, but it is actually built according to the same principle as his simple plywood chairs. Three moulded plywood elements are joined together by metal components and, with a lower frame, form the basic structure. This chair represents a particularly convincing synthesis of modern technology and the human need for comfort. At last, an avant-garde form was not an end in itself but served the needs of the user.

Charles Eames, "Lounge chair", Rio polisander with black leather upholstery, designed in 1956. The armrests connect the seat to the backrest. The technique of bending plywood, with which Eames had experimented for arm splints and stretchers, is very highly developed here.
Vitra, Weil am Rhein

SCENE THREE
CUSHION LANDSCAPE

THE CAST:

HELMUT BÄTZNER
JOE COLOMBO
GUIDO DROCCO
PIERO GATTI
PIERO GILARDI
WILLIE LANDELS
PAOLO LOMAZZI
VICO MAGISTRETTI
INGO MAURER
FRANCO MELLO
VERNER PANTON
CESARE PAOLINI
GIONATAN DE PAS
GAETANO PESCE
CARLA SCOLARI
STUDIO 65
FRANCO TEODORO
DONATO D'URBINO

Joe Colombo, "Central living-Block" of the
"Wohnmodell 1969", shown at Visiona, an
exhibition by the Bayer AG Company,
Leverkusen, as part of the International Furniture
Exhibition in Cologne in 1969. In the background,
an area for sitting or reclining, above it, a rotating
bookshelf with integrated TV set. In the
foreground, a dining table with plastic chairs by
Colombo, which the Italian firm Kartell has been
producing since 1968.

Verner Panton, stackable chair, polyester
reinforced with fibreglass, designed in 1960, first
produced in 1968 by Herman Miller.
WK-Wohnen, Leinfelden-Echterdingen

In 1961, the Soviet cosmonaut Yuri Gagarin became the first man to orbit the earth in a spaceship. In 1969, the US astronaut Neil Armstrong was the first man on the moon. This had to have consequences: progressive designers like the Italian Joe Colombo immediately reacted with visionary designs. They created autarkic living units consisting of air-conditioned individual segments, "coordinated machines", as Colombo called them, "which serve life in a new world". He provided an example of the furnishings for space-age homes of this sort with his "Wohnmodell 1969", which he completed in cooperation with the Bayer company. The kitchen was a completely automated "Kitchenbox-Block" and some details were reminiscent of central control panels. There were plastic chairs at the dining room table, and a round sleeping cabin, combined with a "wet cell". The "Central Living-Block" was dominated by a low lounging area consisting of cushioned elements with an inbuilt bar, and a round book shelf with television set, which appeared to be circling freely above it; an ideal place

Verner Panton, room design at the Bayer AG Visiona in 1968, which was held on a Rhine steamer.

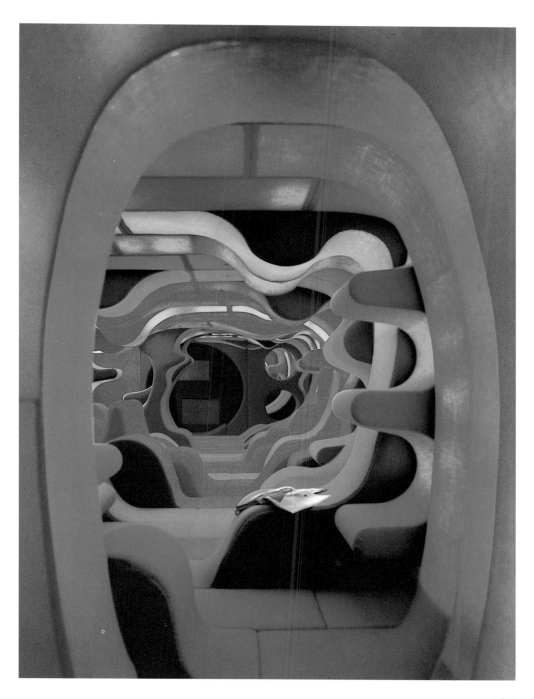

Ingo Maurer, lamps in the shape of giant light bulbs, the "Bulb Opal" model, 1970. Design M Ingo Maurer, Munich

for Barbarella space heroines to stretch out and relax. Now, futuristic furniture was in demand, such as the chairs by the Frenchman Olivier Mourgue, which were used in the Space-Hilton in the famous science-fiction film *2001 – A Space Odyssee* (1968), or the loungers by the Danish architect Jørn Utzon, whose opera house in Sydney might just as well have been an extra-terrestrial station, in which the staff moved around in suits by André Courrèges.

But it was not just industrial technology that had a stimulating effect. It was also claimed that the public needed the support of furniture to snuggle or crawl into, such as the "spherical" chairs designed by the Finn Eero Arnio in 1966, into which people could retreat like a cave. Gaetano Pesce's model "Donna" gave the user the feeling of sinking into a woman's lap. His head rested between large breasts, and the spherical footrest was extremely impractical, but could result in all sorts of games. From a technical viewpoint, this piece was a sensation. The chair was bought as a flat, right-angled package. When the cover was removed, it grew to its full size. But the process was not reversible. In 1968, the Italian manufacturer Zanotta put an inflatable PVC armchair on the market, "a big doll, that will hug you and hold you on her lap", according to the advertisment. An article in the magazine *Form* attempted to analyse this sort of "blow-up" design and the motivation of the designers: "What they are doing goes beyond the conventional idea of solid, permanently assembled furniture. They experiment with air and plastic foil, they speak of closed, flexible cham-

Gaetano Pesce, "UP 5" armchair, known as
"Donna", polyurethane, 1969.
B&B Italia, Novedrate

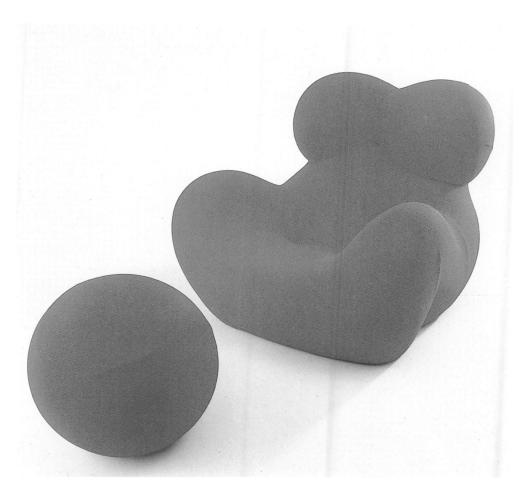

Gaetano Pesce, "UP 1" and "UP 2" armchairs,
polyurethane, 1969. This furniture, like "Donna",
was bought compressed down to a tenth of its
volume and vacuum-packed in a flat, rectangular
box. When the cover was removed, the object
grew to its full size.
B&B Italia, Novedrate

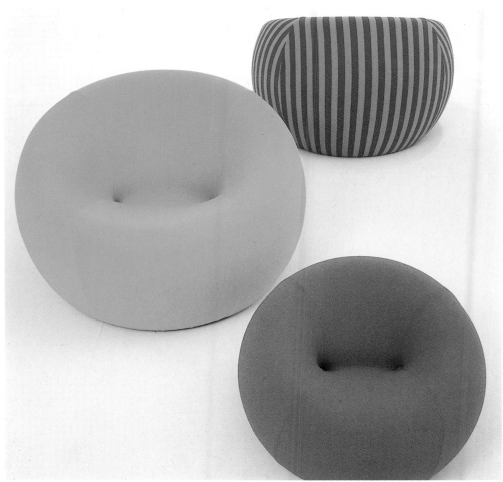

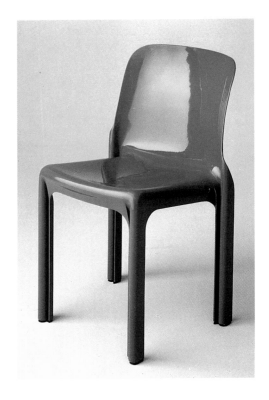

bers and think in terms of pneumatic forms ... It's no longer a matter of chairs, sofa, table, they want ... 'to discover new realms in home furnishings – furniture which stimulates us to new physiological and psychological functions'. These are constructions ... which use optical and acoustic impressions to transport the user to supernatural spheres of relaxation, contentment and love." Increasing human happiness in this way was also the intention of three Viennese "Pneu-Designers" – the architects Laurids Ortner and Günter Zamp, and the painter Klaus Pinter. They called themselves "Love-Protectors", and developed globular structures of clear plastic foil, into which one had to crawl through an airlock. It was claimed that, inside it, one would experience a hitherto unknown sense of harmony. "You will think better and love better, because you will be calmer and more relaxed," the inventors promised.

For joint pleasure, the "Liegewiese" or "lounging area" was invented, for "close, low-level pastimes", as one Swedish manufacturer put it. Usually, it consisted of several cushioned sections, which could be arranged to suit individual wishes. It was in competition to the traditional three-piece suite at a time when Oswald Kolle was teaching the Germans all about sex, and "free love" was not merely being talked about.

The elements of the "Pool" model by Luigi Colani in 1970 made it possible to build a spacious, cosy hollow. The freely combinable cushions to sit and lie on

Vico Magistretti, "Selene", polyester chair, designed in 1967. First, Magistretti worked on a paper model. In order to make the legs stable, he folded them several times. He kept to this principle in the final version.
Artemide, Milan

Helmut Bätzner, chairs, model "BA 1171", polyester reinforced with glass fibres, and matching table, 1966. These "Bofinger" chairs as they were called, after their previous manufacturer, were the first chairs in the world to be made from a single piece of plastic. They were produced in just four minutes on a press, without any manual aid.

*Willie Landels, sofa, "Throw Away", 1965/66.
The piece was made entirely of synthetic material
in white, black, pink, red and yellow. Fabric and
leather covers were used on later models. The
name given to the sofa indicated the deliberate
intention of bringing cheap, consumer furniture
onto the market, which could easily be disposed
of when the owner tired of it.
Zanotta, Milan*

*Joe Colombo, utensil trolley with swing-out
drawers, "Baby" model, made of ABS plastic,
designed 1968. An intelligently designed piece of
furniture, it is popular to this day with designers
and architects.
Bieffeplast, Padua*

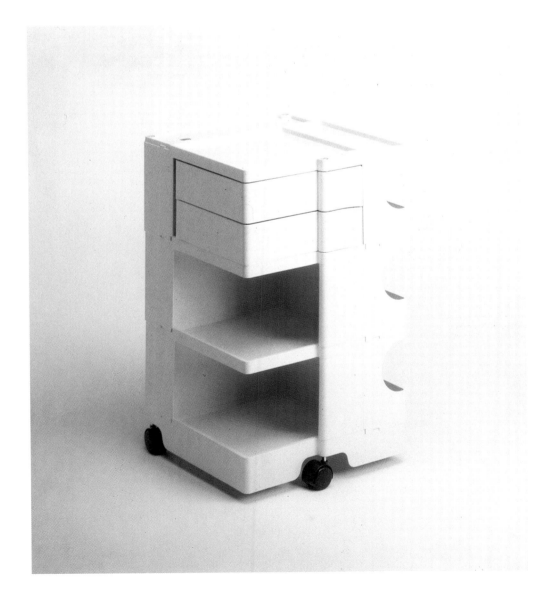

by Cini Boeri and Laura Griziotti, which were marketed the same year by the Arflex company, had soft, quilted covers, the model "Malitte", from the Gavina collection, designed by Roberto Sebastian Matta, was put together like a jigsaw: components of various shapes formed a rectangular block when put together. The "lounging area" was developed not only in the form of a landscape of cushions, but also as a piece of overdimensional "lawn", where one could curl up between thick blades of rubber grass, by the designer team Ceretti, Derossi and Rossi.

This sort of "furniture" was the result of a concept of design which radically broke away from all the conventional rational and functional theories of Industrial Design. The Munich architect Werner Nehls commented in an essay in 1968: "The new shapes are a painted, shaped, constructed protest against the past era with its mechanistic, rational, puritanically utilitarian, soulless, inhuman way of forming the environment, whether it be the unimaginative and endlessly uniform, monotonous glass cubes of architecture or the cold, machine-like, technoid objects of design which lack any trace of humanity. Any further func-

Piero Gatti, Cesare Paolini, Franco Teodoro,
"Sacco" armchair, a cover filled with little balls of
polystyrene, designed 1968/69. It may be
convincing at first glance, but it did not actually
provide the comfort promised. The polystyrene
filling also made a horrible noise when sat upon.
Zanotta, Milan

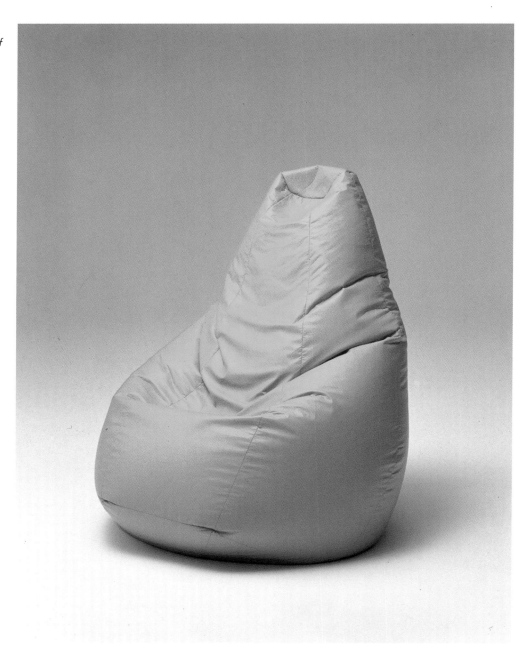

tionalisation of our surroundings and so of man himself is no longer seen just as a fault today, but as a danger which jeopardises the very existence of elementary human values and so of man himself."

Youthful pieces of furniture in Pop-Art colours, which were offered to combat "inhospitableness", turned out to be shortlived, which was quite in keeping with the manufacturers' sales strategies. The UFO-like capsule houses of synthetic materials, for instance the "Monsanto-Haus", which was intended to combat monotony in architecture, or the shell-shaped plastic caps which were put on top of busstops to "humanise everyday life" were also shortlived. These ideas, words and plastic chairs turned out to be bubbles which burst all too soon in the critical light of the functional sun.

Studio 65, design for the furnishings of an apartment in Turin, 1971. The team of designers had to furnish a relatively small flat – see the ground plan in the middle – implementing all sorts of daredevil ideas. An armchair became a throne with a background of clouds, seats in the shape of flower petals combined to form an intimate circle, the shower was built into the stump of an oversized pillar.

203

Piero Gilardi, floor elements, "Pavè Piuma" model, in the form of a bed of gravel, painted polyurethane foam, designed in 1965. Gufram, Cirié-Torino

Carla Scolari, Donato D'Urbino, Paolo Lomazzi, Gionatan de Pas, PVC-foil chair, "Blow", designed in 1967. Zanotta, Milan

"Pneu-Design" furniture was extremely fashionable for a short period. It was produced in all sorts of shapes, from flat moulded seats for "down-to-the-ground" cosiness, which were on the market at low prices, to large plastic foil spheres to crawl into.

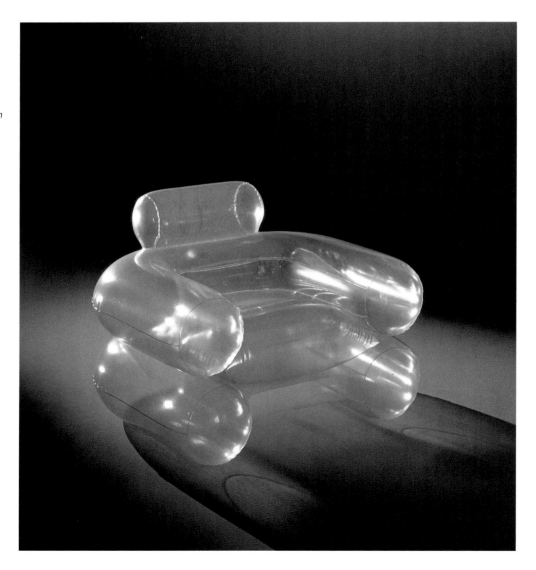

Studio 65, "Bocca", lip-shaped sofa, more than two metres wide, a type of polyurethane foam with elastic fabric cover. It is based on a lip sofa designed by Salvador Dalí back in 1936.
Gufram, Cirié-Torino

Guido Drocco, *Franco Mello*, "Cactus" clothes stand, painted polyurethane foam, designed in 1971.
Gufram, Cirié-Torino

Studio 65, two "Capitello" armchairs shaped like
an Ionic capital, painted polyurethane foam,
1971. The prototype was made by Piero Gilardi.
When someone hesitantly sits down on the curved
surface, he sinks in surprisingly deeply.
Gufram, Cirié-Torino

ACT III

SCENE FOUR
PHOTO STUDIO

THE CAST:

ALCHIMIA
MARTINE BEDIN
MARIO BOTTA
ACHILLE CASTIGLIONI
PAOLO DEGANELLO
NORMAN FOSTER
HANS HOLLEIN
MASSIMO IOSA-GHINI
RODNEY KINSMAN
TOSHIYUKI KITA
MICHELE DE LUCCHI
PETER MALY
XAVIER MATEGOT
ALLESSANDRO MENDINI
MASSIMO MOROZZI
PENTAGON
GAETANO PESCE
CHARLES POLLOCK
FRANZ ROMERO
ETTORE SOTTSASS
PHILIPPE STARCK
SUPERSTUDIO
MATTEO THUN
STEFAN WEWERKA

constantly produce new styles and the relative perfection of what already existed. One consequence of "good design" was that there could not really be better design, just as a washing powder which washes completely white cannot suddenly wash even whiter or "properly white for the first time". Thus the present constantly declares the past to be a liar. One means of escape seems to be in negating one's predecessors. For many young designers, the trail-blazing designs of the 1930s became the icons of a religion which was no longer convincing, which they tried to dislodge from their pedestals with clever-sounding empty phrases. The market, and their own market value, depended on being able to keep arousing the interest of the satisfied, wealthy industrial society with new inventions. Products dated very fast. This explained an attitude fluctuating between irony and cynicism on the part of many designers. If everything has already existed at some point, then anything goes. This does not mean that convincing theories cannot be set up around ideas, abstract concepts discussed, criteria exchanged and values doubted. What used to be described as function was complemented by values which cannot be rationally judged. For instance, the Italian architect Alessandro Mendini spoke of replacing the rational method by a romatic one and defined new design by means of the meaning which the user attributes to the object.

As Friedrich Achleitner put it: "As far as the modern world of consumer goods is concerned, people had to realise that there are other considerations than just logic, reason, minimal expenditure and technical efficiency, and that the 'sublimation of the artificial' was one of man's elementary needs. Very reluctanty,

Achille und Pier Giacomo Castiglioni,
"Allunaggio" (moon landing) metal stool, painted aluminium alloy, nylon feet, designed in 1965, in production since 1980.
Zanotta, Milan

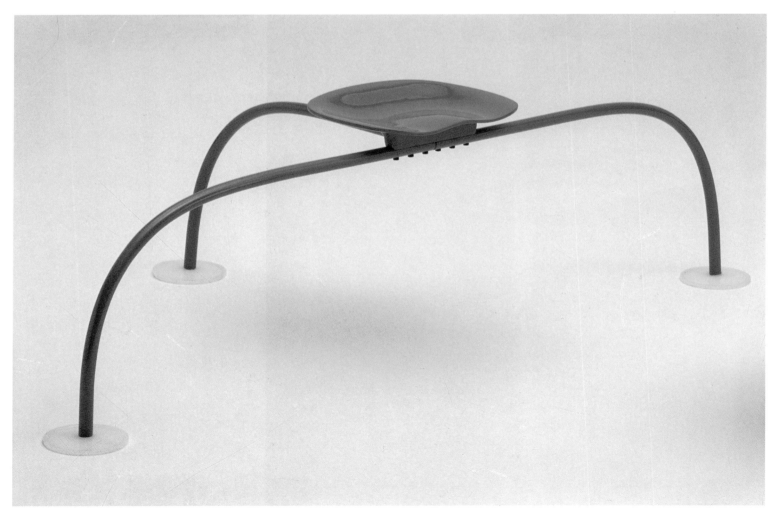

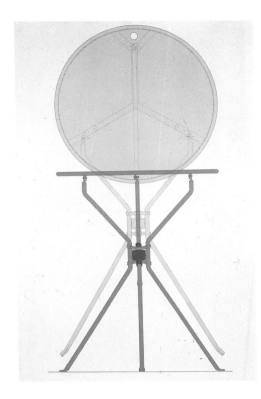 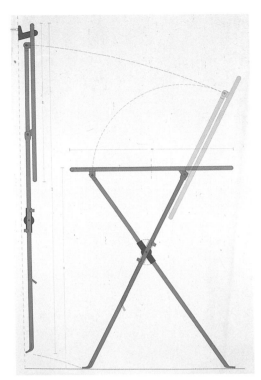 

people were forced to accept that socialised man did not buy objects for their own sake, but for the illusion he associated with them."

Once more, important design initiatives originated in Italy, from groups whose members came mostly from the Faculty of Architecture in Florence. They wanted to distance themselves from the designs of the established old masters, but failed to see that the latter were often far ahead of them in terms of wit and innovation. There were certainly plenty of statements on modern social life, but no real development of a new style of housing and furnishing. There is a good reason for this. It can be observed that the organisation of the home has never really changed in principle. Rooms are still allocated for eating, sleeping, living, cooking and physical hygiene. There are certain pieces of furniture which correspond to these. Chairs remain chairs, tables tables and beds beds, no matter what a designer tries to do with them.

The Italian old masters included the brothers Pier Giacomo, Livio and Achille Castiglioni from Milan, three architects who did design buildings, but became famous for their lamps and furniture – Livio also for his audio-visual environments. They re-discovered forgotten designs and turned them into forms suitable for mass production, reproduced familiar ideas in new, up-to-date materials. A lightweight table with a round top, which could be folded away thanks to an ingenious nylon hinge and hung up on the wall, was reminiscent of garden tables used in the last century. And the "Servomuto" or dumb servant was a repetition in an industrial guise of an accessory from the gentleman's rooms of the 1870s. The Castiglionis' wit and resourcefulness is best demonstrated by objects which they put together from existing separate components, which was described as ready-made design. This included models like the chair "Stella" in 1957, a bicycle saddle mounted on a bar with a semispherical cast-iron base, which functions like a tumbler toy, or the lamp, "Tonio", in 1962. It is composed of a car headlight, an uncovered transformer, components from industrial suppliers and loops designed for fishing rods. Behind the apparent incongruity, on close inspection the design reveals a lot of calculation.

Achille Castiglioni, folding table, "Cumano", painted steel, 1978/79.
Zanotta, Milan

Achille Castiglioni, "Servomuto" (dumb servant) model, occasional table, synthetic material, painted steel and laminate. It goes back to designs from the early sixties and has been in production since the mid-seventies. Castiglioni designed it for a small, cramped restaurant.
Zanotta, Milan

Alchimia, furniture garden, 1982
Zanotta, Milan

"Cinismo abitativo (cynicism you can live in)
A house has a floor, as sticky as honey, your feet stick to it and it's impossible to escape.
A house is an orderly place, because it has a wash-hand basin, a rubbish bin and a tin of peeled tomatoes.
A house is never a place of departure, but a place of arrival, where the view is a print of a work by Cézanne.
A house is a spy, which notes our secret actions.
A house is a rucksack, which rests so huge and blown-up on our shoulders that any movement is impossible . . .
A house allows us to be lazy only on a Saturday morning.
A house always has another house beside it, from which we can nostalgically hear music.
A house always has an alarm clock, to send us to work.
A house is a diagram that represents the condition of our immobility.
A house is a hypocritical refuge for those who fear the storms of life.
A house is not an object of relaxation, because it has too many gutters, porches, aerials and pillars.
A house is the sacrosanct temple that shuts out the actions that take place in other houses.
A house always harbours a terrorist.
A house is the fiction of a lost idyll, which will never come again."
(Alessandro Mendini)

In the mid sixties, the Radical Design movement was formed, to combat the growing degrading trend for inventors to become dogsbodies to industry. Different disciplines cooperated to develop ideal designs, with the aim of breaking open old, encrusted structures and at least throwing a harsh light on and paraphrasing the industrial crisis it had diagnosed, if it could not actually overcome it. The Italian groups of the *disegno radicale* or *architettura radicale* movements were formed around the school of architecture in Florence. Other groups which gained an international reputation were the English Archigram group, the German Haus-Rucker-Co and Superstudio. This name was an obvious choice, as Adolfo Natalini, one of the initiators, later explained: "At that time, everything was super, Superman was flying around, supermarkets were rapidly gaining customers, and we wanted to be a Super-studio. We wanted to have an effect on the world". In their utopian designs, they covered whole towns and landscapes with giant monuments in an arithmetic-jotter pattern. Design was reduced to small squares, which were put together in an unending number and used to cover everything. Natalini explains: "We had no opportunities to work in architecture or to make models, unless we financed them ourselves. In the seventies, thirteen thousand students studied at the Faculty of Architecture in Florence. It was a giant factory, but there was no production. "We could only manufacture small objects as prototypes and offer them to companies like Poltronova, Zanotta or Abet Print." Between 1969 and 1971, the idea of the universal grid system led to a furniture programme called "La Serie Misura", consisting of a bed, cupboard, various tables and shelf systems, which all appeared to be covered in tiles.

Some members of the Florence radical design group Archizoom, which made an appearance no less spectacular than that of Superstudio in the late sixties, succeeded in making a name for themselves in the seventies and eighties as virtuoso soloists. They include Andrea Branzi, Massimo Morozzi and Paolo Deganello. Their designs, for instance Morozzi's "Tangram" table or Deganel-

Alchimia, cupboard from the 1981 "Mobile infinito" project, which involved approximately thirty designers: Ugo la Pietra designed handles, Denis Santachiara feet, Andrea Branzi figures and Kazuko Sato flags, which were put onto the furniture. The decorations, which could be attached to the magnetic surfaces at random, were designed by Francesco Clemente, Sandro Chia and Enzo Cucchi, amongst others.

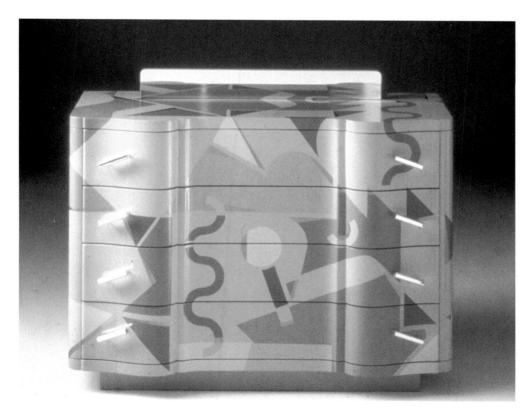

Nuova Alchimia, Alessandro Mendini, chest of drawers, "Cetonia", 1984.
Zabro, Milan

213

lo's "Aeo" chair and "Torso" sofa, were manufactured as part of Cassina's range, the model "Squash" was produced by Driade.

In 1976, the Studio Alchimia was founded in Milan as a "project for the image of the 20th century", as a "laboratory for new iconography". The initiators and active members included Alessandro Mendini, who became editor of *Domus* in 1980, and Ettore Sottsass, the Nestor of a new and different style of design, as well as Michele de Lucchi, Trix and Robert Haussmann and others. Their statements always contained something mystical. Just as the alchemists experimented to try to make gold, in the Alchimia catalogue *Elogio del Banale*, in 1978, Mendini described their hope of being able to make works of art from all sorts of collages, and to deliberately employ kitsch as "the Trojan horse of the masses". "The main characteristic [of new design] is perhaps to regard the objects not in their functional connection, which can more or less be taken for granted, but to think in terms of a ritual and relative expressivity. It's a question of the relation between person and object." In this process, the designer himself is his best observer, when he takes his unresolved relationship to the classicists

Martine Bedin, lamp, "Super" model, from the first Memphis collection, 1981. It calls to mind childrens' brightly painted pull-along wooden animals.
Memphis, Milan

Ettore Sottsass, high table, "Le strutture tremano", from the "Bauhaus Collection" by Studio Alchimia, 1979.
Paolo Curti, Brescia

Ettore Sottsass, room divider, "Carlton", covered with laminated plastic. With the "Casablanca" sideboard, it is one of the "programmatic pieces" designed by Sottsass for the first Memphis Collection in 1981.
Memphis, Milan

as a theme. In 1978, Mendini presented "Metamorphoses" of established objects of design: he covered a plastic chair by Joe Colombo with a marble-style pattern, attached little flags and pennants to Mackintosh's "Hill House" chair and the "Superleggera" by Gio Ponti, turned the wooden back of Gerrit Rietveld's "Zick-Zack" chair into a cross, and decorated Thonet's Model No. 14 and Marcel Breuer's "Wassily" with brightly coloured cardboard clouds and antenna-like structures. But this sort of artistic manipulation was not new, indeed fairly well-known from the Dada movement. Still, Mendini did not only trivialize objects, he also exalted some. He painted a series of old chests of drawers in Kandinsky style, and alienated a neo-baroque armchair with pointillistic painting. This "banal design" hinted "at the natural, intimate and mythical relation" which Mendini sensed between man and the object. Trix and Robert Haussman gave a slightly different accentuation to their presentation of the tension between form and function: a mannerist cupboard in the shape of a Greek pillar could be taken apart to reveal drawers. The user is forced to destroy classical ideal forms in a grotesque fashion.

In order to emphasise the arbitrariness of design and to experiment further with possibilities for alienation, in 1981 there was a sort of "Design Happening", entitled "Mobile infinito". Some thirty designers supplied decorations which could be attached to magnetic surfaces in any order and exchanged at

Masanori Umeda, seating podium, "Tawaraya" model, 1981: clear the ring to sit down. This is one of the most spectacular designs in the first Memphis Collection. "Tatami" mats and iridescent silk cushions rest on a black and white striped wooden base. The "ring" area is surrounded by ropes. The opaque spheric lamps on the four corner posts provide subtle lighting. Memphis, Milan

Michele de Lucchi, occasional table, "Kristall", laminated plastic, painted wood and metal, also from the first Memphis Collection in 1981. Memphis, Milan

Matteo Thun, tea and coffee pot designs, studies for completed models such as "Lesbia Oceanica" or "Passer Passer", both 1981. Objects of this sort were displayed for instance at the exhibition organised by the Anthologie Quartett company, Bad Essen with the theme "Old and new suggestions for a table that is wealthy once more".

random, and designed feet, handles, figures and flags, which were put onto the models. At this time, the avant-garde scene was changing not only in Italy, but also in the United States. This was the beginning of what we now describe as the post-modern movement.

"Architectural quotations" and a deliberately absurd use of basic elements, broken gables, upside-down pillars, and disproportionate ornamentation gnawed at the foundations of traditional architecture. Buildings were like paper patterns put together wrongly. Works such as the Piazza d'Italia in New Orleans by Charles Moore (1977–78), the Public Services Building in Portland/Oregon by Michael Graves (1980–82) or the multi-storey block for the American telephone company A. T. & T. by Philip Johnson (1978–1984) followed Robert Venturi's earlier works like the old people's home, Guild House in Philadelphia (1963).

217

Toshiyuki Kita, "Wink" easy chair, steel structure, upholstery of polyurethane foam and polyester wadding, 1980. The knob at the side is used to adjust the back. The two headrests, which look like Mickey Mouse ears, can be adjusted to any position. The foot can be folded underneath or pulled out to form a lounger. Many different covers are available to provide individual variations.
Cassina, Meda/Milan

The "quotation" as a design element was also transferred to other fields. The "Bauhaus Collection" by Alchimia played openly, as the name suggests, with introducing historical pieces as blocks in a style construction kit. Objects like the table "Le strutture tremano" confused ideas people had become fond of in a sophisticated manner. The designer, Ettore Sottsass, was one of the leading forces behind the commercialisation of the experiments. In 1981, the furniture company Memphis, which he founded with people who shared his views, introduced itself at the Milan Furniture Exhibition. But its furniture, by comparison with that of Alchimia, displayed a "smooth, catchy mixture" – as Volker Fischer describes it – "basically, a boutique version of protest, which can be sure from the very beginning of winning the approval of the middle-class public after an initial show of hesitation."

Memphis had invited well-known architects like Michael Graves or Hans Hollein to contribute. Graves, an American, designed one of the collection's masterpieces, the "Plaza Dressing Table", a mixture of Art Déco elements, "quotations" from post-modern architecture and reminders of old Hollywood films. In five years, just two of these were sold north of the Alps. Programmatic pieces in the first Memphis collection included the models "Casablanca" and "Carlton" by Sottsass. They consisted of small boards covered in laminated plastic in all sorts of shapes, put together like a children's game. Lamps and small pieces of furniture in bright, children's fun colours, with a deliberately naive construction are reminiscent of children's cuddly toys. Their colour and shape transmit what could be described as "impertinent optimism", without regard for historic dignity, cheeky compared with the lofty values of traditional design. It was the patterns presented by Memphis which had the longest-lasting effect, for instance "Bakterio" by Ettore Sottsass, a microscopic swarm of cocci, spores and spirochetes, which he used for the base of the "Carlton". All of a sudden these designs became the signet of companies which wanted to acquire a super-modern image, for instance the fashion concern Esprit, which opted for Memphis designs all over the world.

Ettore Sottsass says of himself: "People say I am a designer because I have made pottery instead of sky-scrapers or tables instead of ministries, that is because I have designed small things for private use, instead of large and monumental objects for public use, although I believe the difference between a designer and an architect always remains primarily a quantitative, dimensional difference: It's always a matter of actions which are carried out, of the scene, and of developing the tools for the comedy of human life; sometimes you know what the comedy will be like, sometimes, you don't." When he designed stage props, he imagined "tearing the geometrical forms and mathematics away from

Massimo Morozzi, "Tangram" table, 1983. The individual elements which make up the table are the triangle, parallelogram and square, as in the Chinese game of the same name.
Cassina, Meda/Milan

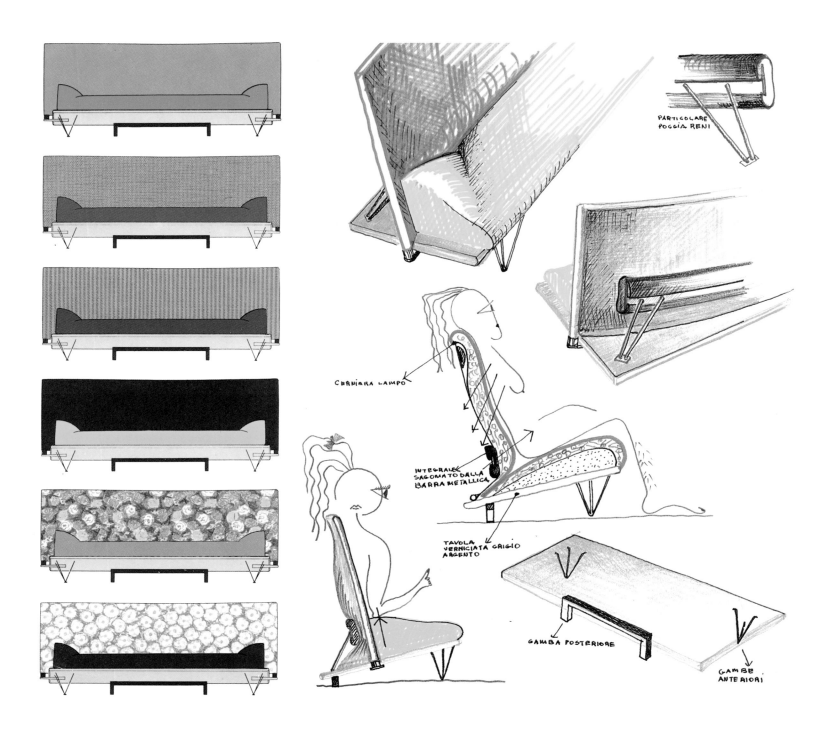

Labels within the drawings:
PARTICOLARE POGGIA RENI
CERNIERA LAMPO
INTEGRALE SAGOMATO DALLA BARRA METALLICA
TAVOLA VERNICIATA GRIGIO ARGENTO
GAMBA POSTERIORE
GAMBE ANTERIORI

*Paolo Deganello, drawings for the sofa
"Squash", which the Driade company has been
producing since 1981.
The ecstatic advertising blurb runs:
"Lifestyle – contradictory. Interested in everything
that happens in the world, stimulated by it ... uses
strong perfumes; accustomed to luxury and a
casual style; dresses with a speedy elegance.
Feels attracted by glitter, but is not put off by the
cold, rational atmosphere of a waiting room.
Faces the flashlights of photographers and TV
cameras as a successful personality, appearing to
be slightly annoyed. Despises interviews, prefers
to keep people guessing."*

intellectual strictness and tracing them back to the ancient symbols in which history recognises itself."

Sottsass belonged to the generation of Italian designers that helped to build up their country's leading position in the sixties; his precise, ergonomically thought-out pieces for Olivetti made their way into every well-known collection and every history of design. In the mid-sixties, he was occupied with social and political events in America. He saw an alternative to the violence he experienced everywhere in a "Design of Tolerance". He advocated a "non-culture", which was not supposed to be class-specific and so was supposed to belong to nobody and at the same time everybody. Even Sottsass designs from his Alchimia period – for instance chairs with lanky, awkward chrome legs, screwed-on metal handles, like those used for filing cabinets or public transport, and little boards, covered with laminated plastic – oscillated between poor and rich, cheap and expensive.

Paolo Deganello, "Torso" sofa, steel frame,
polyurethane foam and polyester wadding for the
upholstery, 1982.
Cassina, Meda/Milan

<u>*Archizoom*</u>*,* <u>*Paolo Deganello*</u>*, "Aeo" armchair,*
1973. The chair can be taken apart. The bar which
supports the back and the base for the seat are
pushed into the plastic base. The cover is pulled
over the back and the cushion placed on the seat
to complete the chair.
Cassina, Meda/Milan

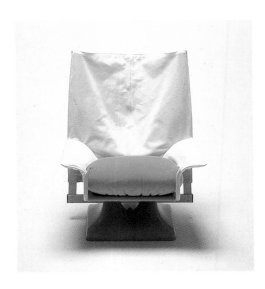

But, for the most part, post-modern decor followed a different course. When the Alessi company tried in 1983 to transfer the ideas to tableware, the result was extraordinarily luxurious objects. Its "Tea and Coffee Piazza" project led many renowned artists to create small materialisations of architectonic dreams in silver and other exquisite materials. Amongst a lot of trivia, one striking piece was a tray in the shape of a small aircraft-carrier, "armed" with severe and aggressive pots and jugs. It was by the Viennese architect, Hans Hollein.

For the first Memphis Collection, Hans Hollein had contributed a table with a layered surface. The top, which had a root wood veneer, appeared to be balanced precariously on the rounded legs. In some of his early sixties drawings, Hollein had emphasised ironic elements. In a collage, he arranged monolithic rock structures above the urban area of Vienna, and hung a giant caterpillar from the skyscrapers of Manhattan. From this "monumentalisation of the banal", the path led to a form of architecture which again allowed for symbolic

Hans Hollein, "Marilyn" sofa, maple root wood, upholstery covered with satin, 1981. It represents a sophisticated furniture version of a pose adopted by Marilyn Monroe on a photo, covered only by a large fan; the whole piece is in the Art déco style.
Poltronova, Montale

Hans Hollein, dressing table, designed for MID, 1981. It was originally designed for series production, but only three were manufactured. The circular segment also appears in the "Schwarzenberg" table in the 1981 Memphis Collection, and in the interior of the Beck Company's shop.

content: the front of a jeweller's shop is broken up to show golden stalactites looking out from the granite fassade; in the public rooms of the Austrian tourist office, stylised palms, fragments of Greek pillars and Far Eastern pavilions aroused colourful dreams of travel.

Hans Hollein, interior of the shop for the Ludwig Beck Company, Munich, in Trump Tower in New York, 1981–83. Like the central office of the Vienna Tourist Office, this interior no longer exists.

Different motifs keep re-appearing, for instance the canyon-like fissures, which cut into level surfaces at irregular intervals. His Museum Abteiberg in Mönchengladbach is a landscape of buildings, consisting mostly of underground sections. A tower with a wavy, fractured surface, forms the focal point, around which elements as different as square shed-roofed buildings with a cheap sheet zinc façade and a marble entrance pavilion are grouped.

For his interiors, Hollein usually used already existing but carefully selected pieces of furniture, for instance Eames' moulded armchair, plastic chairs by Magistretti or Thonet's bentwood chairs. But he also designed some furniture of his own, for instance for the Siemens Casino in Munich.

In the late sixties, the artist and architect Stefan Wewerka had begun to modify classical chair models. This did not result in usable furniture, but rather in comments on seating habits, for instance "classroom chairs", at an adventurous, oblique angle, to avoid an imaginary slap. A sculpture made of two half chairs put together later became a usable article; this was the beginning of Wewerka's first asymmetrical chair, which also became his trade-mark. This was followed by asymmetrical armchairs, sofas and tables. Just as the gondolas

223

Mario Botta, "Quinta" chair, round bar steel and filigree sheet steel, mounted under tension, 1985. Alias, Milan

Mario Botta, "Seconda" chair, steel, perforated sheet iron, cylindrical polyurethane back support, 1982. Alias, Milan

When Botta was asked whether he would design a chair, his initial reaction was: "Another chair? After the hundreds of thousands of chairs we have already?" But then he realised that the history of humanity is the history of the continuing new design of utility objects, which are always the same, and at the same time always different. (From an interview by Dieter Bachmann, 1985)

Matteo Thun, perforated metal cupboard, "Settimanale", 1985. The diamond-shaped pattern was cut using a laser. Bieffeplast, Padua

aim once more at clear contours. They include the Italian architect Mario Botta, the Milan Zeus group of designers, the Frenchman Philippe Starck and Matteo Thun, who also worked on the first Memphis Collection. He dissociated himself from these "gymnastic warming-up exercises" and took back some of his ideas: "It's not a question of replacing the modern movement, but of revitalising it, providing it with new symbols and fresh air." From an early stage, he turned his attention to Japan, and succeeded in getting a lot of orders from there. At the same time it can be observed that Japanese designers are becoming popular in Europe. The new meeting between the cultures led, as it did a hundred years before, to a turn to stricter forms.

Japanese elements can also be discerned in chair designs by Mario Botta. This student of Le Corbusier attempted to integrate a meditative element into his

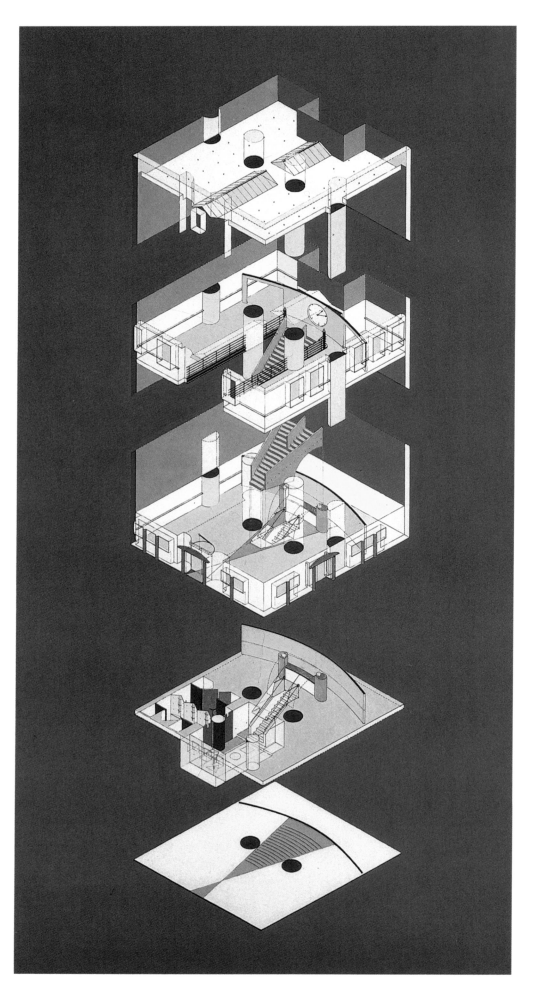

Philippe Starck, isometric drawing for the Café "Costes" in Paris, opened in 1984. Starck was made famous by the interior of this Café, which "was to appear as lavish, barnlike and melancholic as the station restaurant in Prague", and by the rooms he designed in the Elysée Palace.

Philippe Starck, armchair, "Pratfall", 1982. This is the big brother to "Costes", a cafe chair related in structure, but more delicate. The curved woodenform is reminiscent of Art déco designs. Starck also used the chair in a conference room for the French President François Mitterand. Driade, Piacenza

Philippe Starck, "Tippy Jackson" folding table, 1982. The legs, which are curved with different radii, can be folded flat by means of the joint under the table top. The loose top rests only on the vertical supports attached to the legs. Driade, Piacenza

Norman Foster, table from the "Nomos" furniture
system, chromium-plated steel frame with a glass
top, 1986. The feet are adjustable to give a
working height of between 64 and 72 cm.
Tecno, Milan

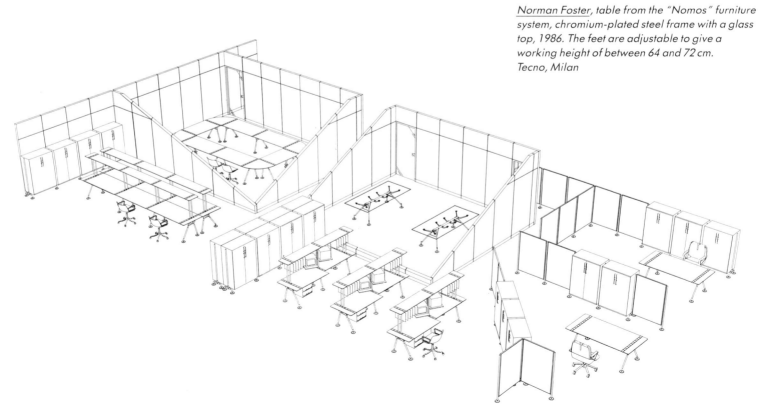

Computer aided design illustrating the use of the
"Nomos" system.

Norman Foster, a working area using the "Nomos" system. The upper level is added as an independent element and can hold small platforms for computers. Plastic cable ducts complete the system, which is specifically designed for electronic data processing equipment. But so far no-one has designed a matching computer. Their yellowish-white casing reflects little of the effort expended by the manufacturers on their inner components. Tecno, Milan

Norman Foster, Hong Kong and Shanghai Bank, schematic representation of a façade.

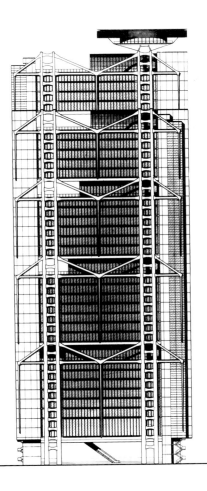

produced metal constructions. This sort of aestheticisation of construction obviously outlasted all trends in fashion. More recent examples are the Centre Pompidou by Piano and Rogers (1974), and the Hongkong and Shanghai Bank by the British architect Norman Foster (1985). This building, the "most expensive building in the world", made Norman Foster known to a wider public. The visible steel skeleton of the multi-storey re-appears in Foster's office furniture. Here, the idea of a flexible structure has been developed to a new high-point. Its predecessors included the office furniture programmes by the Olivetti company and by George Nelson and Bruce Burdick. They had already clearly formulated the basic idea of Norman Foster's "Nomos" programme: tabletops, containers etc. are suspended in a supporting structure, which can also take telephone and computer tables. This office construction kit was no longer intended to fit the walls of small rooms, but the large, undivided areas of modern office architecture. There is one particularly interesting idea of making use of the space above the working area: "The question is no longer how many desks need one monitor, but how many monitors fit on each desk." And Foster's model also takes account of the user's desire to be able to make changes and adaptations himself. A study conducted in London had shown that traditional office systems were not flexible enough, as the cost of alterations was too high. Foster tried to take account of this with useful details, for instance open cable ducts.

While on the international scene the architect Norman Foster is supplying highly professional designs more or less as a by-product, especially in Germany trained designers are producing verbally embroidered dilettantism. In an

233

Gallery room with furniture by the Swiss group Vorsprung and the Cologne group Pentagon. "Pentagon" provided the cupboards in the middle, which consist of steel, maple wood veneer and rubberised material, the "Wagon-lit" model, designed by Detlef Meyer-Voggenreiter in 1987 and the wooden crate sculpture "Mai 68". This display in the "Atoll" gallery in Kassel was on show in parallel to the "documenta 8".

article on new German design in the periodical *Form*, the Moscow designer Dimitri Tchelkunov wrote in 1987 that the "antifunctional design" in the wake of Alchimia and Memphis had as much of "a relation to design as a china pig painted with flowers has to cattle breeding". He fittingly remarked "that these works... always have to be accompanied by a written key, that is by wordy commentaries, which make them sound significant. Often, one even gets the impression that these texts are the main course rather than a side dish...". What was going on in some designers' heads around 1980, and perhaps emerged most clearly in Memphis, was not so much the discovery of the necessity for a new style of design as the recognition that this actually hardly exists any more. The way out was to declare things which were created inspite of this realisation to be works of art. In the early eighties, influenced by enterprises such as the "Möbel perdu" gallery, there was a bizarre display of monstrosities in circulation in German museums and galleries, which lacked any serious design intention. In the opening speeches and introductions to the accompanying exhibition catalogues, the same tune always to be heard, referring to the "criticism of over-rational design" and the "general paradigmatic change to the post-industrial society".

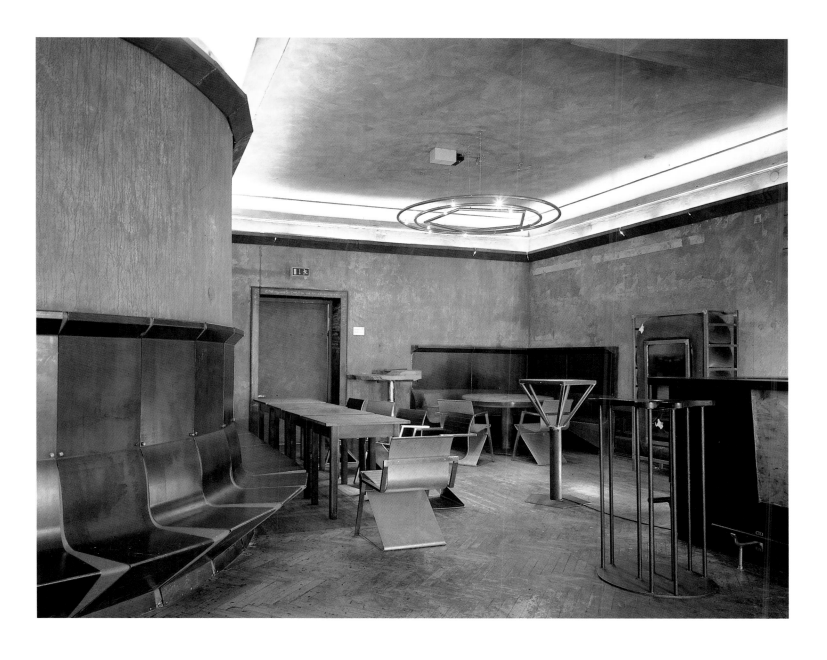

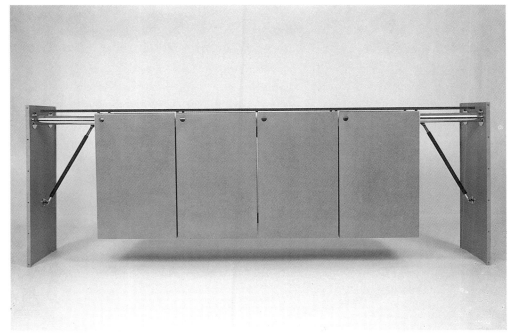

Pentagon, "Casino" Café, furnished for the "documenta 8" in Kassel, 1987.

Xavier Mategot, sideboard, model "M6", tubular steel supports, aluminium plates, wood, 1987. Christian Farjon, Aubusson

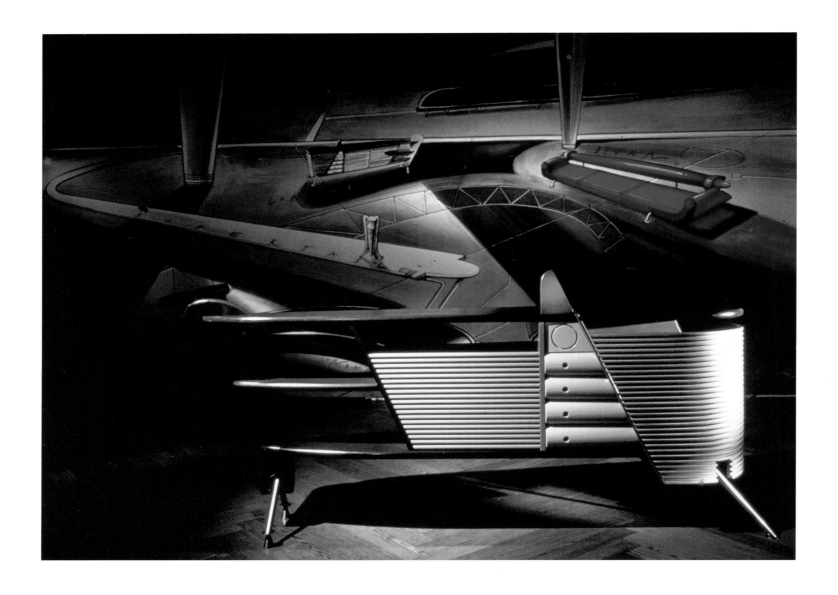

Massimo Iosa-Ghini, sideboard, "Bertrand", wood and metal, from the 1987 Memphis Collection.
Memphis, Milan

One of the numerous groups concerned with furniture design is Pentagon, a cooperative of three sculptors, a neon specialist and an art historian. Pentagon is also the name of their furniture gallery in Cologne. "The gallery sees itself as a base in the mid-west, as a coordinator and distributor of post-modern ideas." In its opening communique, the group wrote: "The general stagnation of the production of ideas, and at the same time the inflationary use of the term 'Design' make it necessary to present radical and individual constructions to the public... If the name 'Pentagon' has military connotations, this is based on "design strategies" which shake up and change the values of relations between objects and their users normally one-sidedly described as 'good design'". The first two exhibitions by the furniture gallery were entitled "Herbstmanöver" (Autumn Manoeuvres) and "Gipfeltreffen" (Summit Meeting). In 1987, Michael Erlhoff, director of the Design Council and at that time design adviser to the "documenta" exhibition, invited the Pentagon "troop" to the exhibition in Kassel at the last minute. Their task was to transform a dilapidated provincial discotheque into an exhibition cafe. The Frenchman Philippe Starck, their only competitor in this project, had given up. The Cologne designers came up with fitted steel wall seats and matching aluminium chairs. "Classical brewery tables with maple-wood tops in a non-name-design" were added.

Pentagon's pieces oscillate between fun and seriousness. The sarcastic box-sculpture "May 68" is really original; so, too, is a cupboard designed for the

236

middle of a room, made up of slim elements, joined by bellows, like train carriages. These objects match the current trend, they fit well into the overall international landscape of slightly sloping furniture. There is also a nostalgic faction which reproduces memories of the stream lined era, up-dated and with a curious way of calling to mind a luxury from the past. We shall have to ask ourselves what will remain of the latest furniture exhibition hits apart from feeling. Anyway, as always, the consumer has already made his decision. His taste remains as obscure as the dark side of the moon.

Franz Romero, armchair, model "DS 57", frame of wood and metal, leather,covered upholstery, 1985.
De Sede, Klingnau

Paris "stage for living", designed by Gaetano Pesce

FINALE

Page 238: apartment of the photographer and art collector Marc André Hubin on the Avenue Foche in Paris, furnished with pieces from the last four decades. In the foreground, a 1940s table by Isamu Noguchi and elements from the "Malitte" "cushion landscape" by Roberto Sebastian Matta from the sixties. By the window, the "Squash" sofa designed by Paolo Deganello in 1981. In the background, a huge prototype for a Memphis-style table clock by George James Sowden. On the gallery above the living room, furniture by Carlo Mollino.

Hannes Meyer, Coop-Interieur, 1926

*Room with a bed and the "Ya Ya Ho" low voltage
lighting system designed by Ingo Maurer in 1984*

Art-déco furniture from the collection in the Musée de la Ville de Paris: cupboard by Maurice Champion, 1937, screen with polar bears by Louis Midavaine, 1932. The table is attributed to Albert Guenot, the chair to Louis Sognot and the sofa to Paul Follot. The 1930 lamp is anonymous.

242

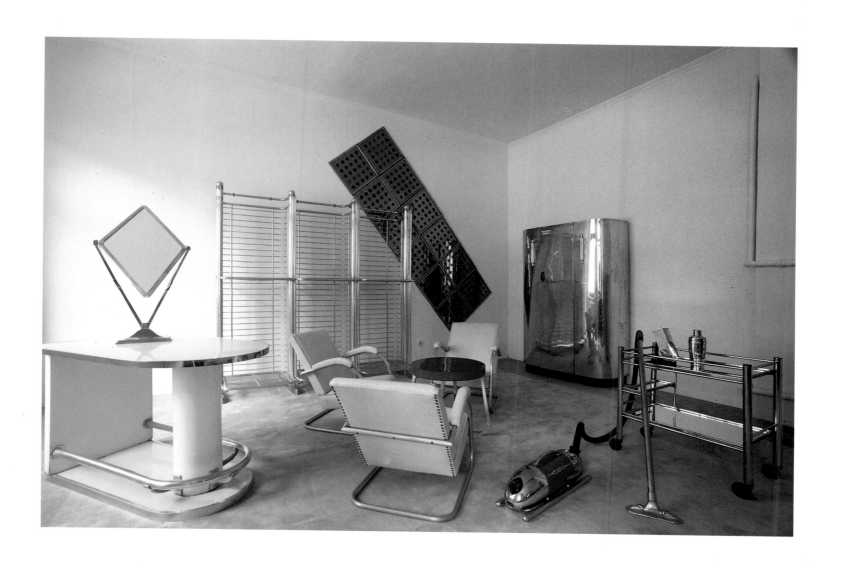

Room in the Stefan Vogdt Gallery in Munich. The aluminium cupboard is said to have been produced for an aeroplane, the work table was originally situated in a motor yacht and the shelf system, which can be dismantled, was part of the interior of a "boulangerie" in Paris. The vacuum cleaner, "Champion", type "OK", is from Holland, around 1930.

243

Living room in the Sorgenfrei house, Schloss Hünefeld, furnished with objects from the extensive design collection belonging to the master of the house, Rainer Krause.

Book shelves, "Suvretta", by Ettore Sottsass from the 1981 Memphis Collection; side tables from George Nelson's model series "5451-53", 1953; on them are two "Jurmo" decanters by Timo Sarpanava and a champagne ice bucket "5052" by Ettore Sottsass, 1979; "Snow" standard lamps by Vico Magistretti, 1974; "Gambadilegno"

(wooden leg) armchair by Enzo Mari, 1976; armchair "406" by Alvar Aalto, 1935–39; table by Isamu Noguchi, 1940–45, on it a pot from the "Rara Avis" (rare birds) series by Matteo Thun, 1981; on the shelves, Matteo Thun's "Passer Passer" pot, 1981, "The Sherry Netherlands" glass vase, also by Thun, 1984, designed for a gourmet restaurant of the same name in New York, and a miniature pillar, a model for the Schröer KG Company in Krefeld, manufactured in a limited edition of 25, designed by Trix and Robert Haussmann, 1983.

Library in the Sorgenfrei house, Schloss Hünefeld.
Re-edition of the "Sant'Elia" armchair, designed
in 1936 by Giuseppe Terragni, 1985; "Cantone"
table by Ettore Sottsass, 1981, with a laminated
top showing the "Bakterio" design, created by
Sottsass in 1978; on the table, a vase for six
flowers from the "Sherry Netherlands" series,
1984, a silver plate, model "5101" by Ettore
Sottsass, 1983, and the "Chad" pot and "Onega"
cups by Matteo Thun, 1982; "Parentesi" lamp by
Pio Manzú and Achille Castiglioni, 1970; side
table by Eileen Gray, 1927.

CARLO BUGATTI

Alvar Aalto, 1898–1976

After studying architecture at the Helsinki University of Technology, Aalto worked in various Swedish architects' offices. In 1927 he opened his own office in Turku, which was moved to Helsinki in 1934. In the mid-30's he founded the Artek company, which produced his furniture. In 1940 he became a professor of architecture at the Massachusetts Institute of Technology in Cambridge. Aalto completed more than 200 buildings and building plans, which included a number of large commissions for community centres, university buildings, hospitals and factories.
Important works: Sanatorium in Paimio, southwest Finland, 1929–33; the town library in the formerly Finnish town of Viipuri, 1930–1935; the Finnish pavilion at the New York World Exhibition, 1938–39; the Baker House student residence in Cambridge/Mass., 1947–48; object No. 16 for the "Interbau" Fair at Berlin, 1955–57.

Peter Behrens, 1868–1940

Born in Hamburg, he studied painting in Karlsruhe and Düsseldorf and lived in Munich from 1890 onwards. There he was one of the founding members of the Munich Secession in 1892 and of the Vereinigte Werkstätten für Kunst im Handwerk (United Workshop for Artist Craftsmanship). From 1899 to the end of 1903 he worked in the Darmstadt artists' colony. Afterwards he became the director of the Kunstgewerbeschule (Arts and Crafts College) in Düsseldorf and was made artistic adviser to the AEG, Berlin, by Emil Rathenau. From 1922 onwards he was the professor responsible for the master's class in architecture at the Vienna Academy. In 1936 he took over a master's architectural workshop at the Berlin Akademie der Künste (Academy of Arts).
Important works: His own house in Darmstadt, 1901; the AEG turbine factory in Berlin, 1908–09; the German embassy in Saint Petersburg, 1911–12.

Harry Bertoia, 1915–1978

Bertoia was born in Italy and emigrated with his father to the United States in 1930. In 1936 he got his degree in sculpture and painting at the Technical High School, Detroit and was awarded a postgraduate scholarship by Cranbrook University, Birmingham/Michigan, where he taught metalwork between 1939 and 1943. In 1943 he moved to California and worked with Charles and Ray Eames on furniture design. From the early fifties onwards he concentrated on metal sculptures.

Marcel Lajos Breuer, 1902–1981

Born in Hungary, he went to Austria is 1920 to study painting at the Vienna Academy of Art. In the same year he matriculated at the Bauhaus and directed its carpentry workshop from 1925 onwards. In 1928 he opened his architect's office in Berlin. In 1935 he went to London, two years later to the United States with Walter Gropius, where the two worked together until 1941. Until 1946 Breuer also taught at the architecture department of Harvard University. Afterwards he opened his own office in New York.
Important works: apartment houses in Doldertal near Zurich, 1935–36; the UNESCO building in Paris, on which he worked together with Pier Luigi Nervi and Bernhard Zehrfuss from 1952 to 1958; the Whitney Museum of American Art, New York, 1966; the IBM laboratories in La Gaude, France, and Boca Raton, Florida.

Carlo Bugatti, 1856–1940

Because of his manifold talents he was called "young Leonardo" by his family. He studied architecture at Milan Academy and was a student at the Ecole des Beaux-Arts in Paris. His father wanted him to become a sculptor like himself and his grandfather, but Carlo was interested in furniture. In 1888 he set up his own workshop in Milan. In 1904 he moved to Paris, where he painted and worked with silver. His son Ettore and his grandson Jean made the name Bugatti world-famous with their cars.

MARCEL BREUER

Achille Castiglioni, *1918

In 1944 Castiglioni got his doctorate in architecture from Milan Polytechnic, and then opened an architect's office along with his brothers, Pier Giacomo and Livio. From 1969 he taught industrial design at Turin Polytechnic and worked for a number of well-known firms, designed exhibitions and still advises on design all over the world.

Pierre Chareau, 1883–1950

After studying architecture at the Ecole des Beaux-Arts and training with an English furniture company in Paris, Chareau became a self-employed architect and furniture designer. In the twenties his firm was represented at most of the important exhibitions and he became a member of the Union des Artistes Modernes. At the beginning of World War II Chareau emigrated to New York, where he lived for the rest of his life. Important works: the golf-club in Beauvallon on the Riviera, 1927; the Grand Hotel in Tours, 1929; the "Maison de Verre" in Paris, 1931.

Charles Eames, 1907–1978

Eames studied architecture at Washington University, St. Louis, and opened his first office in 1930. In 1936 he moved to Cranbrook University, Michigan, and worked in Eliel Saarinen's office at the end of the thirties. In 1941 he and his wife Ray moved to California, where they founded the Plyformed Products Company and successfully tried out new designs and production methods. Later they also made films, including some for IBM and the US government, and designed toys and exhibitions, such as the American contribution to the Moscow World Fair in 1959.

Egon Eiermann, 1904–1970

From 1923–27 he studied architecture at the Technische Hochschule in Berlin-Charlottenburg and attended Hans Poelzig's master class. In 1931 he became self-employed. After World War II he had a joint office with Robert Hilgers and taught at the Technische Hochschule in Karlsruhe from 1947 onwards. In 1951 he was a founding member of

the Rat für Formgebung (Design Council), and in 1962 he was on the planning commission for the building of the new West German parliament and its Upper House, with Paul Baumgarten and Sep Ruf.
Important works: the German pavilion at the Brussels World Fair in 1958; the Kaiser-Wilhelm-Gedächtniskirche in Berlin, 1957–63; the high-rise office building for West German members of parliament in Bonn, 1965–69.

August Endell, 1871–1925

From 1891 onwards Endell studied philosophy and psychology in Tübingen. Between 1892 and 1901 he lived in Munich and taught himself art and crafts, design and architecture. In 1901 he went to Berlin, where he got a number of building commissions. In 1904 he founded the Formschule, which existed until 1914. In 1918 he became Poelzig's successor at the Akademie für Kunst und Kunstgewerbe (Academy for Arts and Crafts) in Breslau.
Important works: the "Elvira" photo-studio in Munich, 1897–98; "das Bunte Theater" in Berlin, 1901; the "Neumann'sche Festsäle", 1905–06; the trotting race-course in Mariendorf, 1911–12.

Eugène Gaillard, 1862–1933

He started his career as a lawyer, then worked as a sculptor for ten years before he took up interior design. At the turn of the century he was one of the most important people to work at Samuel Bing's gallery "L'Art Nouveau" in Paris.

Eileen Gray, 1879–1976

From 1898 she studied at the Slade School of Art in London and learnt the techniques of oriental lacquerwork. In 1902 she went to Paris and continued her art studies at the Académie Colarossi and the Académie Julian. She perfected her knowledge of lacquerwork techniques with the Japanese master Sugawara. As a designer, she had her first successes with a number of well-received interiors in the twenties. Around 1925 she started to experiment with tubular steel for furni-

JOSEF HOFFMANN

HANS HOLLEIN

ture, and turned to architecture. Together with Jean Badovici, she built a few villas. Several projects were not carried out.

Hermann Gretsch, 1895–1950

Gretsch studied architecture with Paul Bonatz and Paul Schmitthenner at the Technische Hochschule in Stuttgart from 1918 on. In 1922, he took up an apprenticeship at the Stuttgart Arts and Crafts College and passed the examination to become a journeyman in ceramics under Bernhard Pankok. In 1930 he became government building officer with the regional industrial inspection board in Stuttgart, and in 1931 artistic adviser for the Arzberg china factory. After the Second World War, he worked as a freelance architect in Stuttgart.

Walter Gropius, 1883–1969

In 1903 he started his studies of architecture in Munich, from 1907 he was Peter Behrens' assistant in Berlin. Together with Adolf Meyer he opened his own office in Stuttgart in 1910. On the recommendation of Henry van de Velde he became the director of the Kunstgewerbeschule and the Hochschule für bildende Kunst in Weimar, and in 1910 director of the Staatliches Bauhaus in Weimar.

He moved to Dessau with the Bauhaus in 1926, and left the institution in 1928. After the Nazis had taken over power he emigrated to the United States via Britain and became professor of architecture at Harvard in 1937. In 1946 he founded the architect's office The Architects Collaborative. Important works: the Fagus factory in Alfeld an der Leine, 1910–11; the model factory for the Werkbund exhibition in Cologne, 1914; the Bauhaus buildings in Dessau, 1925–26; the "Siemensstadt" apartment complex in Berlin, 1929–30; the Harvard Graduate Center, Cambridge/Mass., 1949–50.

Josef Hoffmann, 1870–1956

Hoffmann studied at the Staatsgewerbeschule in Brünn and then, from 1892 until 1895, at the Vienna Akademie der bildenden Künste under Karl von Hasenauer und Otto Wagner. Later he worked in Otto Wagner's studio. From 1899 to 1936 he was a professor at the Vienna College for Arts and Crafts. In 1897 he was one of the initiators of the Vienna Secession, which he left in 1905 together with the Klimt group. Together with Koloman Moser, Hoffmann founded the Wiener Werkstätte (Vienna Workshops) in 1903 and remained the artistic director until 1932. From 1907 until 1912 he was the president of the Austrian Werkbund.

Important works: the Moser, Moll, Henneberg and Spitzer houses in Vienna, beginning of the century; the sanatorium in Puckersdorf near Vienna, 1903; the Palais Stoclet in Brussels, 1905–1911; the exhibition pavilion for the Biennale in Venice, 1934.

Hans Hollein, *1934

Hollein studied at the Akademie für bildende Künste (Academy for the Visual Arts) in Vienna, at the Illinois Institute of Technology in Chicago, and at the University of California in Berkeley. He worked in various architects' offices in Australia, South America, Sweden and Germany. Since 1964 he has had his office in his hometown, Vienna. He is known for his buildings as well as for interior design, environments and exhibitions. Important works: the interior furnishings for the Siemens AG Company in Munich, 1970–75; the Schullin jeweller's shop in Vienna, 1972–74; the main tourist office in Vienna, 1976–78; the Abteiberg Museum in Mönchengladbach, 1972–82.

Victor Horta, 1861–1947

Horta studied at the Académie des Beaux Arts in Brussels and later joined the office of the neoclassicist architect Alphonse Balat. His first major work, the villa designed for the industrialist Tassel in 1893, was the first real Art Nouveau residential

building in Europe. From 1897 onwards he taught at the Brussels free university and from 1912 to 1931 at the Académie des Beaux-Arts.
Important works: the villas "Solvay", 1894, and "van Eetvelde", 1897–1900; the "Maison du Peuple", the headquarters of the Belgian Socialist Party, for which he was commissioned in 1895. All these buidings were designed in Brussels.

Arne Jacobsen, 1902–1971
After an apprenticeship as a bricklayer, he studied architecture at the Royal Academy for Art in Copenhagen, which he later joined as a professor. As an independent designer he designed furniture, cutlery, lamps and textiles, for which he got many prizes and earned worldwide recognition for Danish design. As an architect he built housing, schools, factories, hotels and offices.

Kaare Klint, 1888–1954
Klint studied painting, but later worked as an architect. In 1944 he became professor at the Art Academy in Copenhagen however, his main interest was furniture design. From 1924 onwards he taught whole generations of designers in his furniture class at the School of Architecture at Copenhagen Art Academy. Mogens Koch was one of his students.

Le Corbusier, 1887–1965
The Swiss Charles-Edouard Jeanneret-Gris adopted the pseudonym Le Corbusier in the 1920s. From 1901 he attended the art school in La-Chaux-de Fonds, where he learnt engraving. From 1908–09 he worked with Auguste Perret in Paris, from 1910–11 with Peter Behrens in Berlin. In 1917 he settled down in Paris and in 1920 published the first edition of "L'Esprit Nouveau" with the painter Amédée Ozenfant. In this magazine he published his manifesto "Une maison est une machine à habiter". In 1922 he opened a joint office with his cousin Pierre Jeanneret, who later worked together with Charlotte Perriand. Le Corbusier was a founding member of U.A.M., took

French citizenship and ran his own architect's office in Paris after 1945.
Important works: the pavilion "L'Esprit Nouveau" at the international exhibition in Paris, 1925; two houses on the Weissenhof estate in Stuttgart, 1927; the Villa Savoye in Poissy, 1929–31; the Unité d'habitation in Marseilles, 1947–52; the pilgrimage church of Notre-Dame-du-Haut in Ronchamp, 1950–54; government offices in Chandigarh, India, 1952–64.

Adolf Loos, 1870–1933
After training at the Technische Hochschule Dresden, he went to the USA for three years in 1893, where he survived on occasional jobs. Afterwards, he worked with Carl Mayreder in Vienna for a short time, before he became self-employed. In 1923 he moved to Paris for a few years. He is known for his buildings and interior designs as well as for his publications.
Important works: the shop interior for Goldman & Salatsch, 1898; the "Kärntner Bar", 1908; the Steiner house, 1910; the office block on the Michaelerplatz, 1911, all in Vienna; his entry to the competion to the Chicago Tribune Tower in form of a huge Doric column, 1922; the Tristan Tzara house in Paris, 1926; the Müller house in Prague, 1930.

Charles Rennie Mackintosh, 1868–1928
From 1877–84 he attended Alan Glen's High School and later went to evening classes at the School of Art in Glasgow. He learnt his trade with the architect John Hutchinson and became a draughtsman with John Honeyman & Keppie in 1889. In 1904 he became a partner in the firm. In 1900 he married Margaret Macdonald, a graduate of the Glasgow School of Art, with whom he worked in close co-operation. From 1923 he devoted most of his time to painting.
Important works: the new building for the Glasgow School of Art, 1897–1909; Hill House in Helensburg, 1903; Tea Rooms in Glasgow, 1897–1911.

Bruno Mathsson, *1907

He was an apprentice in his father's carpentry workshop in Värnamo, Sweden, following the family tradition. Mathsson's models were still produced by his father's firm, later, when he worked as a freelance designer. He became known through national and international exhibitions like the one at the Göteburg Rohsska Konstslojd-museum in 1936, the exhibition "Arts et Techniques Appliqués à la Vie Moderne" in Paris, 1937, and the World Fair in New York in 1939. After 1945 he worked mainly as an architect.

Alessandro Mendini, *1931

Mendini studied architecture at Milan Technical College and worked with Nizzoli Assoziati until 1970. From 1970 to 1975 he was chief editor of the magazine "Casabella", from 1977 of the design magazine "Modo" and between 1980 and 1985 the publisher of "Domus". Mendini was an outstanding member of the "Alchimia" group.

Ludwig Mies van der Rohe, 1886–1969

He started off as a designer of stucco decorations with an architect in Aachen. In 1905 he went to Berlin and worked with the already well-known designer Bruno Paul. In 1908 he became a draughtsman in Peter Behrens' office. From 1911 onwards he was a self-employed architect. Between 1926 and 1932 he was the vice-president of the Deutscher Werkbund and was in charge of the overall planning and construction of the Weissenhof estate between 1925 and 1927. From 1930–33 he was the director of the Bauhaus in Dessau, which was closed because of pressure from right-wing radicals in 1932, and only continued as a private institute in Berlin for a few months. In 1938 Mies, who adopted the professional name van der Rohe in the 1920s, emigrated to the USA and became director of the department of architecture at the Illinois Institute of Technology in Chicago. At the same time he had his own architect's office.

Important works: the German pavilion for the International Exhibition in Barcelona, 1928–29; his contribution to the German building exhibition in Berlin, 1931; the Villa Tugendhat in Brünn, 1928–30; the Seagram Building in New York, 1954–58; the new National Gallery in Berlin, 1962–68.

Koloman Moser, 1868–1918

From 1885–1893 he studied at the Vienna Academy for the Visual Arts and then at the Vienna Arts and Crafts College for two years, where he became professor in 1990. He was a founding member of the Vienna Secession, which he left in 1905 together with the Klimt group, and of the Wiener Werkstätte (Vienna Workshops) in 1903.

Joseph Maria Olbrich, 1867–1908

Olbrich studied at the Vienna Academy of Art from 1890 to 1893. He went to Italy and North-Africa on a "Prix de Rome" scholarship, before he joined Otto Wagner's office.
Olbrich stayed with Wagner for four years, contributed to the planning of city railway stations and had the opportunity of designing the Secession building in Vienna. On the invitation of Grand Duke Ernst Ludwig of Hesse, Olbrich moved to Darmstadt in 1899 and directed the building of the "Mathildenhöhe" artists' colony for eight years.
Important works: the Secession building in Vienna, 1898; houses on the Mathildenhöhe in Darmstadt, 1900; the Tietz department store in Düsseldorf, 1906–08.

Bernhard Pankok, 1872–1943

The painter and designer Pankok studied at the Art Academies in Düsseldorf and Berlin from 1889 onwards. In 1892 he opened his own studio in Munich and was a founding member of the Vereinigte Werkstätten für Kunst im Handwerk in 1897. In 1901 he became professor at the newly established Königliche Lehr- und Versuchswerkstätte in Stuttgart, which was amalgamated with the Kunstgewerbeschule (Arts and Crafts College) under his directorship in 1913.

Gaetano Pesce, *1939
He studied design and architecture in Venice until 1965. After that he worked with the "laboratories" of producers like B&B and Cassina on the adaptation of new technical advances for the mass production of furniture. He also experimented with audio-visual montages, kinetic and serial art. Since 1975 he has been working at the department of architecture in Strasbourg.

Giò Ponti, 1891–1979
In 1921 he finished his architectural studies at the Polytechnic in his hometown Milan. After that he worked as a designer for a china manufacturer. Later, he also designed cutlery, espresso machines, sinks, bathtubs etc, furniture and lamps. He designed stage settings and costumes for the La Scala in Milan. He built residential and office buildings, university institutes and churches all over the world. In 1928 he founded the art, architecture, and design magazine "Domus", which he directed until his death.

Eugène Printz, 1889–1948
He learnt his trade in his father's cabinet-making workshop, which for the most part copied "ancien régime" furniture. Later he opened his own studio, but still produced furniture in the Louis Quinze and Louis Seize styles. It was only in the mid-1920's that he started to produce pieces to his own designs. After 1945, he joined other cabinet-makers like Jules Leleu in the "Décor de France" group.

Jean Prouvé, 1901–1984
In 1923 Prouvé, trained in artistic metalwork, opened a workshop in Nancy. He worked for designers like Robert Mallet-Stevens and he himself

GERRIT RIETVELD

designed steel furniture and houses, which were mass-produced in sections which could be easily assembled. In 1939 he made pre-fabs for soldiers, after the war they served as emergency accommodation in Lorraine. In the 1950s and '60s he made curtain walls in metal for numerous buildings in and outside France.

Dieter Rams, *1932
Rams worked as a carpenter and studied at the Werkkunstschule Wiesbaden. He is known for his product-design for Braun AG, for which he has been working since 1955. In 1981 he became professor at the Hamburger Hochschule für bildende Kunst (Visual Arts College). He is one of the board of directors of the Design Council and has been awarded prizes and other tributes both at home and abroad.

Richard Riemerschmid, 1868–1957
From 1888–90 he studied painting at the Academy in his hometown Munich. In 1897 he was one of the founding members of the Vereinigte Werkstätten für Kunst im Handwerk there. From 1903 onwards he worked at the Dresdener Werkstätten für Handwerkskunst. From 1912 to 1924 Riemerschmid was in charge of the Kunstgewerbeschule in Munich and from 1926 to 1931 head of the Werkschule in Cologne.
Important works: the "Kammerspiele" in Munich, 1901; the "Hellerau" garden city near Dresden, started in 1909.

Gerrit Thomas Rietveld, 1888–1964
He learnt his trade in his father's carpentry workshop in Utrecht. From 1906 to 1911 he was a designer for a jeweller. After that he worked as a self-employed carpenter. Rietveld attended courses in architecture with P. J. Klaarhamer, an architect belonging to Berlage's circle, with whom Rietveld worked in later years. Via Robert van't Hoff he came to join the De Stijl movement, to which he adhered until it ended.

GIO PONTI

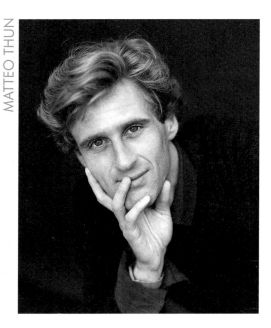

Emile-Jacques Ruhlmann, 1879–1933

He started his career in his father's shop in Paris, which sold pictures, wallpaper and mirrors. In 1910 he presented his own wallpaper design at the autumn exhibition, in 1913 he showed his self-designed furniture for the first time. In 1919, with Pierre Laurent, an expert in paintings, he opened "Les Etablissements Ruhlmann et Laurent", which became known as an exclusive interior furnishings concern within a few years. The Exposition Internationale in Paris, 1925, brought Ruhlmann his breakthrough as a celebrated French furniture designer.

Ettore Sottsass, *1917

In 1919 he finished his architectural studies at the Turin Polytechnic. After the war he set up his own studio in Milan. In 1956 he worked in George Nelson's office in New York. From 1958 onwards he worked as a designer for the office machine manufacturer Olivetti. At the end of the 1970s he was a member of the Alchimia group, in 1980

founder of the Sottsass Associati, in 1981 co-founder of Memphis.

Mart Stam, 1899–1986

After completing his studies at the Rijksnormaal-school voor Tekenonderwijs in Amsterdam, Stam worked for various architects in Amsterdam, Rotterdam, Berlin and Zurich. He concentrated less on individual buildings than on town planning. In this field, he worked in the Soviet Union from 1930 to 1934, in Rotterdam from 1941 on and, after 1949, in Dresden. From 1948 to 1950 he was director of the Dresden Akademie der Bildenden Künste and from 1950 to 1953 director of the Art Academy in Weissensee, Berlin. Stam's reputation as a furniture designer is based on his chair without back legs, 1926.

Gustav Stickley, 1857–1946

He learnt carpentry in his uncle's workshop, which specialized in simple chairs with straw seats. In 1883 he opened his own furniture shop in Binghampton, New York. On a trip to Europe he got to know Charles F. A. Voysey and Charles R. Ashbee and was highly impressed by the ideals and works of the Arts and Crafts movement. On his return to the USA he opened his own Craftsman Workshops. In 1901 he founded the magazine "Craftsman" to promote John Ruskin's and William Morris's ideas and to increase the popularity of the products of his own workshops. After a quick rise to prosperity, his company went bankrupt in 1915 and was bought up by his brothers.

Walter Dorwin Teague, 1883–1960

He came to New York in 1903, attended evening classes at the Art Students League and worked for an advertising agency. In 1911 he opened his own graphics bureau. In 1926 he founded one of the first American "industrial design offices". He designed cameras for Kodak, pianos for Steinway, filling stations for Texaco, car bodies, plane interiors and supermarkets.

Michael Thonet, 1796–1871

In 1819 the carpenter and cabinetmaker Thonet opened his own furniture workshop in Boppard on the Rhine. From 1830 he worked on the production of bentwood furniture. In the early 1840s he showed his first models at exhibitions in Koblenz and Mainz. Prince Metternich invited him to come to Vienna, where Thonet patented his new production technique. In 1853 he handed the firm over to his sons, who went into industrial mass production and sold Thonet products all over the world.

Matteo Thun, *1952

Thun studied in Salzburg at the Oskar Kokoschka Academy and at the Architecture Faculty in Florence. In 1980 he was one of the founders of the Sottsass Associati and from 1981 a member of Memphis. Since 1982 he has been teaching as a professor for product design at the Hochschule für angewandte Kunst in Vienna and has an office in Milan.

Henry-Clément van de Velde, 1863–1957

He studied painting at the academy in Antwerpes from 1881 to 1884. In 1889 he joined "Les Vingt", an avant-garde group of artists in Brussels. From 1901 he was artistic adviser to the court of Grand Duke Wilhelm Ernst in Weimar, from 1906 to 1914 director of the newly founded Kunstgewerbliche Lehranstalten in Weimar. In 1914 he emigrated to Switzerland. In 1925 he founded the Institut Superieur d'Architecture et des Arts Décoratifs in Brussels, which he directed for ten years. The last years of his life were spent in Switzerland.
Important works: the Karl-Ernst-Osthaus-Museum in Hagen, 1898–1902; the theatre at the Deutscher Werkbund exhibition in Cologne, 1914.

Otto Wagner, 1841–1918

Wagner began his studies at the Technische

FRANK LLOYD WRIGHT

Hochschule in Vienna, then went to the Berlin Bauakademie and, from 1861 to 1863, to the Akademie der bildenden Künste in Vienna, where he became professor in 1894. From 1899 to 1905 he was a member of the Vienna Secession. In 1890 he took on the task of redeveloping the city of Vienna and built the urban railway.
Important works: tenement blocks at the Linke Wienzeile, 1898–99; buildings for the city railway, 1894–97; the church at the Steinhof; the Vienna post-office savings bank, 1904–06.

Hans J. Wegner, *1914

After his apprenticeship as a carpenter he went to the Technical College in Copenhagen and studied at the Arts and Crafts College there until 1938. He later worked there as a teacher. In 1942 he opened his own design studio for furniture, lamps, silver and wallpaper in Gentofte and worked as adviser to a number of Danish and German companies.

Frank Lloyd Wright, 1867–1959

After studying architecture at the school of engineering at Wisconsin University in Madison, Wright worked in Louis Sullivan's architect's office from 1888 to 1893. During this time, he was already building his own houses and opened a studio in Oak Park, a fashionable suburb of Chicago. Here he later planned his "Prairie Houses". In 1909 he travelled to Europe and had an important influence on architects like Walter Gropius and Mies van der Rohe through his exhibitions and his book describing his buildings and designs. On his return to the United States he founded the Spring Green community. His house, "Taliesin", became a school of architecture.
Important works: the Coonley House in Riverside, Illinois, 1907–11; the Robie House in Chicago, 1907–09; the Larkin Building in Buffalo, 1904; the "Fallingwater" residential building, Bear Run, Pennsylvania, 1936; the S.C. Johnson office building, Racine, Wisconsin, 1936–39; the Solomon R. Guggenheim Museum in New York, 1943–46,

OTTO WAGNER

Annitrenta. Arte e Cultura in Italia, Comune di Milano, Milano 1982

Rolf-Peter Baacke, Uta Brandes, Michael Erlhoff, Design als Gegenstand. Der neue Glanz der Dinge, Berlin 1983

Albrecht Bangert, Italienisches Möbeldesign. Klassiker von 1945 bis 1985, München 1985

Herbert Bayer, Walter Gropius, Ilse Gropius (Ed.), Bauhaus 1919–1928, London 1975

Vera J. Behal, Möbel des Jugendstils. Sammlung des Österreichischen Museums für angewandte Kunst, München 1981

Peter Behrens und Nürnberg. Geschmackswandel in Deutschland. Historismus, Jugendstil und die Anfänge der Industrieform, Nürnberg 1980

Roger Billcliffe, Charles Rennie Mackintosh, The Complete Furniture, Furniture Drawings & Interior Designs, Guildford 1979

Werner Blaser, Alvar Aalto als Designer, Stuttgart 1982

Willy Boesiger, Hans Girsberger, Le Corbusier 1910–1965, Zürich 1967

Giovanni Brino, Carlo Mollino, München 1987

Bazon Brock, Hans Ulrich Reck, Internationales Design Zentrum Berlin (Hrsg.), Stilwandel als Kulturtechnik, Kampfprinzip, Lebensform oder Systemstrategie in Werbung, Design, Architektur, Mode, Köln 1986

Die Bugattis. Automobile, Möbel, Bronzen, Plakate, Museum für Kunst und Gewerbe Hamburg, 1983

Florence Camard, Ruhlmann. Master of Art Déco, London 1984

Joan Campbell, The German Werkbund. The Politics of Reform in the Applied Arts, Princeton, New Jersey, 1978

Ennio Chiggio (Hrsg.), Studio 65, Milano 1986

Design Dasein. Ausgewählte Objekte zum Sitzen, Stellen und Leben, Museum für Kunst und Gewerbe Hamburg, 1987

Arthur Drexler, Charles Eames. Furniture from the Design Collection. The Museum of Modern Art, New York 1973

Alastair Duncan, Art Déco furniture: the French designers, London 1984

August Endell. Der Architekt des Photoateliers Elvira 1871–1925, Museum Villa Stuck, München 1977

Volker Fischer (Hrsg.), Design heute. Maßstäbe: Formgebung zwischen Industrie und Kunst-Stück, Deutsches Architekturmuseum, Frankfurt am Main, München 1988

Philippe Garner, Twentieth-century furniture, Oxford 1980

Sigfried Giedion, Die Herrschaft der Mechanisierung. Ein Beitrag zur anonymen Geschichte, Frankfurt am Main 1982

Astrid Gmeiner, Gottfried Pirhofer, Der Österreichische Werkbund, Salzburg und Wien 1985

Martin Greif, Drepession Modern. The Thirties Style in America, New York 1975

Tilman Harlander, Gerhard Fehl (Hrsg.), Hitlers sozialer Wohnungsbau 1940–1945. Wohnungspolitik, Baugestaltung und Siedlungsplanung, Hamburg 1986

Ot Hoffmann (Hrsg.), Der Deutsche Werkbund – 1907, 1947, 1987 . . ., Berlin und Frankfurt am Main 1987

Hans Hollein, Architecture and Urbanism (Sonderheft), Tokyo 1985

Richard Horn, Memphis. Objects, Furniture, and Patterns, New York 1985

Industry & Design in The Netherlands 1850/1950, Stedelijk Museum Amsterdam, 1986

Jugendstil. Glas, Graphik, Keramik, Metall, Möbel, Skulpturen und Textilien von 1880 bis 1915, bearbeitet von Irmela Franzke, Badisches Landesmuseum Karlsruhe, 1987

Karin Kirsch, Die Weißenhofsiedlung. Werkbund-Ausstellung "Die Wohnung" – Stuttgart 1927, Stuttgart 1987

Dan Klein, Nancy A. McClelland, Malcolm Haslam, L'Esprit Art Déco, Paris und London 1987

Gabriele Koller, Die Radikalisierung der Phantasie. Design aus Österreich, Salzburg und Wien 1987

Ferdinand Kramer, Architektur und Design, Bauhaus-Archiv, Berlin 1982

Heinrich Kreisel, Die Kunst des deutschen Möbels. Dritter Band: Georg Himmelheber, Klassizismus, Historismus, Jugendstil, München 1973

Ian Latham, Joseph Maria Olbrich, London 1980, Stuttgart 1981

Herbert Lindinger (Hrsg.), Ulm . . . Hochschule für Gestaltung. Die Moral der Gegenstände, Berlin 1987

Howard Mandelbaum, Eric Meyers, Screen Deco. A Celebration of High Style in Hollywood, Bromley/Kent 1985

Karl Mang, History of modern furniture; trans. by J. W. Gabriel, London 1979

Moderne Klassiker. Möbel, die Geschichte machen, herausgegeben von der Zeitschrift Schöner Wohnen, Hamburg 1984

Moderne Vergangenheit 1800–1900. Möbel, Metall, Keramik, Glas, Textil, Entwürfe – aus Wien, herausgegeben von der Gesellschaft bildender Künstler Österreichs, Künstlerhaus, Wien 1981

Walter Müller-Wulckow, Architektur der Zwanziger Jahre in Deutschland. Neu-Ausgabe der vier Blauen Bücher, Königstein im Taunus 1975

Winfried Nerdinger, Walter Gropius, Berlin 1985

Richard Riemerschmid. Vom Jugendstil zum Werkbund. Werke und Dokumente, herausgegeben von Winfried Nerdinger, München 1982

Frank Russell (Ed.), Art Nouveau architecture, London 1979

Frank Russell, A Century of Chair Design, London 1980

Kazuko Sato, Alchimia. Italienisches Design der Gegenwart, Berlin 1988

Wulf Schirmer (Hrsg.), Egon Eiermann 1904–1970. Bauten und Projekte, Stuttgart 1984

Franz Schulze, Mies van der Rohe. A Critical Biography, Chicago und London 1986

Klaus-Jürgen Sembach, Stil 1930, Tübingen 1971

Mildred Friedman (Hrsg.), De Stijl: 1917–1931. Visions of Utopia, Oxford 1982

Die Shaker. Leben und Produktion einer Commune in der Pionierzeit Amerikas. Die Neue Sammlung, München 1974

Allen Tate, Ray Smith, Interior Design in the 20th Century, New York 1986

Robert C. Twombly, Frank Lloyd Wright. His Life and his Architecture, USA 1979

Kirk Varnedoe, Vienna 1900. Art, Architecture & Design, New York 1986

Alexander von Vegesack, Deutsche Stahlrohrmöbel. 650 Modelle aus Katalogen von 1927–1958, München 1986

Otto Wagner. Möbel und Innenräume, Museum Moderner Kunst (Hrsg.), Salzburg und Wien 1984

Hans Wichmann, Industrial Design, Unikate, Serienerzeugnisse: Kunst, die sich nützlich macht. Die Neue Sammlung. Ein Neuer Museumstyp des 20. Jahrhunderts, München 1985

Richard Guy Wilson, Dianne H. Pilgrim, Dickran Tashijan, The Machine Age in Amercia 1918–1941, New York 1986

Wohnen von Sinnen, Volker Albus, Michael Feith, Rouli Lecatsa, Wolfgang Schepers, Claudia Schneider-Esleben (Hrsg.), Köln 1986

Erik Zahle (Hrsg.), Skandinavisches Kunsthandwerk, München und Zürich 1963

Rainer Zerbst, Antoni Gaudí 1852–1926. Antoni Gaudí i Cornet – A Life Devoted to Architecture, Cologne 1988

Bruno Zevi, Frank Lloyd Wright, Zürich und München 1980

PHOTO CREDITS

Front Cover: Cassina, Meda/Milan

Back Cover: Retoria Y. Futagawa & Associated Photographers, Tokyo

Frontispiece: Sotheby's, London

11: Photographer: Marianne Haller, Perchtoldsdorf, Austria

12: Photographer: Sophie Renate Gnamm, Munich

14, 15: Institute for the History of Medicine at the Freie Universtität, Berlin

18: Photographer: Sophie Renate Gnamm, Munich

20: Gottfried Langenstein, Wiesbaden

23: Bastin & Evrard, Brussels

26: Photographer: L. Sully-Jaulmes, Paris

27: Photographers: Frehn & Baldacchino, Hamburg

28: Photographer: Rudolf Nagel, Frankfurt

29: Photographer: L. Sully-Jaulmes, Paris

33: bottom left: Collection, The Museum of Modern Art, New York, Joseph H. Heil Fund

34: Bildarchiv Foto Marburg

37, 38, 39: Library of the "Landesgewerbeanstalt", Nuremberg

40, top right: Bildarchiv Foto Marburg

42, 43: Photographer: Philippe R. Doumic, Paris

44: Foto Archivo Mas, Barcelona

46: Bildarchiv Foto Marburg

47, top: Bildarchiv Preussischer Kulturbesitz, Berlin

49: Library of the "Landesgewerbeanstalt", Nuremberg

55: Retoria Y. Futagawa & Associated Photographers, Tokyo

56, 57: Bildarchiv Foto Marburg

62: Loos-Archiv, Vienna

65, bottom: Paul Asenbaum, Vienna

66: Photo archives of the Austrian National Library, Vienna

67: Paul Asenbaum, Vienna

68, top: Bildarchiv Foto Marburg

68, bottom: Bildarchiv Foto Marburg

71, bottom: Royal Commission on the Ancient and Historical Monuments of Scotland, Edinburgh

72: Bildarchiv Foto Marburg

74, 75: Photographer: Jürgen Regler, Nuremberg

76, top: Architektural Collection, Technical University, Munich

76, bottom: Photographers: Frehn & Baldacchino, Hamburg

77, left: Bildarchiv Foto Marburg

79: Photographer: Rudolf Nagel, Frankfurt

80: Photographer: Bernd-Dieter Roth, Nuremberg

81: Vereinigte Werkstätten, Munich

83: Photographer: Klaus Frahm, Hamburg

84, 85: Bildarchiv Foto Marburg

87, top: Architectural Photographing Company, Chicago

89: The Metropolitan Museum of Art, New York, Photographer: Henry Fuermann

90: Musée des Arts Décoratifs, Paris

94: Bauhaus-Archiv, Berlin

97: Photographer: Günter Derleth, Fürth

98: Musée des Arts Décoratifs, Paris

100, top: Bauhaus-Archiv, Berlin

100, bottom: Photographer: Sophie Renate Gnamm, Munich

101: Baumeister-Archiv, Stuttgart

104, top: Photographer: Emil Leitner, Berlin

104, bottom: Photographer: Günter Derleth, Fürth

106: Bildarchiv Foto Marburg

107: Lore Kramer, Frankfurt

108, top, 109: Bildarchiv Foto Marburg

110: Bildarchiv Preussischer Kulturbesitz

111: Photographer: Günter Derleth, Fürth

115, top: Musée des Arts Décoratifs, Paris

116: Landesbildstelle, Berlin

118, top: Photographer: Sophie Renate Gnamm, Munich

118, bottom, 119: Picture Archives, Austrian National Library, Vienna

120: Triennale di Milano, Milan

124: Photographer: Hans Finsler, Zürich

126, 127, 128 (top): Musée des Arts Décoratifs, Paris

129: Photographer: Philippe R. Doumic, Paris

130: Musée des Arts Décoratifs, Paris

131: Studio Lourmel, Paris

133, bottom, 135, bottom: Eckart Muthesius, Berlin

136: Retoria Y. Futagawa & Associated Photographers, Tokyo

138: Photographer: Klaus Frahm, Hamburg

139: Photographer: Christian Radux, Paris

140, bottom: Photographer: Günter Derleth, Fürth

143: Photographer: Christian Radux, Paris

146: Library of the "Landesgewerbeanstalt", Nuremberg

147, bottom: Museum für Zeppelingeschichte, Friedrichshafen

148, 149: Hedrich Blessing, Chicago

150: Photographer: Bill Rothschild, New York

151: Walter Dorwin Teague Associates, New York

152: Tennessee Valley Authority, Knoxville, TN

157: Photographer: Willi Moegle, Stuttart

158, 159: Regional History Museum, Saarbrücken

160: Lillian Kiesler, New York

162, top: Courtesy Collection, The Museum of Modern Art, New York. Photograph by Samuel Gottscho

163: Courtesy Collection, The Museum of Modern Art, New York. Drawings on white poster board, 30 × 20".

164, top: Courtesy Collection, The Museum of Modern Art, New York. Gift of Charles Eames, 32½" high × 59" wide × 34½".

165: Courtesy The Museum of Modern Art, New York.

168: Photographer: Günter Derleth, Fürth

169, top: USIS, Bad Godesberg

169, bottom: Photographer: Sophie Renate Gnamm, Munich

172: Triennale di Milano, Milan

174: Photographer: Aldo Ballo, Milan

175, top: Yves Gastou, Paris

180: Photographer: Keld Helmer-Petersen, Copenhagen

181: Photographers: Thomas and Poul Pedersen, Arhus

185: Mathsson International, Värnamo

188: Landesbildstelle, Berlin

190, top: Institute for Building History, University of Karlsruhe

191: Knoll International, Murr/Murr

192, top: Paul Swiridoff, Schwäbisch Hall

196, top: Bayer AG, Leverkusen

197: Photographer: Jürgen Kriewald, Cologne

200, top: Rudolf Baresel-Bofinger, Heilbronn

203: Studio 65, Turin

211, top: Achille Castiglioni, Milan

213, top: Occiomagico, Florence

217: Anthologie Quartett, Bad Essen

220: Driade, Piacenza

222, 223: Hans Hollein, Vienna

228: Klaus Stefan Leuschel, Frankfurt am Main

234, 235 (top): Photographer: Klaus Frahm, Hamburg

238: Jahreszeiten-Verlag, Hamburg, Photographer: Roland Beaufre

240: Institute for the History and Theory of Architecture, Eidgenössische Technische Hochschule, Zürich

241: Design M Ingo Maurer, Munich

242: Agence Photographique TOP, Paris, Photographer: Pascal Hinous

243: Burda Syndication, Munich

244, 245: Rainer Krause, Bad Essen

246, bottom: Scheper's estate

247, left: Alessi, Crusinallo

247, right: Vitra, Weil am Rhein

248, top: Picture Archives of the Austrian National Library, Vienna

248, bottom: Ingrid von Kruse, Wuppertal

249: Cassina, Meda/Milan

250, left: Picture Archives of the Austrian National Library, Vienna

250, right: Hessisches Landesmuseum, Darmstadt

251: Cassina, Meda/Milan

252, left: Gebr. Thonet, Frankenberg

252, right: Bieffe, Padua

253, top: Cassina, Meda/Milan

253, bottom: Picture Archives of the Austrian National Library, Vienna

This list contains only sources which are not identical with the owners or manufacturers of furniture already named with the illustrations. Any photographs where an exact source is not given are from the authors' archives.